A Dictionary of
Philosophy

A Dictionary of Philosophy

A. R. Lacey

Department of Philosophy,
Bedford College, University of London

Routledge & Kegan Paul
London, Boston and Henley

First published in 1976
by Routledge & Kegan Paul Ltd
39 Store Street, London WC1E 7DD,
Broadway House, Newtown Road,
Henley-on-Thames, Oxon RG9 1EN and
9 Park Street,
Boston, Mass. 02108, USA
Reprinted and first published
as a paperback in 1978
Reprinted in 1979 and 1980
Set in Monotype Times New Roman
and printed in Great Britain by
Lowe and Brydone Printers Limited
Thetford, Norfolk
© *A. R. Lacey 1976*

ISBN 0 7100 8361 0 (c)
ISBN 0 7100 8362 9 (p)

Preface

This book aims to give the layman or intending student a pocket encyclopaedia of philosophy, one with a bias towards explaining terminology. The latter task is not an easy one since philosophy is regularly concerned with concepts which are unclear. It is one main part of philosophy to clarify them rather than to use them. What I have tried to do is to take some of the commonest terms and notions in current English-speaking philosophy and to give the reader some idea of what they mean to the philosopher and what sort of problems he finds associated with them.

A work of this size cannot do justice to individual philosophers. The entries devoted to them offer only the barest outlines of their work, followed by the most philosophically important of their publications or, occasionally, those of other interest. Where possible, the original title and publication date is given, sometimes followed by the standard title of an English translation, or by a brief indication of the work's topic. Where applicable, each of these entries ends with cross-references to all other entries where the philosopher is mentioned unless cross-references are already given in the text of the entry. It is important to remember that both the description of a philosopher's activity and the list of his writings are by no means exhaustive. The choice of eighty or so philosophers represents, with some inevitable arbitrariness, a compromise between importance and popularity.

In the book as a whole, epistemology and logic occupy far more space than, say, ethics, politics or aesthetics. This is because the former subjects are the central ones. Terms and concepts from them are constantly used in discussing the latter subjects, while the opposite process occurs rarely, if at all. Mathematical logic needs a dictionary to itself, and only those terms are included which occur widely in philosophical and traditional logic. Much the same applies to linguistic theory. I have also generally avoided terms associated with only one author, for which a standard edition or commentary is best consulted.

Many philosophical terms, such as CONFIRMATION, also have a meaning in ordinary language and a technical meaning associated with a particular outlook. I have only occasionally mentioned the ordinary language one and I have not usually mentioned certain fairly obvious ambiguities of a

Preface

kind common to many words. 'Entailment' may mean the relation of entailment, a proposition entailed, and a proposition saying that something entails something else. More important, many words are too complex for even the philosophically significant ambiguities to be covered completely. I have tried to give the dominant sense or senses in current, or currently studied, philosophy, and especially those senses which are technical, or reflect or give rise to philosophical problems. The short definitions that begin many of the longer entries should be taken only as attempts at giving the general character of the term in question.

The wide-ranging reader must be prepared to find almost any term used in ways I have not mentioned. In particular, it can only mislead to offer brief and precise definitions of philosophical '—isms.' I have thus tried instead to bring out something of the general spirit of such terms, which often refer to features or aspects rather than to people or systems. Precision is similarly inapposite in recommending the use of a term like 'the causal theory of meaning' rather than 'causal theories of meaning'. Context or even whim will often decide whether one talks of different theories, or of variants of a single theory. Words like 'principle', 'law', 'rule', 'thesis', 'axiom', again, are usually used almost indifferently in phrases like 'the principle of . . .'.

The cross-references are denoted by small capitals (italic type simply picks terms out), and are of two kinds, within entries and self-standing. The former are given only when they seem useful. The term referred to is often mentioned in an approximate or abbreviated, but obvious, form. For example, the entry called 'conversion' might be referred to as 'converse'. The self-standing cross-references are not a guarantee that a term is treated fully, but they may be thought of as forming a sort of index. Terms with more than one word normally appear only once. RUSSELL'S PARADOX appears under R but not under P.

No single principle underlies the bibliographies. An item may be the original source of a notion, or a good, elementary, or accessible discussion, or a recent discussion from which previous ones can be traced, or a bibliographical source. I have mentioned certain reprintings of articles, but have not tried to be exhaustive, because space forbids and they are constantly being added to. I do not claim to have read everything mentioned, though I hope I have not mentioned things without adequate reason. The absence of a work is not of course a point against it. It may mean no more than that I have not come across it. Readers lucky enough to have access to P. Edwards (ed.), *The Encyclopaedia of Philosophy*, 8 vols, 1967, will no doubt use it anyway, so I have hardly ever referred to it, though I am immensely indebted to it myself. J. O. Urmson (ed.), *The Concise Encyclopaedia of Western Philosophy and Philosophers*, 1960, and D. Runes (ed.), *Dictionary of Philosophy*, 1942 (mainly its logical entries) have considerably helped me, and may also help the reader. The intermittent 'recent work in . . .' surveys in the *American Philosophical Quarterly* may also be mentioned.

Finally it is a pleasure to acknowledge the great help I have received from my friends and colleagues. Mr D. A. Lloyd Thomas, Dr D. M.

Preface

Tulloch, and Dr J. L. Watling have between them offered detailed comments on the entire manuscript, and each has made very significant contributions to both the merits of the work and the morale of its author. For similar comments on smaller portions I am greatly indebted to Dr W. A. Hodges, Miss R. L. Meager, Mr J. D. Valentine, and Professor P. G. Winch. Many other colleagues have helped me by answering queries and discussing individual points. I am also of course indebted to many philosophical publications, especially those mentioned in the bibliographies. The following among my non-philosophical colleagues have gone to great trouble in assisting me to communicate comprehensibly: Mrs J. H. Bloch, Prof. D. F. Cheesman, Dr G. Darlow, Dr D. R. Dicks, Dr M. R. Hoare, Dr E. Jacobs, Mr T. B. Taylor, Miss E. C. Vollans, Dr G. H. Wright. None of these, naturally, is responsible for what I have said, especially as I have occasionally gone my own way, and have made many alterations since they saw it. Mrs Helen Marshall has helped me to make a considerable number of improvements in my style and Dr Ted Honderich has been of great assistance to me in various ways in the later stages. I am also grateful to the Philosophy Department of Bedford College for allowing me two sabbatical terms to work on this book. And I am grateful to numerous typists and secretaries who have come to my aid in time of need.

Note

Cross-references which occur, preceded by 'See also', at the ends of articles may refer to the article as a whole, not just the last paragraph.

A

Abelard (Abailard), Pierre. 1079–1142. Born near Nantes, he lived and worked in France writing mainly on theology, logic and metaphysics, and ethics. His theology is sometimes thought to be rationalistic, subordinating faith to reason, though interpretations differ. He steered a middle course between realism and nominalism over UNIVERSALS, and his ethics particularly emphasized intention. His writings are of uncertain date, but include in theology *Theologia Christiana* and *Sic et Non*, in logic and metaphysics *Logica Ingredientibus* and *Dialectica*, and in ethics *Ethica* (or *Scito Teipsum*).

About. See REFERRING.

Acceptance, Acceptability. See CONFIRMATION, LOTTERY PARADOX.

Access. Philosophers have often claimed either that we alone have access to our own thoughts and sensations (*private access*) or that we alone have access by the most reliable route (*privileged access*). See also PRIVATE LANGUAGE.

N. Malcolm, 'The privacy of experience', in A. Stroll (ed.), *Epistemology*, 1967. (Discusses an ambiguity, and then the issue itself.)
A. R. Louch, 'Privileged access', *Mind*, 1965. (Debate in dialogue form.)

Achilles paradox. See ZENO'S PARADOXES.

Acrasia (Akrasia). See INCONTINENCE.

Action. The doing of something, or what is done. We talk of the action of rain, and of reflex actions, but action of the central kind is what is done by rational beings. Only they can *perform* actions. Acting usually involves moving in some way, or at least trying to move. This raises the problem how actions are related to movements. How is my raising my arm related to my arm's rising? What one intends is relevant here, and this involves the ways in which what happens can be viewed (cf. INTENSIONALITY). The

1

Action

same event may be viewed in many ways, e.g. making certain neurones in the brain fire, tightening one's arm-muscles, flexing one's finger, moving a piece of iron, pulling a trigger, firing a gun, heating a gun-barrel, shooting a man, shooting an ex-farmer, shooting the President, assassinating the President, earning a bribe, grieving a nation, starting a war.

How many of these are actions? How is an action distinguished from its consequence? Are pulling the trigger and starting the war one action, or two actions, or an action and one of its consequences? Actions may be unintentional, as when one frightens a bystander, or involuntary, as when one unwillingly reveals one's feelings by gasping, but perhaps something can only be an action when it is something an agent *could* set out to fulfil. Firing neurones might be an action if deliberately achieved by flexing one's finger, or even if the agent merely knew he *could* achieve it thus.

Further problems concern omissions, and cases of inaction, and negligence. Also can actions be caused? How is acting related to 'inner' mental events like silent thinking, to concepts like choosing, willing and trying? (cf. BASIC ACTION).

The relations between acts and actions are complex and disputed. 'Act' seems more of a technical term, especially in phrases like 'mental act' and SPEECH ACT, and less connected to responsibility, etc. See also EVENT.

G. Langford, *Human Action*, 1971. (Elementary discussion. Extensive bibliography.)

W. D. Ross, *The Right and the Good*, 1930, pp. 6–7.

A. I. Melden, *Free Action*, 1961. (Raising one's arm, etc.)

A. B. Cody, 'Can a single action have many different descriptions?', *Inquiry*, 1967. (Cf. R. E. Dowling's discussion and Cody's reply, ibid.)

A. Kenny, *Action, Emotion and Will*, 1963. (Chapter 7 distinguishes actions from relations.)

W. Cerf, Review of J. L. Austin, *How to Do Things with Words*, *Mind*, 1966, pp. 269–76, reprinted in K. T. Fann (ed.), *Symposium on J. L. Austin*, 1969, pp. 359–68. (Act and action.)

Action (philosophy of). See MIND.

Aesthetics. Roughly, that branch of philosophy concerned with the creation, value and experience of art and the analysis and solution of problems relating to these. Also called *philosophy of art*. The primary topic is the appreciation of art, and major problems centre on what makes something a work of art. Must it exhibit certain formal e.g. geometrical, properties (*formalism*), or express certain emotions, attitudes, etc. (*expressionism*), or do other things? What in fact is the role of pleasure and emotion, and are special types of them involved? Is there a special kind of value involved? Does the work of art embody special properties, like beauty, sublimity, prettiness, and if so, how are these related to its other properties? How relevant are the object's function, the context of production and the artist's intentions? Does it matter how a work was produced, whether difficulties had to be overcome, and whether it was a forgery? These latter questions, involving the artist, are balanced by questions about the appreciation of beauty, and other qualities, in nature, and how this relates to appreciation of art.

Many problems in aesthetics are parallel to problems in ethics. How are aesthetic terms and judgments to be analysed? Can such judgments be true or false, and how, if at all, can they be justified? Are there objective canons of taste? The relations between art and morality are especially relevant in literature, which can portray moral situations, and which has, like other arts, moral or psychological effects. Questions about the moral justification of producing works of art belong to ethics. Aesthetics, however, can ask whether a work's moral or psychological content is relevant to its aesthetic merit, and whether any subject-matters, such as pornography, are intrinsically inimical to aesthetic merit. Further questions cover the relations of art to wit and humour.

Metaphysical issues arise over the nature of a work of art. Is it a UNIVERSAL, or a paradigm, or a particular object, or is the answer different for different arts? Must a work of art be unique, or could it be created independently by different artists? And how is a work of art related to performances of it, where these are relevant? Philosophy of mind introduces questions about emotion, enjoyment, etc., and also about imitation or representation in the various arts: e.g. to what extent does fiction 'imitate' life? Fiction also raises questions of meaning and reference, which involve philosophy of language. What am I referring to when I mention Mr Pickwick? Can statements in fiction be true or false? Other questions concern phrases like 'gay tune', 'imaginative portrait': are the adjectives being used literally here?

Judgments on particular works of art do not properly belong to aesthetics, but general questions, like those about the 'golden section', concerning ways of achieving aesthetics value may. It is, however, no longer as obvious as it once seemed that positions on general aesthetic theory and judgments on particular works are independent of each other. (Cf. ETHICS for some considerations analogous to those in this paragraph.)

E. F. Carritt, *The Theory of Beauty*, 1914. (Introduction from point of view of what makes something a work of art.)

W. Charlton, *Introduction to Aesthetics*, 1970. (General introduction, with some emphasis on metaphysical issues.)

R. L. Saw, *Aesthetics: An Introduction*, 1972. (Rather discursive. Emphasizes more purely aesthetic issues.)

J. Hospers (ed.), *Introductory Readings in Aesthetics*, 1969. (Aimed at non-philosophers.)

E. H. Gombrich, *Art and Illusion*, 1960. (Emphasizes problems about representation.)

R. G. Collingwood, *The Principles of Art*, 1938.

R. Wollheim, *Art and its Objects*, 1968.

Affirmation of consequent. Fallacy of arguing that if the consequent of a

Albert the Great

conditional statement is true, so is the antecedent, e.g., 'If all cats are black, Tiddles is black; and Tiddles *is* black; so all cats are black.'

Albert the Great. c.1200–80. He worked mainly in Germany, where he was born. and in Paris (and taught AQUINAS in the 1240s). He contributed to empirical science, and is important chiefly as a pioneer in reconciling Greek and Arabic science and philosophy with Christianity, and also as translating Aristotle from Greek to Latin. He studied PLATO and ARISTOTLE partly through the eyes of the Neoplatonists and the Arabs. He wrote, among other things, commentaries on Aristotle and other Greek authors, and on the *Sentences* of Peter Lombard and at the end of his life a *Summa Theologiae*.

Alienans. An adjective is called alienans if it cancels the noun it qualifies in either of the following ways: a bogus policeman cannot be a policeman, and an alleged policeman need not be one. See also ATTRIBUTIVE.

Aliorelative. See REFLEXIVE.

Alternation. See CONJUNCTION.

Ambiguity. The property, had by some terms, of having two or more meanings. Ambiguity is not the same as *vagueness*. 'Bald' is vague (how many hairs can a bald man have?) but not ambiguous. An ambiguous term can be quite precise in each of its senses. Also it can be argued that ambiguity applies to terms, vagueness to concepts. 'How ambiguous is "ambiguous"?' is a favourite philosophical question. Ambiguity may apply to words, phrases and sentences, considered in the abstract, or to utterances considered as uttered on a given occasion.

'Bank', connected with rivers and money, may be treated as two words with the same sound but different meanings or as one word with different meanings. Philologists would call 'bank' two words if its uses have different etymologies, but philosophers often arbitrarily treat it as one word or two. Such words, especially in the second sense, are often called *equivocal*.

Phrases or sentences can be ambiguous while none of the words in them is so. In 'little girls' camp' either the girls or the camp may be little. This is sometimes called *amphiboly*.

The ambiguity of 'Jack hit James and Jill hit him' depends not on the *meaning* of 'him' but on who is being referred to by 'him' on the particular occasion of utterance. This and amphiboly are often called *syntactical ambiguity*. 'Ambiguity' itself is sometimes used in wider, sometimes in narrower, senses.

It is often hard to decide when to call a word ambiguous. 'Him' in the 'hitting' example is not really ambiguous, though it is sometimes said to have *ambiguity of reference*. Some words seem to have senses which differ, but are related. A healthy body is a flourishing one, while a healthy climate produces or preserves health and a healthy complexion is a sign of it. 'Healthy' is therefore often said to have *focal meaning* (Owen). Its senses 'focus' on one dominant sense. Words like 'big', which are syncategorematic (see CATEGORIES), have something like focal meaning, in that it makes a difference what standards we use in applying them. Something can be a big mouse without being a big animal, so that to call it simply 'big', without further ado, can be ambiguous.

When the ambiguities of an expression can be predicted according to a rule the expression has *systematic ambiguity*. On the theory of TYPES 'class' is systematically or TYPICALLY AMBIGUOUS because its meaning varies according to the type to which it belongs.

Other kinds of ambiguity include analogical and metaphorical uses of expressions, e.g. God is sometimes called 'wise' in a sense different from, though analogous to, that in which men are wise. Since many terms are ambiguous in this way when applied to God and men, this can be regarded as a case of systematic ambiguity; it is also related to focal meaning.

Some pervasive ambiguities are given special names, such as *process/ product ambiguity* of words like 'vision' which can mean power of seeing or something seen, or 'statement' which can mean act of stating or what is stated. Many philosophically important terms have this ambiguity. See also OPEN TEXTURE.

W. V. Quine, *Word and Object*, 1960, §§ 27-9. (Various kinds of ambiguity. § 26 discusses vagueness.)

W. Leszl, *Logic and Metaphysics in Aristotle*, 1970, part II, chapter 1. (Kinds of ambiguity in Aristotle.)

G. E. L. Owen, 'Logic and metaphysics in some earlier works of Aristotle', in I. During and G. E. L. Owen (eds), *Aristotle and Plato in the Mid-Fourth Century*, 1960, and 'Aristotle on the snares of ontology', in R. Bambrough (ed.), *New Essays in Plato and Aristotle*, 1965. (Discussions of focal meaning and its significance in Aristotle (small amount of Greek). Cf. esp. § 2 of latter, and also (for a related concept) R. Robinson, 'The concept of knowledge', *Mind*, 1971, p. 20.)

Amphiboly. See AMBIGUITY.

Analysis. See PHILOSOPHY.

Analytic. The analytic/synthetic distinction is first explicitly made by Kant. A proposition is analytic, on Kant's view, if the predicate is covertly contained in the subject, as in 'Roses are flowers'. A proposition where the predicate is attached to the subject but not contained in it is synthetic, as in 'Roses are red'. The contradictory of a synthetic proposition is always synthetic whereas the contradictory of an analytic proposition is usually called 'analytically false'. Kant's distinction was partly anticipated by Leibniz, who distinguished 'truths of reason' from 'truths of fact', and had the idea of containment, and by Hume, who distinguished 'relations between ideas' from 'matters of fact'.

Kant's distinction can easily be extended to conditional propositions,

5

Analytic

which are analytic if the consequent is contained in the antecedent, e.g. 'If this is a rose, it is a flower', and otherwise synthetic. Some other kinds of propositions raise difficulties, for instance, existential propositions like 'There exist black swans', and the notion of containment is hard to analyse in general. In 'Red roses are red' the containment is straightforwardly verbal. But in what sense precisely is the predicate 'contained' in the subject in 'Roses are flowers', or the consequent in the antecedent in 'If all men are mortal and Socrates is a man, then Socrates is mortal'?

Because of this difficulty Kant himself proposed an alternative definition now often adopted: a proposition is analytic if its negation is, or is reducible to, a contradiction or inconsistency; otherwise the proposition is synthetic. A proposition which is true because it exemplifies a certain logical FORM, as 'Bachelors are bachelors' exemplifies the form 'x's are x's', can be called *explicitly analytic*. A proposition which is true because of certain definitions, as 'Bachelors are male' is true because of the definition of 'bachelor', is *implicitly analytic* or *true by definition*. Explicitly analytic propositions, and sometimes implicitly analytic ones too, can be called *logically true* or *logically necessary*.

A proposition like 'Nothing is both red and green all over' seems to be true in virtue of the meanings of the words involved, but not true by definition: 'red' is not *defined* in terms of 'not green', nor 'green' in terms of 'not red'. This proposition therefore may be called analytic in a sense even wider than that of 'implicitly analytic'.

Recently the analytic/synthetic distinction has been attacked, especially by Quine, who argues that any clear account of the implicitly analytic would require notions like meaning, definition and synonymy, which themselves presuppose the implictly analytic. He also alleges that the point of calling something analytic is to give a reason why it cannot be revised in the light of experience, and then claims that no statements are immune to such revision; some statements are revisable with little effect on others (suppose 'I see a cat' is taken as true: it could be revised, i.e. rejected as false, by simply dismissing the experience as a hallucination). The rejection of other statements, such as the laws of logic, would profoundly affect our whole way of talking, but Quine thinks it is still possible. Scientific laws form an intermediate case. Thus Quine ends by saying that 'analytic' even in the narrow sense of 'explicitly analytic' cannot be applied absolutely, but at best as a matter of degree to those statements we are least willing to revise. Controversy still rages over this: is it simply that any sentence now expressing a logical truth could one day change its meaning and fail to do so, or is there more to it than this?

The distinction has also been attacked, in a less fundamental way, by Waismann, who claims that it is not a sharp one, and that statements such as 'I see with my eyes' and 'space has three dimensions' cannot be un-ambiguously classified in accordance with it.

A further problem about the analytic/synthetic distinction, for those who accept it, is how it relates to the A PRIORI/empirical and necessary/ contingent (see MODALITIES) distinctions. It is normally assumed that nothing can be both analytic and empirical, or both analytic and contingent (but see Bunge). Kant, though he took 'analytic' in the wider sense, as 'implicitly analytic', treated analytic propositions as trivial and uninformative, like TAUTOLOGIES. He and others have claimed that the propositions of mathematics, etc., must be synthetic a priori, while logical positivists and others have vigorously denied that anything can be both synthetic and a priori. Often the synthetic a priori, which is in practice generally assumed to coincide with the synthetic necessary, is defended merely by interpreting 'analytic' in a narrow sense. Thus the issue at least partly depends on distinguishing senses of 'analytic' and giving reasons for preferring one to another. It is still disputed whether a substantial notion of synthetic a priori is needed for statements like 'Nothing can be red and green all over', or 'If A exceeds B and B exceeds C then A exceeds C'; and also whether the laws of logic themselves can properly be called analytic. How too should we classify the statement itself that no synthetic statement is a priori?

Certain problems concern the relation between sentences and the statements they are used to make. Does 'The fat cow which I see is fat' make an analytic statement, although it apparently implies the synthetic statement that I do see a cow? And does 'I exist', since it cannot be uttered to make a false statement, make an analytic statement?

All the above must be distinguished from the question of the analytic and synthetic *methods*, deriving from Greek mathematics. See also MODALITIES, SENTENCE.

I. Kant, *Critique of Pure Reason*, Introduction, § 4.

W. V. Quine, 'Two dogmas of empiricism', in *From a Logical Point of View*, 1953, chapter 2.

H. P. Grice and P. F. Strawson, 'In defense of a dogma', *Philosophical Review*, 1956. (Defence of analyticity against Quine.)

F. Waismann, 'Analytic-synthetic' (in six parts), *Analysis*, 10, 11, 13 (1949–1953); reprinted in his *How I See Philosophy*, 1968.

D. Mitchell, *Introduction to Logic*, 1962, pp. 159–64. (Claims that 'analytic' properly applies to *sentences*.)

M. Bunge, 'Analyticity redefined', *Mind*, 1961. (Defends notion of analytic a posteriori).

A. Quinton, 'The a priori and the analytic', *Proceedings of the Aristotelian Society*, 1963–4. (Distinguishes several senses of 'analytic' and rejects synthetic a priori for each of them.)

L. Resnick, 'Do existent unicorns exist?', *Analysis*, 23, 1963, pp. 128 ff. ('Fat cow' example. Cf. J. J. Katz, *Linguistic Philosophy*, 1972, pp. 146–73; pp. 156–7 claim analytic sentences are not true.)

R. Descartes, *Reply to Second Objections* (to his *Meditations*), last few pages. (Analytic and synthetic methods.)

R. Robinson, 'Analysis in Greek geometry', *Mind*, 1936, reprinted in his *Essays in Greek Philosophy*, 1969. (Greek origins of analytic and synthetic methods.)

Analytical hypothesis. See TRANSLATION.

And

And. See CONJUNCTION.

Angst, Angoisse. See EXISTENTIALISM.

Anselm, St. 1033–1109. Born in Aosta, he studied in France and became archbishop of Canterbury in 1093. He is best known for originating the 'ONTOLOGICAL ARGUMENT' for God's existence in his *Proslogion* (his *Monologion* contains related proofs of God's existence). He also wrote on truth (*De Veritate*) and on logic and problems such as that of universals (*De Grammatico*).

D. P. Henry, *The Logic of St. Anselm*, 1967. (Henry has also translated the *De Grammatico*, 1964.)

Antilogism. An inconsistent set of three propositions. The two premises of a valid SYLLOGISM with the CONTRADICTORY of its conclusion, or more generally three propositions, any two of which entail the contradictory of the third. Also called *inconsistent triad*. The *principle of antilogism* says that if two propositions together entail a third, then either of them and the contradictory of the third together entail the other, e.g. if 'All men are mortal' and 'Socrates is a man' together entail 'Socrates is mortal', then 'All men are mortal' and 'Socrates is not mortal' together entail 'Socrates is not a man'.

Apodictic. See MODALITIES.

Aporetic. Raising and discussing problems without offering definitive solutions.

A posteriori. See A PRIORI.

Apperception. In Leibniz, reflective consciousness rather than mere passive perception. In Kant, consciousness of oneself as a unity, on the empirical or transcendental level. Other writers use the term in fairly similar senses. Perhaps the unifying thread in its main senses is awareness of the self as that which judges. It plays little part in contemporary philosophy.

A priori. *A priori* and its opposite *empirical* or *a posteriori* apply primarily to concepts, notions or ideas and to propositions, statements or judgments. Roughly, a priori means 'prior to experience' and empirical means 'based on experience', the experience of the five senses and perhaps introspection. However, the terms are ambiguous. An a priori concept may be any of the following: (i) A concept we can acquire without our being presented with an instance in experience, and without having to construct it from concepts so presented. We construct *unicorn* from *horse* and *horn*. (ii) A concept we *must* so acquire because experience could not supply us with it. Here there are the concepts of validity and negation. (iii) A concept we can acquire without any experience at all, or never acquire but have always had. Substance and cause may be examples. (iv) A concept we can apply without using experience. We do not use the senses to find whether an argument is *valid*.

Questions about the temporal order in which we actually acquire concepts are psychological, but they are often confused with philosophical questions about how we can or must acquire them, or what justifies us in applying them. Perhaps some concepts must in some sense be a priori, if we need concepts before having experiences, in order to classify or distinguish the experiences. Much depends here on what we mean by 'having' a CONCEPT. A priori concepts are sometimes called *innate ideas*, and it is disputed how far 'innate' is a justified term. Interest in innate ideas has increased because of the claims of certain linguists, notably Chomsky, to the effect that we have an innate tendency to learn and use certain grammatical structures more easily than others.

With propositions experience may enter in two ways, giving us the concepts involved, and telling us that the proposition is true. An a priori proposition may be any of the following: (i) A proposition we know from birth. (ii) A proposition we know, or can know, as soon as we acquire the relevant concepts. For example, once we acquire the concepts *red* and *green* we can know that nothing is simultaneously red and green all over. (iii) A proposition we cannot understand without knowing it to be true. (iv) A proposition we cannot learn from experience. Kant especially emphasized this. The relations between these senses are complex, and psychology and philosophy can be entangled here. A mere belief, held from birth but which experience could refute, would be instinctive but not a priori.

The concepts in an a priori proposition may or may not be themselves a priori in any one sense. When they are all a priori the proposition can be called *absolutely a priori*, e.g. 'No proposition is both true and false'; otherwise the proposition is *relatively a priori*, e.g. 'Nothing is simultaneously red and green all over'. Relatively a priori could also apply to the everyday sense in which an empirical proposition is knowable independently of a given context, as when a detective says, 'I haven't yet found any clues, but I know a priori that money is a motive for murder'. This use, like that where 'a priori' means 'arbitrary' or 'dogmatic', does not normally occur in philosophy though there are traces of it in Kant.

It has usually been assumed that for any given sense of 'a priori' and the corresponding sense of 'empirical' every proposition is either a priori or empirical. But sometimes a proposition is not derived from experience, nor known a priori, but simply postulated.

Propositions like 'Every event has a cause', when this is simply postulated as a regulative principle to guide scientific procedure can be called *non-empirical*. Often, however, such propositions are classed as a priori or, sometimes, 'weak' a priori. 'Non-empirical' can also cover the a priori in general. A related notion is the *pragmatic a priori* (Lewis), applied to propositions we decide by fiat to make immune to falsification by experience (e.g. 'through a point not on a given straight line infinitely many straight lines parallel to the given one can be drawn', as a postulate of a non-Euclidean geometry).

Special problems concern how the a priori/empirical distinction relates to others, and particularly whether there are any synthetic a priori propositions (see ANALYTIC).

Sometimes, especially in older literature, 'empirical' is used for EMPIRICIST. The restriction of 'empirical' to meaning 'based on simple INDUCTION, or on unsystematic trial and error' is now outdated in philosophy.

Originally, in Aristotelian philosophy, a proposition was a priori if it was based on, or inferred from, something prior to it in the sense of being its cause or ground. A proposition was a posteriori if it was inferred from its effects. When it was later assumed that the main way of knowing a proposition through its effects was to know it through sense-experience, 'empirical' largely replaced 'a posteriori', and 'a priori' took on the meanings described above. See also RATIONALISM.

Aristotle, *Posterior Analytics*, I, 1, 2.

I. Kant, *Critique of Pure Reason*, 2nd edn 1787, B, 1–6.

D. W. Hamlyn, *Theory of Knowledge*, 1970, chapter 9. (General discussion of a priori knowledge.)

J. Locke, *Essay concerning Human Understanding*, 1689, book 1. (Attacks one version of innate ideas. Criticized by G. W. Leibniz, *New Essays concerning Human Understanding*, 1765, written earlier.)

A. Quinton, *The Nature of Things*, 1973, pp. 132–3. (A priori and instinctive.)

C. I. Lewis, 'The pragmatic conception of the a priori', *Journal of Philosophy*, 1923, reprinted in H. Feigl and W. Sellars (eds), *Readings in Philosophical Analysis*, 1949.

J. Lyons, *Chomsky*, 1970. (Elementary introduction to his ideas.)

Aquinas, St Thomas. c.1224–74. Of Italian origin, he worked in the university of Paris and elsewhere. His work largely consisted in continuing the efforts of his teacher ALBERT THE GREAT to reconcile Greek philosophy with Christianity, and he was similarly influenced by the Arabs. He went beyond Albert in the extent to which he created a full-blooded philosophy, based on that of ARISTOTLE but developed so as to fit in with Christian dogma; this involved original treatments of notions like BEING and analogy. He wrote prolifically, but his philosophical work is largely contained in monographs on particular questions, e.g. *De Ente et Essentia* (c.1253), *Quaestiones Disputatae de Potentia Dei* (c.1265), and in more general works like *Quaestiones Disputatae de Veritate* (1256–9), and in commentaries on Aristotle's main philosophical writings. It is summed up in the *Summa de Veritate Catholicae Fidei contra Gentiles* (c.1259–64) and the *Summa Theologica* (c.1265–73). He is also known for his 'five ways' of proving God's existence (see RELIGION). His philosophy, with that of his followers, is called Thomism. See also AUGUSTINE, COSMOLOGICAL, MARITAIN, METAPHYSICS, OCKHAM, ONTOLOGICAL ARGUMENT, PHILOSOPHY, SCOTUS, SUBSTANCE.

Argument. See FUNCTION.

Aristotle. 384–22 BC. Pupil of PLATO, after whose death he travelled round the Aegean (and was tutor to Alexander the Great), and then founded Lyceum in Athens (335 BC; also called Peripatos; hence 'Peripatetics'). His interests were encyclopaedic, and he contributed to most of the main branches of philosophy and natural science, as well as initiating the systematic study of logic. His major works of current interest include the *Organon* (set of treatises mainly on logic), *Metaphysics, Physics, De Anima (On the Soul), Nichomachean Ethics, Politics, Poetics* (fragmentary). See also ALBERT, AMBIGUITY, A PRIORI, AQUINAS, AUGUSTINE, BACON, BRENTANO, BEING, CATEGORIES, CAUSATION, COSMOLOGICAL, DIALECTIC, DIFFERENTIA, ELENCHUS, ENTELECHY, ETHICS, EXPLANATION, FORM, FREEWILL, FUNCTION (bibliography, last item), GOOD, INCONTINENCE, LOGIC, MEANING, METAPHYSICS, MIND, MODALITIES, NEOPLATONISTS, OCKHAM, PLENITUDE, POLITICAL, PROPERTY, REASON, SCOTUS, SENSES, SOCRATES, SPACE, SUBSTANCE, SYLLOGISM, TRANSCENDENTAL ARGUMENTS, TRUTH, UNIVERSALS, ZENO'S PARADOXES.

Arrow paradox. See ZENO'S PARADOXES.

Art (philosophy of). See AESTHETICS.

Assertion sign. The symbol '⊢' invented by Frege, who drew its two parts from a complex system of symbols. It means either that what follows it is being asserted and not merely mentioned for consideration, or, more usually, that what follows *can* be asserted as a truth of logic, or as a theorem in a system. 'p, q ⊢r' normally means that proposition r is assertible if propositions p and q are given as true.

Assertoric. See MODALITIES.

Attributive. An adjective stands in *attributive* position if it precedes its noun ('A *red* house'), and in *predicative* position if it occurs after a verb ('The house is *red*'). It is grammatically attributive if it can only occur attributively ('veritable'), and grammatically predicative if it can only occur predicatively ('well'). It is logically attributive if a significant noun or equivalent must always be understood after it. 'That mouse is *large*' means 'That mouse is a large mouse'—it need not be a large animal. 'Logically predicative' has no application. See also CATEGORIES, GOOD.

J. Brentlinger, 'Incomplete predicates and the two-world theory of the *Phaedo*', *Phronesis*, 1972, p. 71 note 13. (Brief discussion, with references.)

Augustine, St. 354–430. Born in North Africa, he was converted to Christianity in his early thirties, and became bishop of Hippo in 395 or 396.

Austin, John L.

His philosophical interests turned progressively into theological ones, and he strongly influenced medieval thought, in ways somewhat contrasting with the current represented by ARISTOTLE and AQUINAS. His personal religious experience strongly urged him to extricate himself from scepticism, and led him to study the types of knowledge (perception, reason, etc.). He attempted to work out the nature of man in a Christian framework, and studied problems concerning the universe and its creation, the mind/body problem, freewill, and, now often regarded as his most lasting philosophical contribution, the nature of time (see SPACE). He also discussed ethical and (in the *City of God*) political topics. He started from a generally PLATONIC and NEOPLATONIC base. His important writings containing philosophical material include the *Confessions* (400), *De Libero Arbitrio* (freewill, and proof of God's existence), *City of God* (late in life and largely theological), *De Genesi ad Litteram* (late; a commentary on Genesis).

Austin, John L. 1911–60. British philosopher who worked in Oxford, where he was one of the leaders of 'linguistic PHILOSOPHY' after the Second World War. He emphasized the philosophical significance of the nuances of ordinary language, and is mainly noted for his theory of SPEECH ACTS. 'Ifs and Cans', 1960. 'A Pleas for Excuses', 1956. (Two lectures relevant to FREEWILL, and reprinted in his *Collected Papers*, 1961.) *Sense and Sensibilia*, 1962 (attacks AYER'S SENSE-DATUM theory). *How to Do Things with Words*, 1962 (main source for speech act theory). See also CONDITIONALS, EPISTEMOLOGY, LANGUAGE (PHILOSOPHY OF), MEANING, SCEPTICISM, TRUTH.

    John Austin (1790–1859) was a legal philosopher noted mainly for his theory that the law is the command of the soveriegn. *The Province of Jurisprudence Determined*, 1832.

Autological. See HETEROLOGICAL.

Avowals. Certain first-person utterances, like 'I am in pain', which when sincere seem to be infallible. Another person saying 'He is in pain' about oneself could be mistaken. Problems arise about whether avowals can, or need, be justified, and whether they are assertions.

D. Gasking, 'Avowals', M. E. Lean, 'Mr Gasking on avowals', in R. J. Butler (ed.), *Analytical Philosophy*, 1st series, 1962. (Relation of avowals to justification and fallibility.)
F. E. Sparshott, 'Avowals and their uses', *Proceedings of the Aristotelian Society*, 1961–2. (Avowals and their relations to similar utterances.)

Axiology. See ETHICS.

Axiom system. Any system wherein certain expressions are derived in accordance with a given set of rules from an initial set of expressions taken as given (and called *axioms*). The axioms themselves of such a system form an *axiom set*. 'Axiom system' is often used for 'axiom set', as by Tarski.

Ayer, Sir Alfred J.

The *formation rules* specify what elements or symbols the system is going to use and what combinations of them are to count as expressions which can serve as axioms or be tested to see whether they can be derived from the axioms. These expressions are called *well-formed formulae* or *wff*, for short, and those of them which can be derived from the axioms are called *theorems*. The formation rules are like rules of grammar, and the wff like meaningful sentences. The axioms themselves will count as theorems if, as in most systems, they are trivially derivable from themselves. For reasons of economy and elegance the axioms should be *independent*, i.e. not derivable within the given system from each other. The axioms may be infinite in number, provided rules for selecting them are given. Such a rule will define an *axiom scheme* by saying 'All wff of such and such a kind are to count as axioms'. The *transformation rules* say what wff can be derived from others, and so govern what the theorems of the system will be, given the axioms.

In an abstract axiom system the expressions are simply symbols, or marks on paper. But if the system is applied to a certain subject-matter we have a MODEL or *interpretation* of the system, and the subject-matter is said to be *axiomatized*. To axiomatize a subject is thus to systematize it, and show how most of it can be derived if certain selected axioms and transformation rules are taken for granted. These are so selected that the system shall be CONSISTENT and, where possible, COMPLETE. The axioms are therefore either true propositions, which need not be simple or obvious, or propositions which can be postulated as true without leading to contradiction, as in non-Euclidean geometries (see SPACE). The transformation rules are related to VALIDITY as the axioms are to truth. See also MODELS, BOOLEAN ALGEBRA.

A. Tarski, *Introduction to Logic*, 1941, chapter 6.

Ayer, Sir Alfred J. 1910–. British philosopher who has worked mostly in Oxford and London. He introduced logical POSITIVISM to Britain in 1936, and has since then defended a generally empiricist outlook, concentrating mainly on perception and meaning, as well as writing various historical books. *Language, Truth and Logic,* 1936, 2nd edn 1946. *The Foundations of Empirical Knowledge,* 1940 (the book criticized by AUSTIN). *Philosophical Essays,* 1954. *The Problem of Knowledge,* 1956. *Probability and Evidence,* 1972. *The Central Questions of Philosophy,* 1973. See also BASIC STATEMENTS, NEGATION, PHENOMENALISM, PRAGMATISM, PROBABILITY, SENSE DATA, SENTENCES.

B

Bacon, Francis. 1561–1626. Philosopher, essayist and politician, he was born and lived in London, was created Lord Verulam and Viscount St Albans, and appointed Lord Chancellor. His main philosophical work lay in philosophy of science, where he tried to replace what he saw as the a priorism of the Aristotelian tradition by a new and thoroughgoing empiricism. His political writings rely heavily on the scientific optimism which he thought this method justified. *Essays*, 1597, expanded later. *The Proficience and Advancement of Learning*, 1605 (later revised as *De Dignitate et Augmentis Scientiarum* 1623), *Novum Organum*, 1620 (the title contrasts with ARISTOTLE's *Organon*. This and the *De Dignitate et Augmentis* form part of the projected *Instauratio Magna*). *New Atlantis*, 1627 (a scientific Utopia). See also MILL.

Bacon, Roger (died 1292) was a student of sciences and languages, who wrote commentaries on various works of Aristotle and tried to institute a 'universal science'.

Bad faith. In Sartre a kind of self-deception, where this involves behaving as a mere thing rather than realizing, in acts of authentic choice, the true type of being for a man (what Sartre calls 'existence', or being 'pour soi' and not merely 'en soi'). This distinction is metaphysical, but has moral effects, for in 'bad faith' we evade responsibility and 'anxiety' by 'not noticing' possibilities of choice, or behaving in a role others expect of us. See also EXISTENTIALISM, INCONTINENCE.

J.-P. Sartre, *Being and Nothingness*, 1943, transl. 1956, part 1, chapter 2.
H. Fingarette, *Self-Deception*, 1969. (Self-deception in general. Cf. D. W. Hamlyn, H. O. Mounce, 'Self-deception', *Proceedings of the Aristotelian Society*, supplementary vol. 1971.)

Barber paradox. Does a barber who only shaves all those not shaving themselves shave himself? Less important than LIAR PARADOX, etc., because there is no reason impelling us to assert the existence of such a barber.

14

Basic action. Action not involving further action as its cause, or which we do not perform by performing another action, e.g. moving our hands, but not steering our car, which we do *by* moving our hands.

A. Baier, 'The search for basic actions', *American Philosophical Quarterly*, 1971. (Develops and criticizes the notion, giving references.)

Basic statements. Also sometimes called *protocol statements* (*sentences*) or (by Carnap) *primitive protocol statements*. Statements which, according to logical POSITIVISTS in particular, are needed as the basis for the rest of our empirical knowledge. But the various conceptions of them have little else in common. Their subject-matter varies, with different writers, from immediate personal experience to the common world. Their role may be to give a foundation for the individual's own knowledge (Ayer), or for INTERSUBJECTIVELY testable knowledge (O. Neurath). In a variant of the latter role they provide tools for testing universal hypotheses, and are therefore themselves mainly singular existential statements, saying that something exists or occurs at a certain place and date (Popper; e.g. the statement 'There is a black swan in Sydney now' could be used to test the hypothesis 'All swans are white').

R. Carnap, *The Unity of Science*, 1934, esp. pp. 43–4.
A. J. Ayer, *Language, Truth and Logic*, 1936. (See 2nd edn 1946, p. 10.)
O. Neurath, 'Protocol sentences', in A. J. Ayer (ed.), *Logical Positivism*, 1959 (trans. from German original in *Erkenntnis*, vol. 3, 1932–3).
K. R. Popper, *The Logic of Scientific Discovery*, 1934, (transl. 1959), esp. §§ 28–9.

Bayes's Theorem. Theorem of PROBABILITY calculus, variously formulated and developed by and after T. Bayes (1702–61). Briefly, where p and q are propositions, the probability of p, given q, is that of q, given p, multiplied by the independent probability of p and divided by the independent probability of q. The independent probability of a proposition is the probability it has by itself, not its probability 'given' another proposition. 'Bayesian' inductive procedures take the theorem to imply that the increase in probability which a hypothesis gains when its consequences are verified is proportional to the improbability of those consequences. The theorem's validity is undisputed, but its applications and usefulness are controversial (cf. CONFIRMATION). One form of the law of large NUMBERS, unrelated to the above, is also sometimes called 'Bayes's theorem'.

Beauty. Property of an object giving rise to pleasure or approval, the latter requiring justification in terms of the characteristics of the object. Less favoured now in aesthetics because too narrow, unless artificially widened to cover all aesthetic value; ugliness can be valued, as pain can be liked. Various theories of its meaning exist: It may stand for a felt or intuited quality, or for a causal property evoking a special reaction in the speaker, or in people generally; or it may have meaning by expressing non-possessive love (a SPEECH ACT view of its meaning). Kant distinguished beauty into 'free' (pure patterns, etc.) and 'dependent' (where the patterns, etc. which are acceptable are limited by the kind of object in question). Others, from Plato onwards, have seen a similar distinction between formal and expressive or representative beauty, though the whole distinction has been disputed.

I Kant, *Critique of Judgment*, 1790, part 1, § 16.
E. F. Carritt, *The Theory of Beauty*, 1914, chapters 5, 10.

Bedeutung. See MEANING.

Behaviour. What an object, particularly a living creature, does. There are problems and ambiguities: is intention, or at least controllability, needed? Are heart-beats behaviour? Must behaviour affect the outer world and be publicly observable? Is silent thinking behaviour? Must behaviour described in one way (e.g. waving one's arms) also be behaviour when described in another (accidentally breaking a vase)? Can the utterances of a parrot be called verbal behaviour? Should an uncontrollable reflex action, like a knee-jerk, be called behaviour of the knee but not of the man? See also ACTION.

D. W. Hamlyn, 'Behaviour', *Philosophy*, 1953. (Revised on one point in his 'Causality and human behaviour', *Proceedings of the Aristotelian Society*, supplementary vol. 1964.)

G. H. von Wright, *Explanation and Understanding*, 1971, p. 193, n.8. (Knee-jerk.)

Behaviourism. Doctrine or policy of reducing mental concepts to publicly observable BEHAVIOUR. In psychology it involves an experimental, and often physicalist and operationalist approach (see POSITIVISM), which rejects introspection, and is concerned with prediction and control rather than understanding. *Logical* or *analytic behaviourism* defines mentalistic terms using only behaviour and physiology. *Metaphysical* or *philosophical behaviourism* accepts only physical behaviour for claims about the mental. *Methodological behaviourism* insists on behavioural tests but is neutral on the philosophical implications. *Radical behaviourism* is similar, but more rigorous: it rejects hypothetical constructs and intervening variables (see LOGICAL CONSTRUCTIONS).

Being. Roughly, property common to everything that there is. Sometimes different kinds of being are distinguished. Existence is sometimes distinguished from subsistence and other notions. Meinong, for instance, thought that material objects in space and time *exist*, along with other things in space and time like shadows and gravitational fields, while things like UNIVERSALS, numbers and the difference between red and green, *subsist*. Fictional or imaginary objects, which can be concrete (unicorns) or abstract (the prime number between eight and ten), are sometimes said to subsist, but for Meinong they neither exist nor subsist; he says simply that they 'are objects' and have *Sosein* which means, literally, being so, or essence. But 'exist' and 'subsist', like 'existent' and 'subsistent', are often used interchangeably, especially when it is said that certain things, such as universals, do have being in some sense, and are not, as *nominalism* holds, analysable in terms of mere words.

Existence and subsistence, etc. can here be regarded as different grades or kinds of being. One strand of idealism treats being rather as having different degrees. Reality as a whole, the 'absolute', exists fully, while its parts derive their reality from their relations to it and to each other, and exist, but less fully, in proportion to their comprehensiveness.

Carnap divided questions of existence into those internal and external to a given system, e.g. that of arithmetic. 'Is there a prime number between six and nine?' is an internal question and belongs to arithmetic. 'Do numbers exist?' is an external question and belongs to philosophy, along with similar questions about universals, propositions, etc.

These various problems about fictional and timeless objects connect metaphysics with philosophical logic, and two further questions arise here. First, how do we tell to what ontology (i.e. list of things that are) a philosopher has committed himself? What counts as holding that, e.g. universals do or do not exist? Quine introduced this question to replace the traditional question. 'What is there?' He answered with the slogan, 'to be is to be the value of a variable'. I.e. we are committed to the reality of a thing or kind of things if and only if we cannot state our views in formal (i.e. logical) language without using affirmative statements where VARIABLES ranging over the thing or things in question are bound by the existential quantifier (see QUANTIFICATION). The second question is what the laws of logic themselves commit us to. In particular can we prove by logic alone that there must be at least one object? By the predicate CALCULUS (letting 'F' stand for some predicate and '*a*' for any arbitrary individual) the undeniable logical truth 'Everything is F or not F' implies '*a* is F or not F'. This in turn implies 'At least one thing is F or not F', and therefore that there is at least one thing. Various attempts to avoid this have been made. Both these questions are bound up with the interpretation of 'is' in the existential quantifier. Does it signify existence in a substantial sense, and if not, then what does it signify?

A further logical question, particularly important in connexion with the ONTOLOGICAL ARGUMENT, is whether being or existence is strictly speaking a predicate (or property). This involves asking what counts as a predicate or property.

Aristotle insisted that being, like unity, could not be a genus, and also that to call something one or existent is not to add to its description. Out of this arose the medieval doctrine of *transcendentals*. Aquinas listed 'being', 'one', 'true', 'thing', 'something', 'good' as transcending the CATEGORIES and applying to everything. Some other writers, e.g. Duns Scotus, use 'transcendentals' rather more widely, and Aristotle said of 'good' not, with Aquinas, that everything real was somehow good, but that 'good' was predicable in all the categories—a substance, quality,

Being

relation, etc. could be good. These transcendentals are usually included among the syncategorematic terms (see CATEGORIES (end)). They were intended to delineate the characteristics of *being qua being*, another notion originating in Aristotle, who made it the subject matter of metaphysics. This phrase uses the participle 'being' as in 'human being', not the gerund as in 'being fat is unhealthy', and sometimes the plural, 'beings qua beings'. Interpretations of it differ. It may refer to everything that is, considered just as being, or to something which somehow accounts for the being of everything else. This may be substance in general or the highest kind of substance like God, or the movers of the cosmic spheres. On this latter view God and the movers account for the being of other substances, and substance accounts for that of qualities, relations, etc.

A thing's essence, or what it is, can be contrasted with its existence, but in the case of God these have been thought by Aquinas to coincide. But the sense of 'existence' ('esse') here is controversial.

In some forms of existentialism being is contrasted with existence. Being belongs to animals and inanimate things, and existence only to men, who can create themselves and are not mere products of the environment.

A linguistic question concerns the different senses often ascribed to the verb 'to be'. The main senses are: existential ('These things shall be', 'There is . . .'), predicative or copulative ('This is red'), classifying ('This is a shoe'; often subsumed under predicative), identifying ('This is Socrates', 'Tully is Cicero'). Other senses, some rather technical, have been suggested, including constitutive ('This house is bricks and mortar') and presentational ('The meaning of "bald" is: *hairless*'). Sometimes 'is' signifies the present tense as in 'He is hot', but sometimes it is timeless as in 'Twice two is four' or 'Chaucer is earlier than Shakespeare'. What makes these senses different is that different things can be inferred from statements made by sentences containing them. 'Tully is Cicero' implies 'Cicero is Tully', but 'This book is red' does not imply 'Red is this book', where 'red' is the subject. But these differences are complex and controversial in detail, and so is the question what, if anything, links the senses together. (Aristotle thought at least some senses were linked by 'focal meaning': see AMBIGUITY.) Some think the attempt to distinguish definite senses is mistaken. See also SUBSTANCE, REFERRING.

J. Barnes, *The Ontological Argument*, 1972, chapter 3. (Existence.)
L. Linsky, *Referring*, 1967. (Discusses theories of Meinong and later writers.)
Plato. Relevant passages include *Republic*, 476e ff., *Timaeus*, 27d.
C. Crittenden, 'Fictional existence', *American Philsophical Quarterly*, 1966.
R. Carnap, *Meaning and Necessity*, 2nd edn 1956, supplement A, § 2, reprinted in C. Landesman (ed.), *The Problem of Universals*, 1971. (External and internal questions.)
W. V. Quine, 'On what there is', in *Review of Metaphysics*, 1948, reprinted in his book *From a Logical Point of View*, 1953, in L. Linsky (ed.), *Semantics and the Philosophy of Language*, 1952, in Landesman (above), and (with comments and contributions from others on the same theme)

Belief

in *Proceedings of the Aristotelian Society*, supplementary vol. 1951. ('To be is to be the value of a variable'.)

G. J. Warnock, 'Metaphysics in logic', in A. Flew (ed.), *Essays in Conceptual Analysis*, 1956. (Criticizes Quine's use of logic to solve ontological problems.)

W. Sellars, 'Grammar and existence: a preface to ontology', *Mind*, 1960, reprinted in Landesman (above). (Rather more technical criticism of Quine.)

L. J. Cohen, *The Diversity of Meaning*, 1962, § 33. (Does logic prove the universe cannot be empty?)

W. C. Kneale and G. E. Moore, 'Is existence a predicate?', *Proceedings of the Aristotelian Society*, supplementary vol., 1936.

I. Kant, *Critique of Pure Reason*, 1781, revised 1787, B626–9. (Classic attack on existence as predicate.)

Aristotle, *Metaphysics*, 998b22–5 (Being not a genus; cf. *Topics*, 144a32–b4); 1003b26 ('One' and 'existent' not descriptive; cf. 1045a36–b8); Book 4, chapters 1–3; book 6, chapter 1 (Being qua being). *Nicomachean Ethics*, 1096a19–29. ('Good'.)

J. Owens, *The Doctrine of Being in the Aristotelian Metaphysics*, 1951, 2nd edn 1963. (Full discussion of Aristotle on being qua being, and focal meaning (though not so called). Requires Greek.)

P. T. Geach, 'Form and existence', *Proceedings of the Aristotelian Society*, 1954–5, reprinted in A. Kenny (ed.), *Aquinas*, 1969. (Essence and existence.)

D. Wiggins, *Identity and Spatio-Temporal Continuity*, 1967, p. 10. (Constitutive being.)

J. J. Valberg, 'Improper singular terms', *Proceedings of the Aristotelian Society*, 1970–1, p. 132. (Presentational being.)

C. H. Kahn, 'The Greek verb "to be" and the concept of being', *Foundations of Language*, 1966. (Attacks rigidity of distinction into senses.)

Belief. Assent to or acceptance of the truth of propositions, statements or facts. Also acquiescence in the existence or truth of something. We can believe people, books, etc., as well as propositions. But can we believe TAUTOLOGIES, and even contradictions? Where p is a proposition, can we believe p and believe not-p? And does this entail believing p-and-not-p? Also can we believe what we know is false or regard as improbable, and can we be mistaken about whether we believe something? When are beliefs justified? These questions link belief with knowledge and rationality (see EPISTEMOLOGY).

We can 'believe in' the existence, occurrence, truth, validity, or value of something, or in something we think ought to be or occur. We often use 'believe in' for what is good rather than bad; we 'believe in' Smith's generosity but not his malevolence.

To analyse belief is largely to study its connexions with actions, dispositions and inner experiences, and with the mere entertaining of propositions. But 'believe' is often a *parenthetical verb*: 'I believe it's raining' is meant to be about the weather, not about the speaker. Further questions

Bentham, Jeremy

concern how far belief is voluntary, and whether we can have a duty to believe (the *ethics of belief*). See also JUDGMENT.

A. P. Griffiths (ed.), *Knowledge and Belief*, 1967. (Articles and bibliography, with introduction.)

H. H. Price, 'Belief "in" and belief "that"', *Religious Studies*, 1965, reprinted in B. Mitchell (ed.), *The Philosophy of Religion*, 1971.

Bentham, Jeremy. 1748–1832. Moral, political and legal philosopher, who was born in London and worked mainly there. He is generally regarded as the first major UTILITARIAN thinker, though he also had some interest in the theory of meaning, where he held a nominalist position, treating abstract entities as 'fictions'; this position underlay his treatment of moral and legal notions. He also devoted much of his writing to working out the practical applications of his theoretical views, in such fields as prison reform and the writing of constitutions. *A Fragment on Government*, 1776 (attacks the then fashionable legal theorist W. Blackstone). *An Introduction to the Principles of Morals and Legislation*, 1789.

Bergson, Henri. 1859–1941. Worked mostly in his native Paris. He is perhaps most famous for his doctrine of 'creative evolution', which tried to supplement Darwinism by postulating an *élan vital* which causes variations as species develop. He combined this with a double view of time, as time in physics and time as experienced (durée), of which only the latter was continuous and flowing. He also made a famous study of laughter and the comic. *Essai sur les données immédiates de la conscience*, 1889 (time and freewill). *Matière et mémoire*, 1896. *Le Rire*, 1900. *L'Evolution créatrice*, 1907. *Les Deux Sources de la morale et de la religion*, 1932. See also MARITAIN, METAPHYSICS.

Berkeley, George. 1685–1753. Born in Kilkenny he lived mainly in Ireland, though with visits abroad, including one to America, and he became bishop of Cloyne. He is considered one of the 'British EMPIRICISTS', and his philosophy starts from LOCKE's 'new way of ideas', but rejects abstract ideas and the possibility of real existence outside perception. The slogan 'esse est percipi' ('to be is to be perceived') sums up much of his philosophy, which is commonly known as 'subjective IDEALISM', though he himself called it 'immaterialism'. However, among percipients Berkeley included God. *An Essay towards a New Theory of Vision*, 1709. *A Treatise concerning the Principles of Human Knowledge*, 1710. *Three Dialogues between Hylas and Philonous in Opposition to Sceptics and Atheists*, 1713. *De Motu*, 1721 (on motion). *Alciphron, or the Minute Philosopher*, 1732 (largely theological, but with philosophical passages). See also SENSATION, SUBJECTIVISM.

Bernoulli's theorem. See NUMBERS.

Berry's paradox. The phrase 'the least integer not nameable in fewer than nineteen syllables' seems to name a number. But the number concerned must be not nameable in fewer than nineteen syllables since the phrase does name it, yet nameable in fewer since the phrase itself has only eighteen. The paradox is of the kind sometimes called semantic (see PARADOX, and also RUSSELL'S PARADOX, TYPES).

Bertrand's box paradox. Three boxes hold respectively two gold coins, two silver, one of each. A coin drawn randomly is gold. What is the probability that the other coin in the same box is gold? The box chosen must be double gold or mixed, so the probability is a half. Yet the coin must be the first or second in the gold box, or the gold in the mixed box; two of these three alternatives make the other coin gold, so the probability is two thirds. The paradox affects the classical theory of PROBABILITY, by suggesting that it is indefinite what the alternatives are.

Bertrand's paradox. What is the probability that a random chord of a circle exceeds the side of an inscribed equilateral triangle? It is longer if its midpoint lies on the inner half of the radius bisecting it, so, since the midpoint may lie anywhere on this radius, the probability is a half. It is also longer if its midpoint lies within a concentric circle with half the original radius, so, since the area of this inner circle is a quarter that of the original circle, the probability is a quarter. Other answers exist, and the paradox has many variants. It affects the classical theory of PROBABILITY, by showing a difficulty in dividing up infinitely many alternatives.

Best (principle of). See SUFFICIENT REASON.

Better. Not always the comparative of 'good'. Something can be 'better but not yet good', and it may be easier to decide whether one thing is better than another than whether either is good.

A. Sloman, 'How to derive "better" from "is" ', *American Philosophical Quarterly*, 1969. (Makes 'better' more fundamental than 'good', and defines it in logical terms.)

G. H. von Wright, *The Varieties of Goodness*, 1963, p. 36. ('Better' as non-TRANSITIVE.)

S. Hallden, *On the Logic of 'Better'*, 1957. (Full formal treatment.)

Between. Two main senses: (i) That in which a term lies between two other terms in some ordering. (ii) That in which a relation holds between two terms, as in 'difference between' and 'resemblance between'. In 'The Rhine passes between France and Germany' we have (i), but some cases seem less clear: 'The Rhine stretches between Switzerland and Holland', 'The Rhine is the link between Switzerland and Holland', 'The link between these events is such-and-such'. The analysis of 'distance between' is relevant to questions about empty space.

A. N. Prior, 'On a difference between "betweens" ', *Mind*, 1961.

Biconditional. The connective (see CONJUNCTION) 'if and only if', or a sentence comprising two clauses connected by it.

Bivalence

Bivalence (principle, law of). That every proposition is true or false, none being neither and none both. Usually regarded as one form of the law of EXCLUDED MIDDLE (though J. Lukasiewicz contrasts them), and used to reject many-valued logics (TRUTH-VALUE).

Boolean algebra. Algebra or, strictly, set of algebras, invented by G. Boole (1815–64) for the CALCULUS of classes; later developed further and given other applications. It resembles ordinary numerical algebra limited to one and zero (so that $x^2 = x$), but differs from it because classes are not confined to the universal and null CLASSES.

P. H. Nidditch, *The Development of Mathematical Logic*, 1962, chapter 6.
G. E. Hughes and M. J. Cresswell, *An Introduction to Modal Logic*, 1968, chapter 17 (beginning).

Bracketing. See PHENOMENOLOGY.

Bradley, Francis H. 1846–1924. Born in Clapham, he worked in Oxford, and is usually considered the main British IDEALIST. He developed a MONISTIC system whereby the Absolute is the only subject of predicates, and the only fully true proposition would be one completely describing it. No other proposition can be more than partly true. He argued that relations were always internal to their terms (an argument MOORE criticized)—though he also thought that they were illusory. He criticized the psychologism of empiricists like MILL in their use of terms like 'IDEA'. His logic is now particularly known for his views on negation, and his ethics for the anti-utilitarian stance of his essays on 'My Station and its Duties'. *Ethical Studies*, 1876 (contains 'My Station. . .'). *Logic*, 1883 (2nd edn, revised especially on negation, 1922). *Appearance and Reality*, 1893. *Essays on Truth and Reality*, 1914. See also HEGEL, OUGHT, UNIVERSALS.

Brain process theory. See IDENTITY THEORY OF MIND.

Brentano, Franz C. 1838–1917. Born near Boppard, he worked mainly in Würzburg and Vienna and retired to Florence. He was a Catholic priest for a short period. He is particularly remembered for his claim that mental phenomena can be identified as those which are 'intentional' in nature (see INTENSIONALITY). He also studied certain interrelations between ideas, judgments, and emotions of love and hatred, and elaborated a theory of truth which based it on 'evidence' in the sense of evidentness. His analysis of mental phenomena was especially influential on PHENOMENOLOGISTS like HUSSERL, and on MEINONG. He was himself much concerned with the study of ARISTOTLE. *Psychologie vom empirischen Standpunkt* (*Psychology from an Empirical Standpoint*), 1874. *Ursprung sittlicher Erkenntnis* (*the Origin of Our Knowledge of Right and Wrong*), 1889. *Grundlegung und Aufbau der Ethik* (*The Foundation and Construction of Ethics*), 1952 (more elaborate than previous item), *Wahrheit und Evidenz* (*The True and the Evident*), 1930.

Butler, Joseph

Broad, Charlie D. 1887–1971. Born in Harlesden, he worked mainly in Cambridge. Broad's contribution lay chiefly in his systematic exposition and thorough examination of a large number of philosophical theories in widely different spheres, and in his refusal to be browbeaten by current fashions into rejecting unpopular views. Like RUSSELL he appreciated the importance of modern science, and he also, like SIDGWICK, took psychological research seriously. His views tended to have a traditionalist flavour on topics such as causation and induction, perception, and the synthetic a priori; but they were elaborated to take account of current scientific and philosophical thought. Other topics to which he contributed in this way include time, substance, determinism, the body/mind problem, and certain ethical issues. *Perception, Physics, and Reality*, 1914. *Scientific Thought*, 1923. *The Mind and Its Place in Nature*, 1925. *Five Types of Ethical Theory*, 1930. *Examination of McTaggart's Philosophy*, 2 vols, 1933, 1938. See also PROBABILITY, SELF-REGARDING, SPACE.

Burali-Forti's paradox. The ordinal number or ordinal of a series is the number of terms in the series. The ordinal number of a series of consecutive ordinals starting from the lowest exceeds every ordinal in the series. Therefore the ordinal of all ordinals exceeds every ordinal, and so is not an ordinal. One of the logical PARADOXES; cf. RUSSELL'S PARADOX, TYPES.

Butler, Joseph. 1692–1752. Natural theologian and moralist who was born at Wantage and eventually became bishop of Bristol and then of Durham. His contribution to moral philosophy consists in his examination of moral psychology, including the roles of self-love and benevolence, and his treatment of conscience as a principle having overriding authority. In natural theology he claims to see an analogy between the course of events in nature and what religion teaches, and so to derive confirmation of the latter. He also discusses personal identity with reference to LOCKE. *Fifteen Sermons*, 1726 (his moral philosophy). *The Analogy of Religion, Natural and Revealed, to the Constitution and Course of Nature*, 1736.

C _____

Calculus. A general name, applied to a subject, for the body of principles governing reasoning in the subject. One can talk of *an* AXIOM SYSTEM for *the* propositional calculus, etc. Sometimes such systems are themselves called calculi.

The *propositional calculus* (also called the *sentential calculus, calculus of unanalysed propositions, calculus of truth values,* or *calculus of truth functions*) concerns truth FUNCTIONS of propositions, but with the restriction that the propositions are regarded as either the same as each other or completely different. Partial similarities like that between 'All cats are black' and 'Some cats are black' are ignored. Its theorems are the relevant TAUTOLOGIES. When the restriction is lifted and the structure of propositions is taken into account, we have the *functional* or *predicate calculus,* or the *calculus of relations.* When the predicates are limited to MONADIC predicates we have the *monadic predicate calculus.* The predicate calculus is called *extended* or *second-order* (occasionally *higher*) when predicates are quantified over (see QUANTIFICATION). When only INDIVIDUALS are quantified over, it is called *restricted* or *first-order* (occasionally *lower*). There is also an *extended propositional calculus,* where propositions are quantified over.

The *calculus of classes* concerns classes and their members. It is structurally the same as the monadic predicate calculus. ('x is red' is interchangeable with 'x belongs to the class of red things'—though RUSSELL'S PARADOX raises a difficulty for the view that every predicate defines a class.) It is the elementary nucleus of *set theory,* which treats problems arising out of the calculus of classes and goes beyond it by treating, for example, classes whose members are ordered, and problems specific to infinite classes. The relations between set theory and logic are important in connexion with logicism (see philosophy of MATHEMATICS).

For the *calculus of chances* see PROBABILITY.

The *hedonic calculus,* or *calculus of pleasures,* is the set of principles governing any system which claims that pleasures can be measured, added, and in general systematically compared.

D. Hilbert and W. Ackermann, *Principles of Mathematical Logic,* 1928; 2nd edn 1938, transl. 1950. (A standard account of the main logical calculi. Elementary introductions to symbolic logic, covering similar ground, are legion.)

D. C. Makinson, *Topics in Modern Logic*, 1973, chapter 5. (Set theory and logic. Cf. also Introduction to P. Benacerraf and H. Putnam (eds), *Philosophy of Mathematics*, 1964.)

Cancelling-out fallacy. The assumption that where two partially identical expressions mean the same, one can cancel out the identical parts and the remaining parts will mean the same as each other, e.g. if 'Socrates killed Socrates' means the same as 'Socrates was killed by Socrates', then 'killed Socrates' means the same as 'was killed by Socrates'.

P. T. Geach, *Reference and Generality*, 1962. (See index.)

Cantor's paradox. It is provable that any class has more subclasses than members. Suppose there were a class of all classes. Its subclasses, being classes, would *be* members of it. So there can be no class of all classes (and also no greatest cardinal number, not even among infinite numbers).

Carnap, Rudolf. 1891–1970. German logical POSITIVIST, born in Ronsdorf, and a member of the Vienna Circle. He migrated to America where he worked mainly in Chicago and Los Angeles. He tried to show that META-PHYSICS arose through our confusing talk about the world with talk about language (cf. FORMAL MODE). He sought to apply his positivism to scientific method by his physicalism (see POSITIVISM), and later in an elaborate examination of CONFIRMATION and probability. *Der Logische Aufbau der Welt* (*The Logical Structure of the World*), 1928. 'Die Physicalische Sprache als Universalsprache der Wissenschaft, *Erkenntnis*, 1932 (transl. separately as *The Unity of Science*, 1934; physicalism). 'Testability and Meaning', *Philosophy of Science*, 1936–7. *Meaning and Necessity*, 1947, enlarged 1956. *Logical Foundations of Probability*, 1950. *The Continuum of Inductive Methods*, 1952. See also BASIC STATEMENTS, BEING, EXPLANATION, FUNCTION, ISOMORPHIC, MEANING, MEANING POSTULATES, PROBABILITY, REDUCTION SENTENCES, SENTENCES, TRUTH, TYPES.

Cartesian. Connected with Descartes, or his ideas.

Casuistry. See ETHICS.

Categorematic. See CATEGORIES.

Categories. Ultimate or fundamental divisions or kinds. For much of its history the search for categories has wavered between seeking distinctions among things in the world and distinctions among our ways of thinking or talking about the world. Much of the difficulty in each case has lain in knowing what distinctions to count as sufficiently fundamental. It is mainly by being ultimate or fundamental that categories differ from mere classes.

This wavering appears in Aristotle, who first explicitly introduced

Categories

categories. His 'official' list contains ten categories, but the most important are SUBSTANCE, quality, quantity and relation, and his main interest seems to lie in distinguishing substance from the others. The list is clearly derived from different kinds of question that can be asked about a person, like 'How big is he?', 'What is he doing?'.

Sometimes Aristotle seems to take a 'metaphysical' view and to treat categories as the highest genera into which things in general can be divided, so that the world contains substances, qualities, etc., and anything one picks out such as a horse, or red, can be classed under one of these headings. He sometimes lets categories overlap by allowing the same item appear in more than one. At other times he seems to take a 'logical' view and to be classifying the things one can say about something, and in particular about a substance, such as what it is, what qualities it has, how it is related to other things. Here he might be described as classifying predicates, but he often seems to regard predicates themselves as things in the world and not as linguistic expressions, so that the 'metaphysical' and 'logical' approaches are not clearly separate. Aristotle's classification is not very exhaustive. The terms 'one', 'good', 'being', he said, did not belong to any one category. These were later called transcendentals (see BEING). There are many others, some of which he discussed, which have no obvious place, including 'surface', 'sound', 'chance', 'proposition', 'necessity', and complex terms like 'multiple of three', 'knowledge of French'. Aristotle also argues that there cannot be a single all-embracing genus like *being* or *unit*.

Many writers have followed Aristotle in elaborating sets of categories, usually more systematic than his. The Stoics had a set of four and they apparently wanted to classify at least some of the world's contents by examining the questions one can ask about a thing.

Among modern writers the most important contribution is that of Kant, who had a system of four groups of three. He intended these as a classification, whose correctness and exhaustiveness he claimed to prove, of the ways in which any mind recognizably like the human mind necessarily had to perceive and think about the appearances it was presented with. The categories were not a classification of things in themselves (NOUMENA), for Kant thought we could never know these and so never apply categories to them. The categories could only be applied to material given by experience, but they could not themselves be derived from experience, since all use of experience presupposes them. Kant's general idea is that we can only make sense of the world by imposing some structure originating from the mind upon it, e.g. to choose two of his categories, by seeing it as a set of *substances* in *causal* relationships. Many who accept this general idea reject the particular list he gave, and deny that there is some one list valid for all people and times. There is still much dispute about such related questions as whether there are certain features every language must share (cf. philosophy of LANGUAGE).

In this century two converging streams of thought have aroused interest in categories. First there are the logical PARADOXES, which led Russell to construct his theory of TYPES. This theory divides the world up by insisting

Categories

that things of different 'types' cannot be put together into a single class. It leads to corresponding divisions in language, e.g. two sentences of which one refers to the other are on different 'levels', and cannot be joined into a single sentence by 'and'. In fact 'type' and 'category' are sometimes used synonymously. Secondly, thinkers like Husserl and Ryle, among others, have tried to construct a doctrine of categories in order to systematize the ways in which a sentence can go wrong, and in particular the distinction between the false and the meaningless. Roughly speaking, the ideal of this approach would be to divide things into non-overlapping groups so that what could be said truly or falsely, but not nonsensically, of the members of one group differed radically from what could be said of the members of another, rather as most of the things that can be said of a cat differ from what can be said of a wish, or of a day of the week. Sentences which say about a subject in one category something that can only be sensibly said about a subject in another category are called *category mistakes* or type confusions, e.g. 'Saturday is in bed'. Such a doctrine cannot tell us when a sentence makes sense if we must already know this before constructing the doctrine. But the doctrine could systematize the situation, and throw useful light on individual cases through comparisons.

Many difficulties arise concerning categories. It sometimes seems to be thought that, if they exist at all, they must belong to the world and not to language, because they must be found out and not created by us. But even if we create a language, we can still *discover* things about it. We may choose what our sentences shall mean, but once we have chosen we are committed to the implications of our choice, and we do not choose these implications. The main difficulties seem to be of two kinds. First, to think of subjects and predicates that will not go together is perhaps too easy for we may reach so many categories that the doctrine becomes rather trivial, and 'category' becomes a pompous name for 'class' as often happens in ordinary speech. Are spoons and forks in different categories because 'This fork has lost one of its prongs' becomes nonsensical when 'fork' is replaced by 'spoon'? A distinction between absolute and relative categories has been found necessary in facing this problem (Strawson).

The second kind of difficulty, connected with the first, centres round the notion of meaninglessness. There are many ways in which something might be meaningless, nonsensical or absurd, as the following examples illustrate: 'Horse whether the', 'Twice two is five', 'My wish has whiskers', 'I have found', 'I have any apples', 'He sleeps like milk'. Some of these may be given senses in special cases, but which of them serve to distinguish categories? One can ask how clearly in fact is the meaningless distinct from the false? 'Absurd' can cover both. And is *every* kind of predicate relevant? Are two things in the same category merely because the predicate 'being thought about by me now' can apply to both of them? One controversy arising out of all this is whether categories can be ultimately founded on grammatical distinctions (called *syntactical* in logic), or whether considerations of meaning independent of mere grammar must be used (in which case categories will have a *semantic* basis—cf. SEMIOTIC).

Categorial is the proper word for 'having to do with categories'.

Categories

Categorical, though often misused for 'categorial', has something like its ordinary meaning of 'definite' or 'downright', but refers to a certain *form* of proposition, one which says something is the case without reference to conditions or alternatives. 'That's a cat' is categorical. 'If that's a cat, it's an animal' is *hypothetical.* 'That's either a cat or a dog' is *disjunctive.* *Mongrel categorical* is Ryle's name for a statement overtly categorical but covertly including a hypothetical statement, e.g. 'He drove carefully' says, for Ryle, not only that he did something but that he would have done certain things if certain events had occurred. See also categorical IMPERATIVE.

Categorematic, rarely used, refers to words or phrases naming things in categories, especially the Aristotelian categories, substance, quality, etc. *Syncategorematic* applies to words or phrases that somehow link or go 'together with' the categories. Basically, syncategorematic words are all those which are not categorematic, and they have often been regarded as not having meaning independently. The commonest examples are words like 'all', 'if', 'the', which do not name substances, qualities, etc., and are often known as logical words although many other examples are often given, including most adverbs. Also some words which behave grammatically like ordinary categorematic ones, yet which are somehow incomplete in meaning, are sometimes included. Some adjectives, especially, only apply to things when the things are described in certain ways. A big mouse is not a big animal. A thing cannot be big (unqualified) as it can be red (cf. ATTRIBUTIVE). A philosophically important case is GOOD. Bigness and goodness, etc., are therefore sometimes called *syncategorematic properties.* Cf. transcendentals, under BEING.

Aristotle, *Categories,* transl. with commentary by J. L. Ackrill in Clarendon Aristotle series, 1963. (See also his *Metaphysics,* 998b22–7 for argument that being is not a genus.)
J. M. Rist, 'Categories and their uses', in A. A. Long (ed.), *Problems in Stoicism,* 1971. (Stoic categories.)
Kant, *Critique of Pure Reason,* 1781, transl. by N. Kemp Smith in 1929. (See index.)
G. Ryle, 'Categories', *Proceedings of the Aristotelian Society,* 1938–9, reprinted in A. Flew (ed.), *Logic and Language,* 2nd series, 1953. (Attempts to construct theories of categories on semantic basis, resulting in so many category differences that the notion seems in danger of becoming trivial. See also his *The Concept of Mind,* 1949, esp. p. 16 (p. 17 in Peregrine edn), for category mistakes, and esp. p. 141 (p. 135 in Peregrine edn) for mongrel categoricals.)
F. Sommers, 'Types and ontology', *Philosophical Review,* 1963. (One of several articles by Sommers elaborating a semantic theory of categories more rigorous than Ryle's.)
D. J. Hillman, 'On grammars and category mistakes', *Mind,* 1963. (Uses Chomsky's work in linguistics to construct grammatical (syntactical) base to Ryle's theory. Cf. A. D. Carstairs, 'Ryle, Hillman and Harrison on categories', *Mind,* 1971.)

T. Drange, 'Harrison and Odegard on type crossings', *Mind*, 1969. (Brief discussion of two earlier articles.)

P. F. Strawson, 'Categories', in O. P. Wood and G. Pitcher (eds), *Ryle*, 1970. (General discussion of possibility and usefulness of categories, starting from Ryle. See p. 199 (Papermac edn, 1971) for absolute and relative categories.)

J. Passmore, *Philosophical Reasoning*, 1961, chapter 7. (Somewhat sceptical approach.)

T. L. S. Sprigge, *Facts, Words and Beliefs*, 1970, pp. 70–2. (Syncategorematic properties.)

Causation. Roughly, the relation between two things when the first is necessary or sufficient or both for the occurrence of the second. Modern discussions of causation stem primarily from Hume's claim that our idea of causation cannot be gained in any simple way from either reason or observation. It cannot come from reason because reason can only tell us of logical relations, and if the cause and effect were logically related, i.e. if the occurrence of the cause *entailed* (see IMPLICATION) that of the effect, they would be one thing and not two. This is not to deny that causal statements can be ANALYTIC, like 'Whatever causes cancer causes cancer'. If something correctly described as the cause of cancer exists, then cancer must exist—otherwise the first thing could not be called its cause. Hume thought observation can only tell us that some things regularly follow on other things. It cannot reveal that special 'force' or 'necessity' that we feel a causal situation must contain.

Causation may involve regularities (though this is disputed; see Alexander), but is that all it involves? Regularities may be causally significant or they may be accidental, and in trying to distinguish these we meet problems about natural laws and counterfactual CONDITIONALS. Furthermore what regularities are relevant? Perhaps, in the case of singular causal statements, i.e. those about given occasions, to say that *a* caused *b* is to say that *a* was followed by *b*, and that *a*-like things are regularly followed by *b*-like things; but how like *a* and *b* must the things in question be? If I say that striking that match caused it to light, am I saying that all matches light when struck, or only that all dry matches do, or what? One view (Davidson) is that in saying '*a* caused *b*' we imply that there exists some true non-accidental generalization of the form 'Things like *a* in certain respects are followed by things like *b* in certain respects', but we need not know what generalization.

Since the world is an interlocking whole, so that exact repetition of all circumstances is presumably impossible, and the course of events leading to a given event is enormously complex, a looser view of causes has often been taken. Here an event's cause is some condition, or set of conditions, which is either necessary or sufficient, or both, for the event (see NECESSARY AND SUFFICIENT CONDITIONS). This condition is singled out because it is rare or striking in some respect, or is amenable to human control. If matches were usually wet, and so did not light when struck, we might call its dryness the cause when some particular match did light when struck.

Causation

As things are, we call the striking the cause because it is controllable and matches are usually dry.

It is tempting to tighten this up by saying that an event's cause is the set of those things which are separately necessary and together sufficient for its occurrence, perhaps with a proviso that general background conditions (the stars in their courses, etc.) can be excluded as irrelevant. But two difficulties arise. First, this would not distinguish causal from logical relations (see NECESSARY AND SUFFICIENT CONDITIONS). Secondly, if a is a necessary condition of b, b is a sufficient condition of a, and vice versa. Therefore if a is a necessary and sufficient condition of b, so is b of a. But then if a causes b we must say that b causes a, which seems absurd. (Variants of this 'tightening up' procedure are possible, but with similar disadvantages.)

We often feel that a cause should precede its effect, but since time is continuous this seems to imply that there must be a gap between cause and effect. But when 'cause' is being used strictly, and not just to pick out what is striking or unusual, such a gap, whether temporal or spatial ('action at a distance') seems mysterious. It seems no better to say, alternatively, that the gap is filled by a chain of infinitely many causes. Some kinds of causes, however, do seem simultaneous with their effects, e.g. forces or objects: 'Gravity caused him to fall', 'The dog caused the accident'. It has even been suggested that an effect could precede its cause (Dummett).

One way of explaining why causation seems to be a one-way relation, so that things cannot cause each other (though they can sustain each other, like the stones in an arch) is to derive the idea of causation from our experience of our own activity. To cause something is then to bring it about, and we call causes those things that could serve us, at least in principle, as recipes for producing their effects. On a primitive version of this view nature itself does the bringing about, but we need not assume this. Even things clearly outside our control, like stellar processes, can be viewed *as if* they were in our control, and we need not attribute activities to nature. Why we refuse to allow effects to precede their causes may then be because we cannot make sense of bringing about the past, because we have no experience of it in our own activities. We could always explain the case where the later event seems to cause the earlier (Dummett) by saying the earlier causes the later but by a process that has escaped us; but cf. von Wright.

Heisenberg's uncertainty principle (1927) says that we cannot in principle discover both the momentum and the position of a fundamental particle, because the process of discovery will always affect what is being discovered. (Whether the particle *has* both a momentum and a position is disputed.) We can, however, attribute probabilities to the behaviour of such particles, and then use PROBABILITY theory to predict with virtual certainty the behaviour of masses of particles, i.e. of ordinary objects. This, coupled with the fact that physicists usually talk in terms of equations rather than one-way relations, raises three questions: Has physics abandoned or even undermined causation? Does it make sense to suppose that individual sub-atomic movements are caused, even though we cannot in principle discover their causes? Can there be ultimate causal *tendencies*, i.e. cases where a cause is followed by its effect, say, 90 per cent of the time and where this cannot be explained by pointing to an underlying 100 per cent generalization? (If 90 per cent of matches light when struck, this might be because 100 per cent of dry matches light when struck.) Clearly the answers will depend on how we view causation. The 'recipe' view might say causation is irrelevant for physics, not undermined by it, and that *virtual* certainty is all that causation requires.

What sort of things can be causes? Objects, events, forces, facts, states, processes, even absences ('The absence of oxygen caused his death'), can be described as causes. Which, if any, of these has the prior claim to the title of cause is disputable. No doubt the 'strikingness' mentioned above can explain much here. But recently what appear to be near synonyms have been explicitly distinguished, notably 'effects', 'results' and 'consequences'. It has even been claimed by Vendler that, strictly, no effects have causes, except perhaps incidentally, because effects are processes or activities while causes (to which the correlative term is 'results') are facts.

An important question in recent philosophy of mind concerns whether actions can be caused, and if so, whether this affects our notion of responsibility (see FREEWILL). Obviously the word 'because', which we use in giving reasons for our actions, need not be causal. It can, e.g. signify logical relations, as in '141 cannot be a prime number because the sum of its digits is divisible by 3'. But even 'cause' may imply causality less than 'causal' does. We might accept 'My wife's profligacy caused me to sell my house', while rejecting 'The relation between my wife's behaviour and my action was a causal one.'

Aristotle's *four causes*, here illustrated by reference to a man, are the *material cause*, (flesh, etc.), *formal cause* (FORM of man), *efficient cause* (father), *final cause* (end or purpose, e.g. to live in a certain way). The notions are, however, less clearcut than this suggests, and the Greek word is wider than 'cause'. It means something like 'responsible factor'. An *exemplary cause* is a pattern or exemplar playing the role of Plato's 'FORMS'. God was sometimes called the exemplary cause when these Forms were regarded as IDEAS in His mind.

D. Hume, *Treatise*, 1739, I 3, §§ 2, 3, 7. (Classic statement of problem, Cf. his *Enquiry concerning Human Understanding*, 1748, §§ 4, 7.)

B. Blanshard, *The Nature of Thought*, 1939, chapter 32, §§ 10–21. (Thinks causation does involve logical necessity. Criticized by E. Nagel, *Sovereign Reason*, 1954, pp. 387–95.)

M. Bunge, *Causality*, 1959. (Standpoint of science.)

H. L. A. Hart and A. M. Honoré, *Causation in the Law*, 1959. (Standpoint of philosophy of mind.)

P. Alexander, P. B. Downing, 'Are causal laws purely general?', *Proceedings of the Aristotelian Society*, supplementary vol. 1970.

M. Dummett, A. Flew, 'Can an effect precede its cause?', *Proceedings of the Aristotelian Society*, supplementary vol. 1954. Cf. G. H. von Wright, *Explanation and Understanding*, 1971, chapter 2, § 10, and S. Waterlow,

Central state materialism

'Backwards causation and continuing', *Mind*, 1974, which also contains a bibliography, to which add P. B. Downing, 'Subjunctive conditionals, time order and causation', *Proceedings of the Aristotelian Society*, 1958–9.)

B. Russell, *Analysis of Mind*, 1921, chapter 5, esp. beginning. (Can a cause precede its effect? Cf. his *Our Knowledge of the External World*, 1914, chapter 8.)

D. Gasking, 'Causation and recipes', *Mind*, 1955, reprinted in A. Sesonske and N. Fleming (eds), *Human Understanding*, 1965. (Cf. von Wright (above), chapter 2, §§ 8, 9.).

D. Davidson, 'Causal relations', *Journal of Philosophy*, 1967, reprinted in Sosa below. (Singular causal statements.)

Z. Vendler, 'Causal relations', *Journal of Philosophy*, 1967. (Criticizes Davidson and treats causes as facts. Also discusses effects, results and consequences, on which see also Hart and Honoré (above), pp. 25–6, and symposium in R. J. Butler (ed.), *Analytical Philosophy*, 1st series, 1962.)

G. J. Warnock in A. Flew (ed.), *Logic and Language*, 2nd series, 1953. (Discusses 'Every event has a cause'.)

Aristotle, *Physics*, book 2. (Four causes.)

F. Copleston, *A History of Philosophy*, vol. 2, 1950. (Exemplary causes. See index.)

E. Sosa (ed.), *Causation and Conditionals*, 1975. (Readings.)

Central state materialism. See IDENTITY THEORY OF MIND.

C-Function. See CONFIRMATION.

Church's theorem. See DECIDABLE.

Class. Loosely, a group of objects or things. Normally 'class' and 'set' are synonymous. But some theories, associated with J. von Neumann, K. Gödel and P. Bernays, hope to avoid RUSSELL'S PARADOX by saying some classes are not members of any other classes (as the class of cats *is* a member of the class of animal-classes). 'Set' is then limited to those classes which *are* members of other classes. The terms 'set-theory' and 'CALCULUS of classes' are conventional, irrespective of this variation in usage.

A class is *closed* if it has finitely many members and these are theoretically enumerable. It is *open* if it has infinitely many members, or if its membership is and always will be indeterminate (e.g. the class of children I might have had).

It is important to distinguish *class-inclusion* from *class-membership*. A class is included in any class containing at least the same members. The class of cats is included in, but is not a member of, the class of animals for it is not an animal. It is a member of, but is not included in, the class of animal-classes for cats are not animal-classes. Class-inclusion is TRANSITIVE, but class-membership is non-transitive. Smith may be a member of a union, and the union a member of the TUC, without Smith

Complete

being a member of the TUC. For extensional and intensional definitions of classes see UNIVERSALS.

A *unit class* is a class with only one member. The *universal class* is the class containing everything, or everything in a given sphere.

The *null*, or *empty, class* is the one class with no members. '{a, b}' means the class whose members are a and b. '⟨a, b⟩' means the ordered class whose members are a and b, in that order.

Class paradox. See RUSSELL'S PARADOX.

Clusters. See UNIVERSALS.

Cognitive. Concerning or involving knowledge. Theories analysing statements which apparently involve knowledge of facts, especially in ethics, metaphysics and religion, as really involving something else, perhaps expression of emotion or recommendations, are often called non-cognitive (cf. NATURALISM).

Collingwood, Robin G. 1889–1943. Philosopher and archaeologist who was born at Coniston and worked mostly in Oxford. Most of his philosophical work concerns aesthetics, philosophy of mind, philosophy of history and metaphysics. His theory of art, influenced by CROCE, bases art on expression and imagination, which leads him to a treatment of language. In philosophy of history he treats the historian's task as that of reconstructing the thoughts that lay behind or were embodied in historical actions. His later metaphysics is rather similar in nature, in that he sees its task as limited to the reconstruction of the 'absolute presuppositions' of an epoch in the history of thought (see IMPLICATION). *The Principles of Art*, 1938. *Autobiography*, 1939. *An Essay on Metaphysics*, 1940. *The New Leviathan*, 1942 ('an attempt to bring the *Leviathan* [of HOBBES] up to date' (preface)). *The Idea of History*, 1946.

Complete. An AXIOM SYSTEM, in the sense of a set of axioms and rules of inference, is complete in a weak sense if all the truths of the kind it caters for can be derived within the system. It is complete in a strong sense if the addition of any other proposition of the relevant kind as an independent axiom makes the system inconsistent. There are further refinements. In particular, formalizations of the propositional CALCULUS can be complete in both senses; formalizations of the first-order predicate CALCULUS can only be weakly complete. Also a set of axioms in a formal language is called complete if for every sentence S in the language either S or not-S follows from the axioms. In this sense no explicitly definable set of axioms rich enough for elementary arithmetic is complete (see GÖDEL'S THEOREMS); in fact no such set is complete in any sense mentioned above.

A. N. Prior, *Formal Logic*, 1955. (See index.)
A. H. Basson and D. J. O'Connor, *Introduction to Symbolic Logic*, 3rd edn, 1959. (See index.)

Composition and division

Composition and division. 'Someone sitting could walk' might be interpreted in the *composite sense* (*sensus compositus*) to mean 'Someone could walk while sitting', or in the *divided sense* (*sensus divisus*) to mean 'Someone sitting could walk instead'. In a fairly intuitive sense the former puts *walking* and *sitting* together, while the latter keeps them apart. To wrongfully infer the expression interpreted in the composite sense from the same expression interpreted in the divided sense is to commit the *fallacy of composition*. The converse *fallacy of division* occurs if, e.g. we are given 'Everyone is male or female' in the composite sense, that each person is male-or-female, and take it in the divided sense, that everyone is male or everyone is female.

In modal contexts 'composite' and 'divided' have been thought to correspond respectively to 'de dicto' and 'de re' (see MODALITIES). 'Cats may be black' can mean 'Possibly all cats are black' or 'Any given cat may be black'. In the former (de dicto, composite) *cats* and *black* go together, with the modal term ('possibly') outside. In the latter (de re, divided) the modal term comes essentially between *cat* and *black*.

A. N. Prior, *Formal Logic*, 1955. (See 'composition' in index.)

Comprehension. See INTENSIONALITY.

Comte, I. Auguste M.F.X. 1798–1857. Born in Montpellier, he lived mainly in Paris, holding various minor academic posts. From 1817 he was secretary for some years to the social reformer C. H. de Saint-Simon (1780–1825) and was influenced by him. His main work consisted in the development of POSITIVISM. *Cours de philosophie positive*, 6 vols, 1830–42. *Discours sur l'esprit positif*, 1844 (popular exposition). *Système de politique positive, ou traité de sociologie, instituant la religion de l'humanité*, 4 vols, 1851–4. (Comte also applied the title *Système de politique positive* to the second edition (1824) of a small work published in 1822.)

Concept. 'Concept' has taken over some uses of the ambiguous term 'IDEA', perhaps partly because 'idea' suggests images etc. To have a concept of anything is to be able to distinguish it from other things, or be able in some way to think or reason about it.

Concepts are connected with UNIVERSALS. On one view concepts are 'of' universals, so that to have a concept of, say, dog, is to be related to a nonmaterial object like a Platonic FORM. 'Concept of dog' is perhaps best taken as a single linguistic unit, like 'dog-concept', so that one is not tempted to seek some entity that 'dog' stands for.

A closely related view, *conceptual realism*, makes the concept itself a substantial entity, to which one is somehow related when one 'has' the concept. This leads to the 'paradox of analysis'. (See PHILOSOPHY for this and for conceptual analysis.)

Whereas conceptual realism says in effect that concepts are universals, *conceptualism* says that universals are concepts, but leaves open what concepts are. They seem to be mind-dependent but common to many minds.

It may be that to have a concept is to have an ability, if, as suggested

34

Conditionals

above, to have a concept of dog is to be *able* to think about dogs. How much the ability must cover is disputed. Has an animal, or a machine, a concept of dog if it reacts differentially to dogs? Can a man blind from birth have a concept of red? Does having a concept involve being able to use a word? Perhaps 'having a concept' is ambiguous in these respects. We must distinguish between the public concept of dog, or the concept *dog*, and an individual's concept of dog. An individual may include foxes, or think that dogs must by definition have tails; but if he diverges too far his concept will no longer be one of dog.

For Frege 'concept' is a logical term, contrasted with OBJECT. Objects are whatever we can talk about, while concepts can be regarded as what we apply to objects in talking about them. In 'Arkle is a horse' 'Arkle' introduces an object while 'is a horse' introduces a concept. Concepts are thus somehow incomplete: 'Arkle' can stand by itself, as a name, in a way that 'is a horse' cannot. Frege expressed this by calling objects *saturated* and concepts *unsaturated* (but cf. Dummett, pp. 31–3). Frege also defined a concept as 'a FUNCTION whose value (see VARIABLE) is always a TRUTH-VALUE'. Since what is talked about is automatically an object, Frege concluded paradoxically that 'the concept *horse* is not a concept' since we are talking about it.

Concepts are normally general (the concept *dog* covers dogs in general), but there can be *individual concepts* (e.g. the concept of the Atlantic).

Conception normally has only its everyday senses in philosophy. See also POLAR CONCEPTS.

P. T. Geach, *Mental Acts*, 1957. (Discusses nature and acquisition of concepts. Sometimes difficult.)

P. T. Geach and M. Black (eds), *Translations from the Philosophical Writings of Gottlob Frege*, 1952. (Contains his 'Concept and Object'. See also p. 30 for 'concept' and 'function', and J. Valberg, 'Improper singular terms', *Proceedings of the Aristotelian Society*, 1970–1 for discussion of 'horse' paradox. Also M. Dummett, *Frege: Philosophy of Language*, 1973.)

K. R. Popper, *The Logic of Scientific Discovery*, 1934, transl. with additions 1959, §14. (Individual concepts. See also Leibniz, passim.)

Conceptualism. See UNIVERSALS, CONCEPT, IDENTITY.

Conditionals. 'Conditional' and 'hypothetical' are normally used synonymously before terms like 'proposition' or 'statement'. Standardly a proposition of the conditional form, 'If p then q', is taken to entail its CONTRAPOSITIVE, 'If not–q then not–p'. There are cases, however, whatever their ultimate analysis, which seem not to be of this kind, e.g. 'If you want it, there's some bread here' does not entail 'If there's no bread here, you don't want it'. Austin uses this concerning freewill. Also an antecedent may be followed by a question or command as in 'If it rains, stay in'.

As there is a problem about relating entailment to strict IMPLICATION and its 'paradoxes', so there is one about relating the standard 'if' of ordinary thought to material implication and its 'paradoxes'. One cannot

Conditionals

truly say 'If p then q' when p is true and q is false, i.e. when p does not materially imply q. But can one say it in all other cases? Or must p and q be somehow relevant to each other? Or must some other condition be fulfilled? Some say that relevance has nothing to do with the *meaning* of 'If p then q', but that general conventions forbid us to utter it when p and q are mutually irrelevant. 'If that's so, I'm a Dutchman' may be an exception to these conventions, relying for its effect on contrast to the normal case (Strawson). Also should we distinguish between asserting a conditional and conditionally asserting its consequent? Perhaps in saying 'If p then q' we are simply asserting q conditionally, in which case when p is false, 'If p then q' is neither true nor false but simply inapposite.

A particular source of difficulty lies in *subjunctive* and *counterfactual conditionals* or *counterfactuals* (also called *contrafactual* (Quine), *contrary-to-fact, unfulfilled*). Strictly subjunctive conditionals and counterfactuals are not the same. Counterfactuals may be conditionals with a false antecedent. Or they may be conditionals interpreted as entailing or presupposing that their antecedents are false. Or other analyses may be offered. (In the first case they will not have a special analysis, for the analysis of something should not depend on whether it or part of it is true or false; but the fact that a conditional can have a false antecedent will then affect the analysis of conditionals in general.) Subjunctive conditionals are those normally expressed in the subjunctive in English or related languages, and may include some *open conditionals*, which leave open whether or not the antecedent is taken as true ('Were it to rain tomorrow we should get wet'). However, the relevant problems are largely common to counterfactuals and subjunctive conditionals, and so are often expressed in terms of either.

Counterfactuals and subjunctive conditionals seem even more remote from material implication than ordinary conditionals. They also provide problems for the verification theory (POSITIVISM) and the correspondence theory of TRUTH, and have a puzzling element of indefiniteness. After 'If Bizet and Verdi had been compatriots' should we put 'Bizet would have been Italian' or 'Verdi would have been French'?

Counterfactuals are also important in connexion with LAWS of nature, PHENOMENALISM, and dispositional statements like 'This glass is brittle', which seems to imply that had it been struck it would have broken. Some writers distinguish natural laws from accidental generalizations ('All the coins in my pocket are silver', 'All ruminants are, as it happens, cloven-hoofed') by saying laws entail counterfactuals (or '*sustain*' them, a looser term used in case counterfactuals are not, properly speaking, statements, and because on some views laws of nature do not make, and so cannot entail, assertions about the world). Counterfactuals have also, however, been divided into 'purely hypothetical' ones of the Bizet/Verdi type and 'nomological' ones which we accept only if they accord with laws or similar acceptable statements. We accept 'If it were snowing it would be cold (since snow is always cold)' rather than 'If it were snowing snow would be hot (since today is in fact hot)' (Rescher). But obviously one cannot, without circularity, explain natural laws in terms of counterfactuals, and explain counterfactuals in terms of natural laws.

36

Confirmation

Other views about conditionals say that they state relations between propositions. They state that the antecedent proposition implies, in some sense, the consequent. Alternatively, conditionals may be rules or sets of instructions for making inferences. See also CAUSATION.

R. B. Braithwaite, *Scientific Explanation*, 1953, p. 295. (Distinguishes 'conditional' from 'hypothetical'; cf. also P. Edwards (ed.), *Encyclopedia of Philosophy*, 1967, 4, p. 128.)

J. L. Austin, 'Ifs and cans' in his *Philosophical Papers*, 1961, reprinted in B. Berofsky (ed.), *Free Will and Determinism*, 1966. (Relevance of senses of 'if' to freewill problem.)

L. Simons, 'Intuition and implication', *Mind*, 1965. (Analyses 'if' in terms of material implication.)

P. F. Strawson, *Introduction to Logical Theory*, 1952, chapter 2 § 7, chapter 3 § 9. (Distinguishes 'if' and material implication. For 'Dutchman' see p. 89.)

D. Holdcroft, P. Long, 'Conditional assertion', *Proceedings of the Aristotelian Society*, supplementary vol., 1971. (Conditional assertion and assertion of conditional.)

S. Hampshire, 'Subjunctive conditionals', *Analysis*, vol. 9, 1948, reprinted in M. Macdonald (ed.), *Philosophy and Analysis*, 1954. (Problems raised by subjunctive conditionals.)

N. Goodman, *Fact, Fiction and Forecast*, 1954, 2nd (revised) edn. 1965.

F. L. Will, 'The contrary-to-fact conditional', *Mind*, 1947. (These two discuss difficulties in using material implication to analyse counterfactuals.)

P. B. Downing, 'Subjunctive conditionals, time order and causation', *Proceedings of the Aristotelian Society*, 1958–9. (Claims time is relevant to subjunctive conditionals.)

P. Alexander, M. Hesse, 'Subjunctive conditionals', *Proceedings of the Aristotelian Society*, supplementary vol., 1962. (Connexion between them and natural laws.)

N. Rescher, 'Belief-contravening suppositions', *Philosophical Review*, 1961. (Differences among counterfactuals.)

G. Ryle, ' "If", "so" and "because" ', in M. Black (ed.), *Philosophical Analysis*, 1950. (Conditionals as instructions for inferences.)

J. L. Mackie, 'Counterfactuals and causal laws', in R. J. Butler, (ed.), *Analytical Philosophy*, 1st series, 1962. (Counterfactuals as argument forms. Develops Rescher.)

D. Lewis, *Counterfactuals*, 1973. (Offers extended analysis. See especially chapters 1, 3, 4.)

E. Sosa (ed.), *Causation and Conditionals*, 1975. (Readings.)

Confirmation. A weak form of verification. To verify something is to show that it is true, or else to test it in a way that will reveal its truth if it *is* true. Often, however, we can only show that something is more likely to be true than it was, or was thought to be. This is one sense of confirmation. In logic 'confirmation' lacks its everyday senses of verifying or making

Confirmation

definite ('I confirmed the booking', 'The facts confirmed my hypothesis'). The opposite of confirmation is usually called *disconfirmation*, occasionally *infirmation*.

Confirmation is closely related to PROBABILITY, though both terms are used in various senses. Speaking only generally, confirmation is the process by which probability is conferred on a hypothesis, and probability is what is conferred by confirmation. The problems in this area therefore, especially in earlier writings, concern the two notions in this way: Problems about confirmation concern the methods that can make a hypothesis more probable, while problems about probability concern what it is that we are saying about something when we say that it is probable. The two sets of problems overlap, however, and the difference is not clearcut. *Probabilify* means 'make probable to some degree' (not necessarily more probable than not), and so is synonymous with *one* sense (see below) of 'confirm'.

So far we have taken 'confirmation' to cover any process by which a scientific hypothesis is made more probable. In this sense its problems approximate to those of INDUCTION. One way to support a hypothesis is to eliminate its rivals, and through much of its history induction has been viewed as an eliminative process. But a hypothesis can only be established in this way if *all* its rivals are eliminated, which in practice is seldom possible. It is difficult even in theory, unless it can be shown that its rivals are finite in number. Eliminating merely some of them will help only if there is some way of assigning probabilities to those that remain. Only if there is such a way can we talk of confirming by partial elimination. In fact confirmation has sometimes been contrasted with elimination and confined to some real or alleged process of giving positive support to a hypothesis—a process not dependent on eliminating any of its rivals. To find such a process is one aim of confirmation theory. Another aim is to account for how it is we can talk, as we do, of evidence being favourable even to a hypothesis we know to be false. These aims, especially the second, have led recently to technical notions of confirmation as a logical relation holding between a set of evidence propositions and a conclusion. ('*Support*' is often then used for the original notion, though it has other uses too.) One such relation (Carnap, Hempel) holds whether or not the conclusion is true, and even if we know it is false.

Confirmation is here a relation between some evidence and a conclusion, and holds irrespective of any other evidence. (Whether a conclusion is 'probable' in the ordinary sense depends on how far it is confirmed by all the available evidence.) Confirmation in this sense resembles entailment (see IMPLICATION), but is weaker, and the conclusion is not (as with entailment) contained in the premises. (There are further differences, e.g. where p, q and r are propositions, if p entails q then, normally, p- and-r entails q; this does not hold for confirmation.) For other writers (Popper, Swinburne) the confirmation given to a conclusion by some evidence is not the probability the conclusion acquires, but the ratio between that probability and the probability the conclusion had, usually on the basis of all the available evidence. Here confirmation is *increase* in probability.

An enquiry into confirmation can ask three main questions. First, what is confirmation? Second, when is one conclusion more highly confirmed by some evidence than another? Third, can numerical values be given to degrees of confirmation?

In treating the second problem Carnap, like most of those who elaborate a logic of induction, relies on the calculus of chances (PROBABILITY) and BAYES'S THEOREM. He considers a finite model, which can later be extended to an infinite one. He imagines a world containing a definite number of objects and a definite number of properties, and considers the various states that world might be in according to how the properties were distributed among the objects, e.g. if the objects were Tom and Bill and the properties tall and short, four *state-descriptions* could be given of the world, namely 'both tall', 'both short', 'Tom tall, Bill short', 'Tom short, Bill tall'. The confirmation given to a conclusion by evidence is then expressed in terms of a ratio between the number of state-descriptions compatible with the evidence and conclusion together and the normally larger number compatible with the evidence considered by itself. An important complication, however, is that not all state-descriptions need be treated equally, and part of the task is to devise a 'measure' which will give a certain weighting to any given state-description. A favoured way is to give equal weight to different *structures* in the world. In the above example 'both tall' and 'one tall, one short' represent two structures and have equal weight. They are *structure-descriptions* ('both tall' is also a state-description). 'Tom tall, Bill short' and 'Tom short, Bill tall' share the structure-description 'one tall, one short', and so each has half the weight of 'both tall'. The resulting formula by which confirmations are worked out is called a *confirmation-function* or *c-function*.

What ultimately justifies a given c-function is presumably that it gives results that tally with our intuitions of what should confirm what. But there is a difficulty about applying c-functions. If a proposition is entailed by something we know, we can assert it, but if it is only confirmed it may be absurd to assert it. That Smith is twenty no doubt confirms that he will live another forty years, but we would not assert that he will if we knew also that he had acute heart disease. Carnap therefore insisted on the *requirement of total evidence*, that we should not apply a confirmation argument unless the premises represent our total knowledge. This naturally raises practical difficulties over what can be excluded as irrelevant.

It is disputable how far Carnap has cut confirmation adrift from elimination, especially when we turn to the first problem of confirmation and ask when one proposition confirms another.

Two *paradoxes of confirmation* arise here, associated with Hempel and Goodman. Hempel's paradox begins from *Nicod's criterion* of confirmation. This says that 'All ravens are black' is confirmed by a black raven and refuted by a non-black one, other objects being irrelevant. But it is plausible to say that whatever confirms a hypothesis in one formulation should confirm it in any logically equivalent formulation (the *equivalence condition*). A sentence like 'Here is a red shoe' confirms 'All non-black things are non-ravens' since a red shoe is a non-black non-raven. It should therefore also confirm the equivalent sentence 'All ravens are black',

Confirmation

which seems absurd. Various questions arise from this, e.g., is there any difference between satisfying a hypothesis (i.e. being compatible with it) and confirming it? How is confirming a hypothesis related to increasing our knowledge about it, and to testing it?

Goodman's paradox concerns similar problems from a different point of view. Let 'grue' mean 'green if and only if examined before time t, and otherwise blue'. Assuming t is still future, the fact that all emeralds so far examined have been green (and therefore also grue) seems to confirm 'All emeralds are grue' as much as it confirms 'All emeralds are green'. Yet surely it would be absurd to infer the former. (There are variants of the paradox, and also of the definition of 'grue'.) Many who have discussed this have tried to distinguish normal predicates like 'green' from odd ones like 'grue'. They could then rule that only the normal ones could be 'projected', i.e. used in inferences as above. However, it is not obvious that the problem concerns only 'odd' predicates, and it seems to resemble the *curve-fitting problem*: When two independently measurable features, such as temperature and pressure of a gas, are plotted against each other on a graph the resulting set of points must be finite because we can only perform finitely many measurements. They may suggest a simple curve connecting them, but they are compatible with infinitely many curves. What, then, justifies us in choosing the suggested one?

These and similar problems have led to some scepticism about whether there is a logical relation of confirmation at all. Popper replaces confirmation by *corroboration*, which he defines in terms of falsifiability and the passing of tests. He insists that he is not claiming that the hypothesis corroborated is thereby more likely to be true. Others concentrate on *acceptability*, which differs from confirmation because to give rules for when it is rational to accept a hypothesis need not involve any reference to a logical relation and can take account of such things as what the accepter knows already, and what risks acceptance involves him in. (In fact Popper's rules for corroboration are acceptance rules.) Also it may be rational to accept a hypothesis with a low probability, if its rivals have even lower probabilities; if there were just three competing hypotheses, with probabilities respectively of 40 per cent, 30 per cent and 30 per cent, it would be rational to accept the first, even though its probability was less than a half. See also PROBABILITY, INDUCTION, LIKELIHOOD.

R. Carnap, *Logical Foundations of Probability*, 1950. (Full treatment of his views on confirmation and two kinds of probability, with chapter summaries. See pp. 211ff. for requirement of total evidence.)

W. Kneale, *Probability and Induction*, 1949. (Introduction to these subjects, though getting more technical towards end. § 23 discusses confirmation and elimination.)

R. Swinburne, *An Introduction to Confirmation Theory*, 1973. (See first chapter for confirmation and probability.)

C. G. Hempel, 'Studies in the logic of confirmation', *Mind*, 1945, reprinted with addition in his *Aspects of Scientific Explanation*, 1965. (Starts with discussion of his paradox and then elaborates his own theory of confirmation. See index of *Aspects* for discussion of requirement of total evidence.)

N. Goodman, *Fact, Fiction and Forecast*, 1954, 2nd (revised) edn. 1965. (Introduction and discussion of 'grue' paradox.)

J. Hullett and R. Schwartz, 'Grue: some remarks', *Journal of Philosophy*, 1967. (Survey of ways of treating Goodman's paradox. Several other relevant articles in same and preceding volume.)

I. Scheffler, *The Anatomy of Inquiry*, 1964. (Contains discussion of Hempel and Goodman paradoxes.)

K. Popper, *The Logic of Scientific Discovery*, 1959, (German original 1934). (Chapter 10 introduces corroboration.)

L. J. Cohen, *The Implications of Induction*, 1970. (Develops theory of confirmation not based on calculus of chances, though he prefers to call it 'support'. Also discusses acceptability.)

Conjunction and disjunction. A compound sentence is a *conjunction* if its component sentences are joined by 'and'. It is a *disjunction* if they are joined by 'or'. The component sentences are, respectively, *conjuncts*, which are *conjoined*, and *disjuncts*, which are *disjoined*. 'Conjunction' and 'disjunction' can also mean the logical operations of forming such expressions. 'And' and 'or' here have only their joining force, without signifying, e.g. temporal order (as in 'He came and went'). 'Or' is usually *inclusive* ('either and perhaps both'), but can be *exclusive* ('either but not both'). Sometimes *alternation* replaces 'disjunction', with *alternant* and *alternate* for 'disjunct' and 'disjoin'. Occasionally 'disjunction' and 'alternation' are distinguished. Conjunctions in the ordinary sense ('and', 'or', etc.) are in logic called *connectives*, and are among constants (see VARIABLE) and OPERATORS.

P. F. Strawson, *An Introduction to Logical Theory*, 1952, pp. 77–92. (Connectives in logic and ordinary language. Cf. R. E. Gahringer, 'Intensional conjunction', *Mind*, 1970.)

Connected. A relation is connected or connective if it holds, one way or the other, between any two objects which can, without absurdity, have the relation to something. It is *connected in a domain* (i.e. sphere, class) if it is connected when only the objects in that domain are considered, e.g. *earlier than* is connected in the domain of years: of any two years one is earlier than the other.

Connective. See CONJUNCTION, CONNECTED.

Connotation. See MEANING.

Consequences. See CAUSATION.

Consequential characteristics. Those qualities or properties which depend on some other quality or property. Also called *supervenient characteristics*, sometimes *tertiary qualities*. Two things can be exactly alike except that

Consequentialism

one is red and the other not. They cannot be exactly alike except that one is good and the other not. A thing is only good as a consequence of having some other characteristic, and one can always ask 'What's good about it?' Characteristics like *good*, as against *red*, are therefore called consequential. *Good*, however, may not be consequential in statements like 'Pleasure is good'.

W. D. Hudson, *Modern Moral Philosophy*, 1970. (Chapter 5 discusses supervenience (as he calls it) and UNIVERSALIZABILITY.)

Consequentialism. Doctrine that the rightness of an act is to be judged solely in terms of its consequences, either actual or expected. A weaker form holds that there are no moral principles which cannot at least sometimes be legitimately overriden because of the consequences of applying them.

UTILITARIANISM is one form of consequentialism. On the difficulty of distinguishing acts from their consequences see ETHICS.

J. Cargile, 'On consequentialism', *Analysis*, vol. 29, 1969.

Consistent. One or more propositions form a consistent set if no contradiction can be deduced from the set. An AXIOM SYSTEM is consistent if no contradiction can be derived within it, i.e. by the rules it specifies. For some purposes, e.g. for systems without negation, other definitions are given, such as that a system is consistent if not every well-formed formula (see AXIOM SYSTEM) of the relevant kind can be derived in it. But the equivalence of different definitions cannot be taken for granted. Usually it is held that a logically false proposition or a contradiction is inconsistent with every proposition since every set it belongs to will imply a contradiction. But some have rejected this and insisted that whether two propositions are consistent with *each other* cannot be determined on the basis of either alone (Nelson); they would say, e.g. that 'Twice two is five' is consistent with 'Twice three is seven', but not with 'Twice two is seven'. See also VALID (for 'sound').

A. H. Basson and D. J. O'Connor, *Introduction to Symbolic Logic*, 3rd edn, 1960. (See index.)
E. J. Nelson, 'Intensional relations', *Mind*, 1930. (Consistency as involving both of two propositions.)

Constant. See VARIABLE.

Constatives. See SPEECH ACTS.

Constructivism. See INTUITIONISM.

Contextualism. In aesthetics, the doctrine that a work of art can only be appreciated in terms of its context. In philosophy of science, the doctrine that theoretical terms like 'electron' have meaning (*contextual meaning*) only by appearing as terms in deductive systems containing theorems which are empirically testable. In ethics, the doctrine that all values are instrumental (see GOOD), or that moral problems both arise and can be solved only when we already accept some moral principles. These principles can be questioned only in the light of further principles.

Contingent. Normally, neither necessary nor impossible. See MODALITIES.

Contradiction. A proposition false on logical grounds. The *law* or *principle of contradiction* (also called that of non-contradiction) says that nothing can simultaneously have and lack the same property, or that a proposition and its negation cannot both be true. Two propositions are *contradictories* if one is the negation of the other, or if they cannot both be true nor both false ('X is black', 'X is not black'). They are *contraries* if they cannot both be true but can both be false ('X is black', 'X is white'), and *sub-contraries* if they cannot both be false but can both be true ('X is not black', 'X is not white'). These terms can also be applied to predicates. 'Black' and 'white' are contrary predicates because 'X is black' and 'X is white' are contrary propositions. But contraries need not be opposites. 'Red' and 'yellow' are contraries. Of two contradictory terms one and only one must apply to anything in their range of significance, but neither need apply to things outside that range. 'Black' and 'not black' are contradictory predicates even if neither is true (or false) of, say, numbers. But if we insist that both are false of numbers they become contraries. In a loose sense a proposition contradicts its contraries, since it entails (see IMPLICATION) their contradictories. 'X is black' contradicts 'X is white', if it entails 'X is not white'.

Contraposition. Replacement of a proposition by a logically equivalent one (its *contrapositive*) having as subject the negation of the original predicate. The contrapositive of 'All cats are animals' is 'All non-animals are non-cats'. The contrapositive of a conditional or hypothetical proposition negates its antecedent and its consequent and interchanges them. 'If grass is green, snow is white' has as contrapositive 'If snow is not white, grass is not green'. This latter process is occasionally called *transposition*.

Contraries. See CONTRADICTION.

Contravalid. See VALID.

Conventionalism. In logic and mathematics, any doctrine according to which a priori truths are thought to be true by linguistic convention. Applied to science, conventionalist views emphasize that the laws and hypotheses we accept or postulate depend on convention (though we may have good reason for adopting one convention rather than another): We *can* explain the data of astronomy by Ptolemaic epicycles, it is claimed, though at the price of extreme complexity. For a conventionalist, a law found to be successful for predicting, etc., becomes analytic, i.e. nothing is any longer

Conversion

allowed to count as falsifying it. On some views it is only at this stage that it becomes a law. The real issue is perhaps *how far* convention enters in?

Conventionalism is close to INSTRUMENTALISM and PRAGMATISM. See also MODALITIES.

K. Britton, J. O. Urmson, W. C. Kneale, 'Are necessary truths true by convention?', *Proceedings of the Aristotelian Society*, supplementary vol., 1947.

H. Poincaré, *Science and Hypothesis*, 1902, transl. 1905. (Supports a conventionalist view of science.)

K. R. Popper, *The Logic of Scientific Discovery*, 1934, transl. 1959. (Critical of some aspects (only?) of conventionalism in science.)

Conversion. In traditional formal logic, replacement of a proposition by a logically equivalent one (its *converse*) having as subject the original predicate (*simple conversion*). 'No dogs are cats' is the converse of 'No cats are dogs'. In *conversion per accidens* the converse is implied by, but does not imply, the original. 'Some pets are dogs' is the converse per accidens of 'All dogs are pets'.

Corroboration. See CONFIRMATION.

Cosmological argument. An argument for God's existence, originating with Aristotle but taking various forms. Some versions of it are called the *first cause argument*. This is that everything requires a cause and God must exist to be the first cause—usually not first in time (Aristotle thought the universe was eternal) but as a sustaining cause. Aristotle gives the example of a stick moving a stone but itself simultaneously moved by a man. Another version of the cosmological argument, which is due to Aquinas, is that the universe exists only CONTINGENTLY (see MODALITIES), and therefore must depend on something which exists necessarily, namely God. Kant claimed that this version shared the main defect of the ONTOLOGICAL ARGUMENT. The argument is called cosmological because it argues from the nature of the cosmos or universe, which the ontological argument, and that from religious experience, do not. However, the argument from DESIGN, which also argues from the nature of the universe, is usually treated as distinct from the cosmological argument.

A. Flew, *An Introduction to Western Philosophy*, 1971, chapter 6.

A. Kenny, *The Five Ways*, 1969. (Aquinas's arguments for God's existence. First three are relevant.)

Counterfactuals. See CONDITIONALS.

Count noun. Roughly, *count nouns* have plurals and can take numerical adjectives (e.g. 'cat'), while *mass nouns* (*mass words, mass terms*) do neither of these things (e.g. 'snow', in its main sense). Many words are both, in different senses (e.g. 'tin'). Count nouns, if defined in this grammatical way, need not provide a principle of counting (see SORTAL). 'Thing' is grammatically a count noun, but one cannot unambiguously count the things in a room: what constitutes one thing? Mass nouns may or may not include some abstract nouns.

V. C. Chappell, 'Stuff and things', *Proceedings of the Aristotelian Society*, 1970–1. (Some of the complications.)

Covering law model. See EXPLANATION.

Criterion. Something providing a conclusive way of knowing whether something exists, or whether a word is used correctly. Criteria must be logically, and not merely inductively, evidence for what they are criteria of. Philosophical interest in criteria stems mainly from Wittgenstein, though what precisely he meant by the term is disputed. If some disease is defined as the presence of a certain bacillus, then finding that someone has the bacillus gives us a criterion for saying he has that disease, while finding simply that he has an inflammation gives us only a symptom. A symptom is something that we know from experience always accompanies the thing in question, but it does not have to do so by definition. Symptoms are therefore one kind of evidence of the thing's presence. Another kind is what only sometimes accompanies the thing. Wittgenstein emphasizes that criteria and symptoms fluctuate as circumstances differ or alter.

But a criterion, though linked by definition with what it is a criterion of, need not be present in every case. Horses are by definition quadrupeds, so that being a quadruped is part of a criterion for being a horse, but occasional freaks may have five legs. More importantly, we only have a concept of pain, Wittgenstein thinks, because there are publicly accessible criteria for telling when someone is in pain—but pain or its absence can be simulated. This suggests that criteria are important for applying a concept in general rather than in particular cases (see Hamlyn). Cf. also Wittgenstein's 'family resemblance' view of UNIVERSALS. A concept may have more than one criterion.

A feature is often loosely called a criterion of something if it is one of a set of features which jointly constitute a criterion of it in the strict sense. If being maned, neighing and a quadruped is a criterion of being a horse, being maned is loosely a criterion of it, though not all maned things are horse. See GOOD for meaning and criteria, which some writers (e.g. Hare) relate differently in the case of value terms like 'good' than in the case of other terms.

L. Wittgenstein, *The Blue and Brown Books*, 1958, written much earlier, pp. 24–5. (Nearest Wittgenstein comes to defining 'criteria'. Cf. section on criteria in N. Malcolm's review of Wittgenstein in *Philosophical Review*, 1954, revised and reprinted in his *Knowledge and Certainty*, 1963, and in G. Pitcher (ed.), *Wittgenstein*, 1966.)
R. Albritton, 'On Wittgenstein's use of the term "criterion" ', *Journal of Philosophy*, 1959, reprinted with afterthoughts in Pitcher (above). (Thinks Wittgenstein had two views on criteria. Many detailed references to text.)
D. Locke, *Myself and Others*, 1968, chapter 6.

Croce, Benedetto

J. W. Cook, 'Human beings', in P. Winch (ed.), *Studies in the Philosophy of Wittgenstein*, 1969. (Both these discuss criteria and their use in philosophy of mind.)

D. W. Hamlyn, *The Theory of Knowledge*, 1970, pp. 68–75. (Concepts and criteria.)

R. M. Hare, *The Language of Morals*, 1952, chapter 6. (Meaning and criteria, with reference to 'good'.)

Croce, Benedetto. 1866–1952. Born in Abbruzzi, he worked mainly in Naples. Though he wrote also on economics, ethics, politics and history, he is now best known for his work in aesthetics and literary criticism, in which he influenced COLLINGWOOD. His system was idealist in flavour, influenced by HEGEL and VICO, and centred on art as the expression of 'intuition', which is a certain kind of knowledge. Croce claims that aesthetics ends up as the general study of language. *Estetica come scienza dell'espressione e linguistica generale* (*Aesthetic*), 1902. *Breviario di Estetica* (*The Essence of Aesthetic*), 1913 (shorter work, originally published in translation in America (Houston), 1912).

Curve-fitting problem. See CONFIRMATION.

Cybernetics. See MIND (especially Anderson reference in bibliography).

D

Dasein. See EXISTENTIALISM.

Decidable. Theories, in the sense in which arithmetic is a theory, are decidable if formalizations exist for them which are COMPLETE. In systems without CONTINGENT (see MODALITIES) propositions, such as formalizations of arithmetic, a well-formed formula (see AXIOM SYSTEM) is decidable if and only if its negation is a theorem. Where contingent propositions enter, as in formalizations of the propositional CALCULUS, a well-formed formula is decidable if and only if one can prove whether it is logically true, logically false, or neither. A *decision procedure* decides this mechanically by simply following a rule in finitely many steps. Decision procedures exist for the propositional and monadic predicate CALCULI, but not, in general, for more complex systems. Proof that such a procedure exists, or does not exist, for a given sphere is called a *positive* or *negative solution*, respectively, to the *decision problem*. The negative solution for the predicate calculus (beyond the monadic) is *Church's theorem* (1936).

Decision problem. See DECIDABLE.

Decision procedure. See DECIDABLE.

Decision theory. The mathematical theory of how it is rational to act when confronted with alternatives which have various utilities and various probabilities. Sometimes called *game theory* or *theory of games*, though this is often limited to where one is playing against rational opponents, not against nature or 'blind chance' (e.g. in taking account of the weather).

M. D. Davis, *Game Theory*, 1970. (Elementary.)

Deduction. An argument is deductive if it draws a conclusion from certain premises on the grounds that to deny the conclusion would be to contradict the premises. But 'deduction' is used more loosely by early philosophers and outside philosophy. See also NATURAL DEDUCTION.

47

Defeasible

Defeasible. Concepts, and claims about where they apply, are called defeasible when they are always open to objection, and the objections are irredeemably heterogeneous, e.g. it is sometimes held of concepts like freewill and responsibility that no definite criteria can be given for when they apply. Compare the notions of *imperfect* and *prima facie duties* (see OUGHT).

H. L. A. Hart, 'The ascription of responsibility and rights', *Proceedings of the Aristotelian Society*, 1948–9, reprinted in A. Flew (ed.), *Logic and Language*, 1st series, 1951. (Hart has since withdrawn this paper, for reasons not affecting this reference.)

Definist fallacy. See NATURALISM.

Definition. In a definition a *definiens* or defining expression is given for a *definiendum* or what is to be defined. 'Definition' itself can stand for the sentence doing the defining, for the process of doing it, or for the definiens. Various rules for definitions have traditionally been given, but these are now widely regarded as either unduly restrictive, or as mere practical guides.

In a *real* or *essentialist definition* the definiendum is an essence or concept. A real definition is therefore an analysis of a concept (but see Mill). In a *nominal definition* the definiendum is a term or word. 'Real' here means 'applying to the thing or concept, as against the word'. 'Nominal' means 'applying to the word, as against the thing or concept'. The phrase 'real definition' is little used now. However, even a nominalist (i.e. here, one who accepts only nominal definitions) may reserve a word for a certain concept and then use a definition of the word to analyse the concept.

A definition may aim to clarify the meaning of an already existing term (*lexical* or *dictionary definitions*, e.g. ' "Puppy" in English means "young dog" '.) Or it may introduce an abbreviation or stipulate how a term is going to be used (*stipulative definitions*, e.g. 'By "puppy" I shall mean any dog shorter than twelve inches'.) Stipulative definitions are *prescriptive* in that they prescribe how a word is to be used as are lexical definitions in so far as they do not merely report usage but prescribe standards of 'good' usage. Normally it is not the case that any explanation of a term counts as a definition. A definition must have a certain adequacy, completeness, and universality. A definition should normally state NECESSARY AND SUFFICIENT CONDITIONS for applying the definiendum. 'A puppy is a dog' is true, but not a definition for not all dogs are puppies.

Contextual definitions or *definitions in use* define a term indirectly by giving an equivalent for a whole context in which it occurs. One might define 'average' by explaining how it is used in sentences like 'The average man has two and a half children'. Two rather technical notions may be briefly mentioned. In a *recursive definition* the term defined occurs in the definiens, but in a way that avoids circularity. The term 'ancestor of' might be recursively defined as 'parent of, or ancestor of a parent of'. Cf. RECURSIVE. An *inductive definition* or *definition by induction* defines the possession of a property by a term x in terms of its possession by all the terms preceding x in a series, together with a definition of its possession by the first term in the series. Recursive and inductive definitions thus come to the same thing. (In the above example, considered as defining what it is for x to be an ancestor, the first term in the series would be someone's parent, the second his grandparent, etc. x might be, say, his fourteenth ancestor.)

In an *ostensive definition* an instance of what the term applies to is physically pointed to ('Red is that colour there', or just 'Red!', said while pointing to a tomato). For *impredicative definitions* see theory of TYPES. In *persuasive definitions* an emotionally charged term is given a revised factual significance, to which the emotional charge then attaches. If one dislikes those who live on rent, one might redefine 'fascist' to include them. For *extensional* and *intensional definitions*, see UNIVERSALS.

What kinds of words can be defined will largely depend on the kind of definition, and on how rigorously 'definition' is interpreted. Problems often arise about whether a given term can be defined without going outside a specified set of terms, e.g. can 'life' be defined in chemical terms?

R. Robinson, *Definition*, 1950. (Full-scale study, taking very liberal view of what counts as definition.)

J. S. Mill, *A System of Logic*, 1843, book 1, chapter 8. (See § 5 for real definitions.)

A. Tarski (see bibliography to TRUTH AND FALSITY. *Inter alia*, distinguishes formal correctness and material adequacy of definitions.)

C. L. Stevenson, *Ethics and Language*, 1945, chapter 9. (Persuasive definitions.)

Denial. See NEGATION.

Denial of antecedent. Fallacy of arguing that if the antecedent of a conditional statement is false, so is the consequent, e.g. 'If all cats are black, Tiddles is black; but not all cats are black; so Tiddles is not black.'

Denotation. See MEANING, INTENSIONALITY, DESCRIPTIONS.

Denoting phrases. See DESCRIPTIONS.

Deontic. See ETHICS.

Deontological. See ETHICS.

Descartes, René. 1596–1650. Born at La Haye in France and educated by the Jesuits, he travelled in his youth and then lived mostly in Holland, but finally at the Swedish court. Usually known as the first of the 'continental RATIONALISTS', he contributed to mathematics, as well as philosophy, inventing 'Cartesian co-ordinates' and analytical geometry. In philosophy he aimed to pursue SCEPTICISM as far as possible, using a 'method of

Descriptions

doubt' until he reached something he could not doubt, his principle 'Cogito ergo sum' ('I think therefore I am'), on which he built up a systematic philosophy. He is particularly noted for his body/mind dualism. *Discours de la méthode pour bien conduire sa raison et chercher les vérités dans les sciences (Discourse on Method)*, 1637. *Meditationes de Prima Philosophia (Meditations on the First Philosophy)*, 1641. *Principia Philosophiae (Principles of Philosophy)*, 1644. See also ANALYTIC, CARTESIAN, HOBBES, INCORRIGIBLE, MALEBRANCHE, RYLE, SPACE, SPINOZA, SUBSTANCE, THINKING.

Descriptions (theory of). Theory devised by Russell to analyse sentences containing 'denoting phrases'. Russell originally recognized two ways of picking something out in discourse. One could name it. Or one could *denote* it, pick it out by using terms with a general meaning. 'Socrates' names Socrates. 'That man' does not name Socrates, or anyone, but might serve to pick Socrates out because of general rules for the use of 'that' and 'man'. Russell therefore recognized what he called *denoting phrases*. These were of two kinds. *Definite descriptions* begin with the definite article or its equivalent. ('That man' equals 'The man over there'). *Indefinite descriptions* begin with the indefinite article. But because definite and indefinite descriptions can occur in meaningful sentences where there is nothing for them to denote, as in 'The present king of France is bald', he concluded that they cannot really function by denoting after all, and that the grammatical form of sentences containing them is misleading as to their logical form. In fact he abandoned denoting, though he temporarily kept the term 'denoting phrase'. The theory of descriptions says that the logical form of the above example is: 'There is one and only one person now reigning over France, and there is no one now reigning over France who is not bald.' Variant alternative formulations exist. Since what a sentence means should not depend on what happens to exist, Russell applied this analysis to all denoting phrases, including 'the queen of England' as well as 'the king of France'. These phrases are then called *incomplete symbols* (see LOGICAL CONSTRUCTIONS).

Contrasted with denoting phrases are *logically proper names*, whose meaning is what they name. Ordinary proper names which do not name anything (and ultimately, for various reasons, all ordinary proper names) he regarded as disguised descriptions, and so as incomplete symbols, e.g. 'Apollo' stands for 'The Greek sun-god'.

B. Russell, 'On denoting', *Mind*, 1905, reprinted in his *Logic and Knowledge*, 1956, and elsewhere. (Original version of theory of descriptions.)

R. J. Butler, 'The scaffolding of Russell's theory of descriptions', *Philosophical Review*, 1954. (Background to the theory.)

P. F. Strawson, 'On referring', *Mind*, 1950, often reprinted. (Attacks the theory. Cf. also Strawson's 'Identifying reference and truth-values', *Theoria*, 1964, reprinted (with 'On referring') in his *Logico-Linguistic Papers*, 1971. Russell replies in 'Mr Strawson on referring', *Mind*, 1957, reprinted in his *My Philosophical Development*, 1959.)

L. Linksy, *Referring*, 1967. (Mediates between Russell and Strawson.)

Descriptivism. See NATURALISM.

Design (argument from). Argument, with many versions, for God's existence, relying on apparent pattern, design or purpose in the universe. Also called the teleological argument, and, by Kant, the *physico-theological argument*. See also COSMOLOGICAL ARGUMENT.

A. Flew, *An Introduction to Western Philosophy*, 1971, chapter 6.

Designate. A name designates its bearer, and so only designates at all if it has a real bearer, though it may be quite intelligible without one ('Pickwick'). Its bearer is not nowadays regarded as its MEANING. Occasionally 'designates' means 'connotes' (see MEANING). A *rigid designator* is a term which, if it designates an object at all, would designate it in any situation provided only that the object still exists and language remains the same. 'Square of three' is a rigid designator of nine. 'Victor of Waterloo' is a non-rigid designator of Wellington, since he could have lost the battle.

S. Kripke, 'Identity and necessity' in M. K. Munitz (ed.), *Identity and Individuation*, 1971. (See pp. 144-9 for rigid designator.)

Designated values. See TRUTH-VALUE.

Determinism. See FREEWILL.

Dewey, John. 1859–1952. Educationalist and philosopher who was born in Vermont and worked in various American universities, the last being Columbia. His philosophical views are usually classed as PRAGMATIST and INSTRUMENTALIST. In particular, he is noted for his use of *warranted assertibility* in connexion with the notion of truth. Much of his work was concerned with applying his pragmatist views to the study of educational theory and reform. *How We Think*, 1910. *Democracy and Education*, 1916. *Reconstruction in Philosophy*, 1920. *Human Nature and Conduct*, 1922. *The Quest for Certainty*, 1929. *Logic: The Theory of Inquiry*, 1938.

Diagonal procedure. See RICHARD'S PARADOX.

Dialectic. Literally, 'a method of conversation or debate'. 'Dialectic' originally referred to debating tournaments, but Socrates and, at first, Plato thought that the cultivation of philosophy, and discovery of philosophical truths, could best be achieved by the interplay of opinions in co-operative enquiry by question and answer. Plato therefore used 'dialectic' for philosophical method in general, and came to apply it to whatever method of enquiry he favoured at the time, or to the highest stage thereof. Aristotle kept the sense of conversational interplay; but though he confined dialectic to serious enquiry rather than *eristic* or argumentativeness, he thought it an inferior method of enquiry because it had to start from premises which were agreed to by the interlocutors rather than those which could be demonstrated to be true.

The use of 'dialectic' for debates where one reduced an opponent to

Dichotomy paradox

contradiction helped to make 'dialectic' largely synonymous with 'logic' for the Stoics and the Middle Ages. The Aristotelian feature whereby dialectic relies on inadequate premises is seen again in Kant. In many later writers, notably Hegel, the sense of 'interplay' is transferred from the development of thought to that of the world itself. The world develops dialectically by the interplay of opposites.

G. E. L. Owen (ed.), *Aristotle on Dialectic*, 1968. (Essays on dialectic up to Aristotle. Varying in difficulty. Most accessible are items by Ryle (controversial), Moreau and Moraux (both in French).)

Dichotomy paradox. See ZENO'S PARADOXES.

Differentia. What distinguishes a species from other species of the same genus. For Aristotle there was a problem about which CATEGORY the differentia of a substance-species (man, horse, etc.) belonged to.

Disciplinary matrix. See PARADIGM.

Disjunction. See CONJUNCTION.

Distribution. In traditional SYLLOGISTIC logic the subject of a universal proposition (see QUANTIFIER WORDS) and the predicate of a negative proposition are said to be distributed. This has been taken to mean that a universal proposition and a negative proposition say something about every member of the classes which their subject and predicate, respectively, denote. 'No cats are black', which is both universal and negative, would say something about all cats and something, though it is unclear what, about all black things. On the other hand 'All cats are black' says something about all cats but nothing about all black things. The *laws* or *rules of distribution* say that in a valid SYLLOGISM the middle term must be distributed at least once, and any term distributed in the conclusion must be distributed in its premise. It is disputed whether any coherent rationale of distribution can be given, and how far the rules are in fact needed or effective.

This notion is unconnected with the *distributive laws* or *rules* of modern logical and mathematical algebras, which govern the interchange of 'and' and 'or' (or analogous notions).

P. T. Geach, *Reference and Generality*, 1962, chapter 1. (Attacks distribution.)
D. Makinson, 'Distribution in traditional logic', *Nous*, 1969. (Defends and generalizes distribution. Moderately technical.)
W. C. Wilcox, 'Another look at distribution', *Mind*, 1971. (Another criticism. Moderately technical.)

Division. See COMPOSITION.

Double aspect theory. Theory that mind and matter as a whole (Spinoza), or that individual minds and their corresponding bodies, are two aspects of a single substance. See also IDENTITY THEORY OF MIND.

Double effect. See ETHICS.

Duhem, Pierre M. M. 1861–1916. Born in Paris, he worked in various French universities. He did important scientific work, notably in thermodynamics, and also engaged in the history of science. In philosophy his chief contribution was to philosophy of science. His position was akin to positivism and to conventionalism, but while he insisted on the separation of science from metaphysics, he gave metaphysics the role of providing explanations and, it might be relevant to add, he remained a Catholic. Science itself, he thought, should elaborate theories, whose purpose was not to explain but simply to systematize phenomena in ways which science found convenient. *La Théorie physique, son objet et sa structure* (*The Aim and Structure of Physical Theory*), 1906.

Duty. See OUGHT.

Dyadic. See MONADIC.

E

Education (philosophy of). The study of general theoretical problems, of an A PRIORI kind, about the possibility, nature, aims and methods of education.

The ancient *paradox of learning* (you can't learn what you don't know, because you won't know what to seek, and won't recognize it when found) is now dead, but one can still ask whether things like moral education are possible.

How does education differ from indoctrination, training and programming and must indoctrination etc. be totally, or only partially, excluded? What is presupposed in the learner, e.g. what degree of rationality? Is a teacher needed, or can one educate oneself, deliberately or accidentally? Can one be educated to be rational, in any sense, and what is involved in acquiring one's first language (cf. PRIVATE LANGUAGE)?

These questions about the nature of education affect questions about its aims and methods. Is the primary aim to instil knowledge, or to instil the ability to acquire knowledge, or neither? How far is education concerned with FACTS, and of what kinds? What is involved in education in morality and (aesthetic or other) taste? Does education aiming at knowledge differ from education aiming at action?

Questions of method largely belong to the theory and practice of education rather than to its philosophy, but answers to the above questions are relevant both here and to traditional questions on the roles of nature, training, practice, play, example.

W. Jaeger, *Paideia*, 1934 and after, transl. 1939–45. (Extended treatment of education and related topics in and before the age of Plato.)

Plato, *Meno*. (Can 'virtue' (or excellence) be taught? (For paradox of learning see §§ 80–81.) Cf. also *Protagoras, Republic*, books 2, 3, *Laws*, books 1, 2, 7.)

R. S. Peters (ed.), *The Philosophy of Education*, 1973. Readings, with annotated bibliography.)

Effects. See CAUSATION.

Egocentric particulars. See TOKEN-REFLEXIVES.

Eidos. See FORM.

Eleatics. Parmenides and his disciple Zeno (not Zeno the STOIC) started a philosophy of extreme monism in Elea in south Italy in the early fifth century BC. Parmenides held that reality must consist of a single, undifferentiated and unchanging object. Zeno, as usually interpreted, defended him by revealing paradoxes in rival views. With their follower Melissus of Samos (mid fifth century), who developed Parmenides, they influenced PLATO among others. See also PARADOX, SPACE, SUBSTANCE, ZENO'S PARADOXES.

Elenchus. Usually, especially in Socratic context, an attempted refutation by questioning. In Aristotle it means refutation, sometimes limited to refutations in SYLLOGISTIC form. *Ignoratio elenchi:* ignoring the issue.

Emotivism. See NATURALISM.

Empirical. See A PRIORI.

Empiricism. Any of a variety of views to the effect that either our concepts or our knowledge are, wholly or partly, based on experience through the senses and introspection. The 'basing' may refer to psychological origin or, more usually, philosophical justification. For some of the complexities see A PRIORI. Extreme empiricists may confine our knowledge to statements about SENSE DATA, plus perhaps ANALYTIC statements. Less extreme empiricists say that such statements must form the basis on which all our other knowledge is erected. Other empiricists, however, may simply deny that there are any a priori propositions, or any synthetic or non-analytic, a priori ones. Or they may say that if there are any a priori propositions, there are still no a priori concepts. A weak form of empiricism may say only that we can acquire some knowledge through the senses. An empiricist view of some given concept or proposition bases it somehow on experience.

Recently empiricism has often taken the form of a doctrine of meaning, saying that a word or sentence has meaning only if rules involving sense experience can be given for applying or verifying it. Analytic sentences are excepted. Such rules may further *constitute* the meaning. This is often called *logical empiricism*. For this and *consistent empiricism* see POSITIVISM.

Radical empiricism is a name for the philosophy of W. James; cf. PRAGMATISM.

'British empiricists' is a traditional label for Locke, Berkeley and Hume, in particular, and for sundry lesser or later figures regarded as sharing their general outlook. See also RATIONALISM.

D. Odegard, 'Locke as an empiricist', *Philosophy*, 1965. (Discusses senses of 'empiricist', in connexion with Locke's philosophy.)

Empiriocriticism. See POSITIVISM.

Enantiomorphs. See INCONGRUENT COUNTERPARTS.

En soi

En soi. See BAD FAITH.

Entailment. See IMPLICATION.

Entelechy. In Aristotle, actuality as against potentiality. He defines soul as the first entelechy of an organic body, meaning, roughly, the set of things the body can do when active. The second entelechy is the actual doing of these things. It is unclear how far entelechy is general or particular, i.e. whether each individual animal, etc. has its own entelechy, or only has that of its species. In Leibniz 'entelechy' means sometimes MONAD and sometimes the dominant monad in a complex. The term also occurs elsewhere.

Aristotle, *De Anima* (*On the Soul*), book 2, chapter 1.
G. W. Leibniz, *Monadology*, 1714, esp. §§ 18–19, 63, 70.

Enthymeme. Argument in which one or more premises, or interim conclusions, are silently assumed.

Epicureans. Epicurus of Samos (342–271 BC) founded a school (sometimes called the Garden, from its meeting-place in Athens) which rivalled the STOICS till Roman times, though producing few famous names. Like the Stoics, they were materialists, but they added the concept of empty space and were atomists (following Leucippus and Democritus of the fifth century). They also rejected determinism by allowing an uncaused 'swerve' to their atoms, though its role in their system is obscure. Like the Stoics they were interested in epistemology, but were less interested in logic. In ethics, as well as rejecting determinism they advocated HEDONISM, but of a very restrained kind: their hedonism was largely a matter of emphasizing the role of feeling, but their stress on the pains that followed excess led to their recommendations differing little in practice from those of Stoicism. A version of the system is eloquently expounded in Lucretius' (c.99–c.55BC) poem *De Rerum Natura* (*On the Nature of Things*). See also PHILOSOPHY, SUBSTANCE.

A. A. Long, *Hellenistic Philosophy*, 1974.

Epiphenomenalism. Doctrine that mental phenomena are entirely caused by physical phenomena in the brain or central nervous system, and themselves have no effects, mental or physical.

Epistemic. Concerning knowledge.

Epistemology. Enquiry into the nature and ground of experience, belief and knowledge. 'What can we know, and how do we know it?' are questions central to philosophy, and knowledge forms the main topic of epistemology, along with other cognitive notions like BELIEF, understanding, REASON, JUDGMENT, SENSATION, imagination, supposing, guessing, learning, forgetting. See philosophy of MIND (last paragraph, for philosophy of mind and epistemology). Also called *theory of knowledge, gnoseology*.

Questions about knowledge can be divided into four main, though overlapping, groups, concerning its nature, its types, what is known, and its origin. Knowledge clearly differs in its nature from purely psychological states like feeling sure, for in straightforward contexts the word 'know', like 'realize', 'REFUTE', and many other words, can only be used by a speaker who himself has certain beliefs on the matter in question. If I say 'Smith knows (or, Smith does not know) that fairies exist' I commit myself to their existence, which I do not if I say 'Smith believes (feels sure, is sure) . . .'. Knowing is usually thought to involve believing, though some say that it *replaces* belief, or that one can believe one thing while somehow knowing the opposite.

It is often thought that knowledge is justified true belief, but even if belief *is* involved there are objections to this view. No agreed account has yet been produced of what counts as justification, and sometimes no justification seems called for: do we have to justify claims to know our own intentions, or where our limbs are? Some say we have a special *knowledge without observation* of certain things, e.g. (in normal health) where our limbs are, which others can only know by observing us. Also has one knowledge if one is regularly right but can give no reasons, though the subject-matter seems to demand them (e.g. successful sooth-saying)?

Obviously if one is in error one does not have knowledge, but must error be not only absent but impossible (cf. INCORRIGIBLE)? If so, knowledge will be a rarity. Some philosophers on the other hand, notably Wittgenstein, claim that we cannot have knowledge unless the idea of our being mistaken makes sense, e.g. we cannot know, nor not know, that we are in pain.

Other accounts of knowledge introduce causation, or make 'know' a performative verb (see SPEECH ACTS), or say that to know is to be able to tell.

Does knowing involve knowing that one knows? How far do knowledge and the other cognitive notions involve consciousness and rationality: can humans have unconscious knowledge? Can animals and machines have knowledge at all?

The types of knowledge often occur in pairs. A PRIORI and empirical knowledge have long been contrasted (see also below on origins), and the ANALYTIC/synthetic distinction is relevant here. If a priori knowledge is analytic it risks having no content. Kant postulated synthetic a priori propositions, known by TRANSCENDENTAL ARGUMENTS, but their existence is controversial.

Knowing propositions or facts (propositional knowledge, e.g. knowing that Paris is the capital of France) is contrasted with knowing objects (e.g. knowing Paris). 'OBJECTS' must presumably be wide enough to include things like someone's character, and knowing objects may anyway involve knowing facts about them.

Russell distinguished *knowledge by acquaintance* from *knowledge by description*, a distinction only intelligible in the light of his theory of DESCRIPTIONS. If I am acquainted with an object it can be a constituent of a proposition I understand, and its logically proper name will be the subject of that proposition. If I know such a proposition to be true I have

Epistemology

knowledge by acquaintance of the object. If on the other hand I know the proposition *that the last French king was beheaded*, whose subject is a description, I have knowledge by description of that king, whether or not I am also acquainted with him. By acquaintance Russell apparently means a form of immediate knowledge which is not propositional but consists in confrontation. 'Immediate knowledge' might cover some propositional knowledge like knowledge without observation, some perceptual knowledge, telepathy and intuition, but there are difficulties over just what acquaintance, in Russell's sense, consists in.

Ryle contrasts *knowing how* and *knowing that*, and this distinction has been widely used in, for example, ethics and philosophy of mind, e.g. moral knowledge might consist in knowing how to behave.

Some types of knowledge are partly defined in terms of what is known, including memory, of the past, and precognition, of the future.

The objects we have knowledge of are legion, and apart from the general problems of SCEPTICISM some of these objects raise special problems about how, rather than whether, we know them. One such sphere is knowledge about ourselves, especially about our existence, our feelings and their locations (when they have them), our mental states and characteristics, and the position of our limbs (see above). Two controversial notions relevant here are private and privileged ACCESS. Other such spheres include the past (including dreams), the future, general facts and scientific laws, logical and mathematical facts, philosophical, religious, moral and aesthetic facts. In many of these cases it is disputed whether, strictly, there are any such facts to be known.

RATIONALISTS and EMPIRICISTS have traditionally battled over the origin of knowledge. Can the mind to any degree actively originate its contents, or are those contents entirely built up from what it passively receives through the senses or introspection, as the *tabula rasa* or blank tablet theory suggests? The strong empiricist and sceptical trend in English-language philosophy earlier in this century is now breaking down as the issue becomes less clearcut. Here too belong questions about conceptual schemes, or basic ways of looking at the world. How fundamental can differences between them be? e.g. must we view the world in terms of substances and attributes, etc., or could we substitute an alternative scheme? Cf. CATEGORIES.

Epistemology includes further questions somehow related to knowledge. Rigour and provability concern the acquisition of knowledge. TRUTH and PROBABILITY concern the assessment of it. MEANING and other notions relating to language concern the vehicle of it. METAPHYSICS, LOGIC, and the philosophies of MATHEMATICS, SCIENCE and LANGUAGE are all relevant here.

Genetic epistemology, associated largely with J. Piaget (1896) and his followers, studies empirically the acquisition of concepts and mental abilities by children, and belongs to psychology rather than philosophy. For *Moral Epistemology* see ETHICS.

A. D. Woozley, *Theory of Knowledge*, 1949. (Elementary introduction.)
D. W. Hamlyn, *Theory of Knowledge*, 1970. (More advanced introduction.)

A. P. Griffiths (ed.), *Knowledge and Belief*, 1967. (Articles and bibliography, with introduction. Note E. Gettier's objections to the 'justified true belief' definition of 'knowledge'.)

A. J. Ayer, *Problem of Knowledge*, 1956. (Empiricist approach.)

G. N. A. Vesey, *The Embodied Mind*, 1965, chapter 7, § 5. (Discussion of knowledge without observation.)

N. Malcolm, 'The privacy of experience', in A. Stroll (ed.), *Epistemology*, 1967. (Wittgensteinian view of knowledge and error. Compare (and contrast) his article in Griffiths, above.)

A. I. Goldman, 'A causal theory of knowing', *Journal of Philosophy*, 1967. (Cf. also B. Skyrms, 'The explication of "X knows that *p*" ', ibid.)

J. L. Austin, 'Other minds', in his *Philosophical Papers*, 1961. ('Know' as performative verb.)

B. Russell, 'Knowledge by acquaintance and knowledge by description', in his *Mysticism and Logic*, 1918. (Cf. INTUITION.)

G. Ryle, *The Concept of Mind*, 1949, chapter 2. (Knowing how and that. For criticism see D. G. Brown, 'Knowing how and knowing that, what', in G. Pitcher and O. Wood (eds), *Ryle*, 1970, and for use in ethics J. Gould, *The Development of Plato's Ethics*, 1955.)

G. Ryle, 'Epistemology', in J. O. Urmson (ed.), *The Concise Encyclopaedia of Western Philosophy and Philosophers*, 1960. (Brings out breakdown of rationalist/empiricist contrast.)

Epoche. See PHENOMENOLOGY.

Equivalence. Reciprocal implication, in any sense of 'IMPLICATION'.

Equivalence relation. Any SYMMETRIC and TRANSITIVE relation, e.g. *equal in size to*. Its terms are equivalent in the sense that there is some determinable property, like size, which they all have to the same degree or in the same determinate form, and whatever any of them has the relation to, so do the others. If *a* is equal in size to *b*, then if *a* exceeds *c*, *b* also exceeds *c*.

Equivocal. See AMBIGUITY.

Eristic. See DIALECTIC.

Erotetic. Concerning questions.

Essence (nominal and real). A *nominal essence* is a group of terms used to define a concept. For example, if I define a horse as 'anything with a mane and four legs that neighs', then this phrase or group of terms forms the nominal essence of *horse*. A *real essence* is either a group of concepts or UNIVERSALS objectively given in nature independently of our definitions (e.g. Socrates' question 'What is courage, really and truly and irrespective of mere human opinions?' presupposes that courage has a real essence); or

Essentialism

else (with Locke) it is an underlying structure of an object, e.g. an atomic structure. See also FORM.

J. Locke, *An Essay concerning Human Understanding*, 1690, book 3, chapters 3–6.

Essentialism. See MODALITIES.

Eternal recurrence. See METAPHYSICS.

Ethics. Perhaps on the dominant view an enqiry into how men ought to act in general, not as means to a given end. Etymology supports this; see MORAL. The primary concepts are then ought, obligation, duty, right, wrong, though not in all their uses. For the other main view the primary topic is value and the primary concepts are the valuable, the desirable, the good in itself. These notions are normally included under ethics, though they can also be excluded as belonging rather to *axiology*, the study of value in general (in aesthetics, economics, etc., as well as ethics). An ethics based primarily on value can be called an *axiological ethics*.

These two views *of* ethics correspond closely to two outlooks *in* it. For *deontologists* (notably Kant, W. D. Ross, H. A. Prichard) duty is prior to value, and at least some of our duties, such as promise-keeping, are independent of values. *Deontological* properly means connected with, or favouring, this outlook. *Deontic* means, simply, connected with duty and related notions, as in 'deontic LOGIC'. For *teleologists*, notably UTILITARIANS, our only duties have reference to ends and are to produce value, or perhaps to distribute it in certain ways. These views may not be sharply distinguishable, since deliberate action must always aim at some end; and even Kant emphasized moral worth. Also the slogan 'Do right, whatever the consequences' faces difficulties over distinguishing acts from their consequences (cf. CAUSATION).

The distinction between views *of* ethics and views *in* ethics is reflected in two groups into which ethical questions are often divided. These are usually contrasted as *ethics/morals*, *metaethics/ethics*, or *philosophical ethics/normative ethics*, the subject as a whole being called *ethics*, *moral philosophy*, or sometimes *morals*.

In the first group are conceptual questions, which introduce other branches of philosophy, notably logic, philosophy of language, and epistemology. During this century questions about the meaning of ethical terms and the CRITERIA for applying them have been emphasized. How do the terms relate to each other, including the 'bad' terms, like 'bad', 'evil', 'wrong', etc., though in practice these 'bad' terms receive much less attention? How do moral uses of all these terms relate to non-moral uses, and in general what distinguishes the MORAL as such? Other questions concern how we should analyse sentences contining these terms. Cf. NATURALISM, on the prescriptivist/descriptivist issue and the fact/value distinction. A connected question is whether there are any objective moral truths, and whether moral conclusions can be objective even if not strictly

60

describable as 'true'. Questions about how such conclusions might be known, and, in general about how moral arguments can be justified, what part is played in them by reason, feeling and intuition, and about the nature and role of conscience, belong to *moral epistemology*. An important notion in this area is that of UNIVERSALIZABILITY, and the MORAL sphere can often be compared with others, e.g. the aesthetic or that of rational action in general. Cf. also GOOD, OUGHT.

Questions of the second main group mentioned above concern actual moral issues, like: What things are good, right, etc.? What are our duties? Are there any natural rights?

These two groups were sharply distinguished (and the first preferred) both by logical POSITIVISM because of its restrictions on what could be true or false, and by the succeeding linguistic PHILOSOPHY because in rejecting the restrictive dogmatism of the positivists it also thought the philosopher should avoid dogmatizing on substantial issues. However, this all implies that every position on questions of the first group is compatible with every position on those of the second. This compatibility results from the particular answers positivism and linguistic philosophy gave to questions of the first group. These answers, and therefore the sharpness of the distinction, have been attacked because of doubts on the fact/value distinction and more willingness to allow reason a role in moral arguments, not just in factual or logical preliminaries.

Many questions seem not to belong to either group alone, such as analyses of particular virtues and vices, and questions about merit and responsibility and about moral ideals. Questions belonging to philosophy of mind rather than ethics, but clearly relevant here, concern FREEWILL, psychological HEDONISM and INCONTINENCE. Such borderline questions are often classified as *moral psychology*, along with analyses of notions like motive, intention, desire, voluntary, deliberation, pain, pleasure, happiness; ethics proper examines their moral relevance. Interest is a more specifically ethical notion, and the distinction between one's own and others' interests leads to questions about egoism and altruism.

One question involving both moral psychology and ethics concerns the Catholic *double effect* doctrine: we may not intentionally produce evils, but we may sometimes rightly do what we foresee will produce evils, provided we do not intend these. Does this make sense? If so, is it psychologically possible? And is it morally acceptable?

Metaphysical and religious justifications for ethical positions are uncommon now, but one concept deserving mention is that of the FUNCTION of man, appealed to especially by Aristotle.

A distinction is sometimes made between *agent ethics* and *spectator ethics* because things like motives, and the difference between what is right and what the agent thinks is right, may play one role when one is deciding what to do, and another role when one is judging what someone else does or should do.

Casuistry is the application of moral principles to particular cases or types of case. Here it contrasts with *situational ethics*, which insists on considering each moral situation as it arises, in isolation from others, and

Event

rejecting general principles. Casuistry has fallen into disrepute largely from the possibility of using ever more subtle features of a situation to reach a desired moral conclusion in the face of allegedly inadequate moral principles—'inadequate' can be stretched to cover 'inconvenient'.

Descriptive ethics examines what moral views are actually held by various people or societies, and whether any are universally held. Though such questions are, strictly speaking, scientific rather than philosophical, they often involve analysis and interpretation as well as mere fact-finding.

Aristotle, *Nicomachean Ethics*. (Very influential, for methods rather than conclusions, on post-war British ethics; cf. R. Sorabji, 'Aristotle and Oxford Philosophy', in *American Philosophical Quarterly*, 1969. See book 1 for functions, books 2–5 for virtues and responsibility, book 7 for incontinence.)

A. Gewirth, 'Metaethics and moral neutrality', R. C. Solomon, 'Sumner on metaethics', *Ethics*, 1968. (Discussions of relations between metaethics and normative ethics. Cf. G. H. von Wright, *The Varieties of Goodness*, 1963, esp. chapter 1.)

W. Frankena, *Ethics*, 1963. (Short introduction, from modified Utilitarian standpoint.)

R. B. Brandt, *Ethical Theory*, 1959.

J. Hospers, *Human Conduct*, 1961. (Two extended introductions, emphasizing normative ethics as well as metaethics. Both have bibliographies. Hospers has exercises.)

G. J. Warnock, *The Object of Morality*, 1971. (Brief. Reacts against positivist deprecation of normative ethics.)

H. A. Prichard, *Moral Obligation*, 1949. (Modern version of intuitionism.)

R. M. Hare, *Freedom and Reason*, 1963. (Includes discussion of moral ideals. Cf. J. O. Urmson, 'Saints and heroes', in A. I. Melden (ed.), *Essays in Moral Philosophy*, 1958, reprinted in J. Feinberg (ed.), *Moral Concepts*, 1969.)

A. C. MacIntyre, *A Short History of Ethics*, 1966.

J. N. Findlay, *Axiological Ethics*, 1970. (Discusses some less fashionable writers.)

Event. Generally regarded as a change, usually of short duration, in the qualities or relations such as spatial relations of a thing. Many of the problems about events concern how they are related to other things, e.g. OBJECTS, particulars (see UNIVERSALS), INDIVIDUALS, UNIVERSALS, FACTS, states of affairs, propositions (see SENTENCES), changes, ACTIONS. Can events be classed under any of these? Also are events of radically different kinds? Are some events recurrent (e.g. 'annual events' perhaps?) and some unique, some instantaneous and some enduring, some mental and some physical? An important ambiguity is that sometimes 'event' means 'kind of event'. How should we individuate events (i.e. tell when we have one and when another)? Are events always datable? A murder is presumably an event, but if I murder someone by slow poison, does the murder occur when

Existentialism

I administer the poison or when the victim dies, perhaps years later? And can events move or change?

R. Chisholm, 'States of affairs again', D. Davidson, 'Eternal versus ephemeral events', *Nous*, 1970. (Events, propositions, particulars. Further references in Davidson.)
Z. Vendler, 'Causal relations', *Journal of Philosophy*, 1967, pp. 707–8. (Events and facts.)
D. Davidson, 'Mental events', in L. Foster and J. W. Swanson (eds), *Experience and Theory*, 1970.

Evidence (paradox of ideal). Suppose we assume that the a priori PROBABILITY of a certain penny falling heads on the next toss is ½, and that therefore it is rational to half-expect heads. Suppose we then find that in the past it has fallen heads and tails equally often. This evidence seems ideal justification for the rationality of this half-expecting. Yet the half-expecting was already the perfectly rational state of mind to adopt. Therefore the evidence seems superfluous. Offered by Popper as objection to (what he calls) subjectivist theory of PROBABILITY.

K. R. Popper, *The Logic of Scientific Discovery*, transl. 1959, pp. 407–10.
R. H. Vincent, 'The paradox of ideal evidence', *Philosophical Review*, 1962. (Criticizes Popper.)

Examination pararadox. See PREDICTION.

Excluded middle. A is B or A is not B or, in the propositional calculus, P ∨ ~P. Each thing either has or lacks any given property. Various formulations exist. In particular, there is a strong formulation, 'Every proposition is true or false', and a weaker formulation, 'Every proposition is true or not true'. In standard logic the weaker form follows from the law of CONTRADICTION, but in INTUITIONIST logic, which rejects the double negation principle, it does not. Alleged exceptions to the first mentioned formulation also include vague predicates (must Smith be either bald or not bald?). For J. Lukasiewicz (1878–1956) the law says that two contradictory propositions cannot both be false (cf. BIVALENCE). 'Middle' here has no connexion with the middle term of a syllogism.

P. T. Geach and W. F. Bednarowski, 'The law of excluded middle', *Proceedings of the Aristotelian Society*, supplementary vol. 1956.
J. Lukasiewicz (see bibliography to FREEWILL.)

Existential import. See QUANTIFIER WORDS.

Existentialism. A movement primarily associated with Kierkegaard, Jaspers, Heidegger, Sartre, Marcel, though many others are often included. Its exponents have widely differing outlooks, in religion and politics as well as in philosophy, but share certain general themes.
The most important of these themes is an interest in man as such and his relations to the world, and in the notion of BEING. Existentialists normally

63

Explanation

contrast the sort of being that applies to men, what Heidegger calls *Dasein*, with that which applies to things, and to men only in so far as they are things. Existentialists tend to regard the being which applies to men as something which men only attain sometimes, and ought to struggle for. Sartre contrasts the *être-pour-soi* which partly does, and partly should, belong to men, with the *être-en-soi* which belongs to things but which men fail to escape from when they live in BAD FAITH. There seems therefore to be a certain tension in existentialism about whether what is described is the inevitable human condition, or an ideal, perhaps never fully attainable. The two poles of this tension give existentialism its two philosophical footholds, in metaphysics and ethics.

A feature of human existence, for existentialists, is that men are active and creative while things are not. Things are simply what they are, but men might be other than they are. Men must choose, and (at least on some versions) must choose the principles on which they choose. They are not, like things, already determined. 'Existence precedes essence' for men: men make their essences as they go along, and do not live out a predetermined essence or blue-print. Men are free, and the reality and nature of freedom is a major concern for existentialists. Furthermore, men are conscious of the contrast between themselves and things, of their relations with other men, of their eventual deaths, and of their power to choose and become what they are not. All this leads to a notion of not-being, or 'Nothing', which, to the despair of logicians, existentialists tend to treat as a thing or condition in its own right. Sometimes this 'Nothing', and sometimes the contingency of things in general, provokes an emotion or condition of dread (despair, anguish, Angst, angoisse).

In elaborating what being is for men, and how men are related to the world, recent existentialists have been strongly influenced by Husserl's PHENOMENOLOGY.

N. Langiulli (ed.), *The Existentialist Tradition*, 1971. (Selections from many writers, with brief biographies and full bibliographies of them. Very difficult. Items by Abbagnano, Buber, Marcel, Sartre perhaps easiest.)

M. Warnock, *Existentialism*, 1970. (Elementary introduction, though limited in coverage.)

A. Manser, *Sartre*, 1966. (General philosophical study. Fairly elementary; but cf. hostile review in *Mind*, 1969.)

J. Collins, *The Existentialists*, 1952. (Critical appraisal. Difficult.)

D. M. Tulloch, 'Sartrian existentialism', *Philosophical Quarterly*, 1952.

A. R. Manser, A. T. Kolnai, 'Existentialism', *Proceedings of the Aristotelian Society*, supplementary vol., 1963. (Critical discussions of existentialist ethics.)

Explanation. The process of making something intelligible, or saying why certain things are as they are, or the account used to do these things. The account is sometimes called the *explanans*, and the thing to be explained is called the *explanandum*. An explanation may do things like reducing the unfamiliar to the familiar, thus enlightening people. Things it does in this way are called its pragmatic features, and they are relevant to the question of whether an explanation should be relative to the receiver. A child, a lay adult, and an expert seem to require different explanations of the same thing, since what is already familiar to them will differ. Yet a scientific explanation may be in terms hitherto unfamiliar even to the scientist, the layman may study science to find 'the' explanation of something, and the familiar itself may need explaining, as Newton explained the falling of an apple. Many writers have therefore regarded the pragmatic features as subjective and incidental, and have concentrated rather on various views of the logical form an explanation should take.

On one view, the *covering law model*, an explanation should state general laws and initial conditions which together logically entail the explanandum. 'All water heated at normal pressure to 100°C boils' and 'This water was so heated' together explain why this water boiled. The model can be adapted to explain laws themselves, and may have more complex applications, where covering laws are distinguished from supporting laws. However, not just any covering law will do. 'Whenever water is about to turn to steam it boils' and 'This water was about to turn to steam' do not explain the boiling. This suggests that an explanation must present what is 'more knowable absolutely' even though perhaps not 'more knowable to us' (Aristotle), and that pragmatic features are relevant, though they need not be subjective (cf. Dray, p. 74). An explanation therefore might present a cause, or something logically prior to the explanandum in the relevant system, as when the explanandum is a mathematical fact.

Often, however, scientific laws say not that all A's are B's, but that a certain proportion are. When the covering law model is extended to use laws of this type, explanations are called *statistical* or *probabilistic*. The previous kind, all A's are B's, are called *nomological*. Nomological explanations are DEDUCTIVE. The explanandum is deduced from the premises. Statistical explanations are usually (not always: see Hempel) INDUCTIVE. For reasons given under CONFIRMATION statistical explanations must be supplemented by Carnap's *requirement of total evidence* (or Hempel's weaker form, the *requirement of maximal specificity*).

It is disputed whether any but deductive explanations are properly called explanations at all, and also how many kinds of explanation there are. In particular can the covering law model apply to subjects like history and psychology, and can teleological explanations, i.e. those in terms of purposes or final causes, be reduced to causal explanations? Also do questions beginning with Why?, How?, etc. call for the same type of explanation? Is there a basic difference between explaining why-necessarily and how-possibly (Dray)? Can the covering law model account for explaining what something is, or what people are doing?

Further, how is explaining something related to describing it, and also to predicting it? Darwinism explains the variety of species, but does not seem fitted for predicting new species. Thales allegedly predicted the eclipse of 585 BC by consulting records but he could certainly not explain it. Do explanation and predictability nevertheless ultimately go together?

Explication

So far we have left the explananda vague. When not themselves laws, are they events, states, processes, situations, actions, forbearances, or are they statements describing these? To explain a statement one needs to explain one or more features of the relevant event, while to explain the event itself in its infinite richness would seem a hopeless task. Explaining meanings raises special problems.

After asking what an explanation is, we can ask when one is adequate, and whether the same explanandum can be given more than one explanation.

Explication, when not simply a synonym for 'explanation', is the process whereby a hitherto imprecise notion is given a formal definition, and so made suitable for use in formal work. The definition does not claim to be synonymous with the original notion, since it is avowedly making it more precise. (This is a form of logical analysis: see PHILOSOPHY.)

J. Hospers, 'What is explanation?', *Journal of Philosophy*, 1946, reprinted in A. Flew (ed.), *Essays in Conceptual Analysis*, 1956. (Elementary defence of covering law model as adequate for explanations-why of events.)

Aristotle, *Posterior Analytics*, 71b33–2ab. ('More knowable absolutely' and 'to us'. See also early chapters for when scientific argument is explanatory.)

C. G. Hempel, *Aspects of Scientific Explanation*, 1965. (Chapter 12 has full account of covering law model, and defends its adequacy in all fields. Chapter 9 (also in *Journal of Philosophy*, 1942) defends it regarding history. Cf. also his 'Explanation in science and in history', in R. G. Colodny (ed.), *Frontiers of Science and Philosophy*, 1962, reprinted in P. H. Nidditch (ed.), *The Philosophy of Science*, 1968, and in W. H. Dray (ed.), *Philosophical Analysis and History*, 1966.)

S. T. Goh, 'Some observations on the deductive-nomological theory', *Mind*, 1970. (Covering and supporting laws.)

W. H. Dray, *Laws and Explanation in History*, 1957. (Opposes covering law model for history.)

A. Donagan, 'Explanation in history', *Mind*, 1957. (Defends deductive model regarding history, but without general laws.)

C. Taylor, *The Explanation of Behaviour*, 1964. (Distinguishes, and defends need for, teleological and purposive explanations. T. L. S. Sprigge, 'Final causes', *Proceedings of the Aristotelian Society*, supplementary vol., 1971, assimilates teleological to causal explanations.)

G. H. von Wright, *Explanation and Understanding*, 1971. (Causal and teleological explanations regarding human action, etc. Good bibliography.)

R. Carnap, *Logical Foundations of Probability*, 1950, chapter 1. (Explication. Cf. W. V. Quine, *Word and Object*, 1960, §§ 53–4.)

Explication. See EXPLANATION.

Extension. See INTENSIONALITY.

Extensionality thesis. See LEIBNIZ'S LAW, INTENSIONALITY.

F

Fact. Usually, that which corresponds to a statement or makes it true (cf. the correspondence theory of TRUTH). As such a fact has seemed somehow to exist in the world, independent of thought and language. Since statements have a structure, consisting of subject and predicate, etc., it has been thought that facts must also have a structure, so that the elements in the statement can correspond to elements in the fact. Facts may simply be sets of objects in the world related in certain ways. If so, a cake will be a fact, which is philosophically implausible and not supported by common usage: while we might call the existence of a cake a fact, we would not normally call the cake itself one—we do not talk of having facts for tea. Nor are facts quite the same as situations or states of affairs, for one can be 'in' these, and it is natural to talk of a situation, but less natural to talk of a fact, as enduring or being altered.

The view that facts are things in the world corresponding to parts of thought and language has led to difficulties about whether there are any facts corresponding to statements involving words like 'not', 'or', 'all', 'some', 'if', since these statements seem to be less directly about the world than are simple statements (cf. LOGICAL ATOMISM).

If we abandon strict correspondence theories of truth, which need facts as entities in the world for statements to correspond to, we can tie facts more closely to thought and language. Are facts simply true propositions, or 'truths'? 'It's true that ...' and 'It's a fact that ...' mean much the same, and we can say 'What he says is a fact'. But expressions like 'His statement is borne out by (corresponds to) the facts' raise some difficulty. Facts can be causes ('The fact that the match was struck caused it to light'); but could we substitute 'true proposition' for 'fact' here? (On propositions see SENTENCES.) Perhaps one should no more ask what facts *are* than what cases are when something 'is the case'.

Brute facts are either facts in general considered as given independently of how we see the world, or facts about the world not involving values, rules, or institutions, e.g. 'Grass is green', 'I like beer', but not 'Beer is good for you'. 'Smith scored a goal' is an example of an *institutional fact*, depending on rules or institutions.

'Factual' is used in various ways and in each case false statements as

Fact/value distinction

well as true ones can be called factual. Contrasted with 'fictional' it refers to the real world. Contrasted with 'evaluative' it refers to what is objectively and decidably there and not merely contributed by human attitudes as evaluation may seem to be. Contrasted with 'theoretical', it refers to what is decidable, directly even if not conclusively, by observation. Contrasted with 'logical' or 'necessary', it refers either to what concerns the world rather than thought or discourse, or to what is merely contingently true or false. However, since statements in logic can normally be proved to be true or false, one can also talk of facts of logic or mathematics (cf. MODALITIES). See also SENTENCES, EVENTS.

J. O. Urmson, *Philosophical Analysis*, 1956, part 1, esp. § 5. (Facts and logical atomism.)

P. F. Strawson, 'Truth', *Proceedings of the Aristotelian Society*, supplementary vol., 1950, § 2, reprinted in G. Pitcher (ed.), *Truth*, 1964, and in Strawson's *Logico-Linguistic Papers*, 1971.

D. W. Hamlyn, 'The correspondence theory of truth', *Philosophical Quarterly*, 1962.

G. E. M. Anscombe, 'On brute facts', *Analysis*, vol. 18, 1958.

Fact/value distinction. See NATURALISM.

Fallibilism. Doctrine that nothing or nothing about the world can be known for certain.

False. See TRUTH AND FALSITY.

Fatalism. See FREEWILL.

Feeling. Any one of an indefinitely large number of ways of experiencing situations, real or imaginary, in the world or in oneself. One can feel external things (tables, the warmth of the fire), impingements of things (pin-pricks, the touch of a hand), internal things (lumps in the throat), the effects of situations (the lack of a counsellor), physical or mental feelings themselves, which do not exist independently of being felt (twinges of rheumatism, stabs of remorse), desires, etc. One can feel in a state (sick, angry, uneasy), or in a relation (constricted, insulted), or in a position regarding something (unable to run faster). To feel queasy, or angry, seems close to being queasy, or angry, but one can feel ill, better, or a failure, without being ill, etc. One can feel that something is so, either perceptually (that one's hand is warm, whether one feels this internally or by using the other hand), or intellectually (that the Government will fall), or emotionally or intuitively (that his friendship was cooling). One can feel like a fool —or feel like a cup of tea. Also an object can be said to feel ('This feels hot') and 'feel' corresponds to 'look', 'listen', 'sound', as well as to 'see' and 'hear'.

The noun 'feel' is largely used for the immediate or direct object of feeling, considered as external ('the feel of velvet'). 'Feel' in this sense is to 'feeling' *somewhat* as 'SENSE DATUM' is to 'SENSATION'. But 'feel' is general

First cause argument

('I felt the feel of velvet'), and seldom follows verbs like 'sense' or 'have'. In 'Have a feel at it', 'feel' refers to the act of feeling, not to what is felt. 'Raw feels', however, is sometimes used technically like 'sense data'. Cf. SEEING for the noun 'look'.

Philosophical problems involving feelings largely concern how they are to be identified and described, e.g. how far can they be distinguished from each other intrinsically and without reference to causes or accompanying inclinations or dispositions? How far can they be used to elucidate concepts like emotion, consciousness, PLEASURE? How far do these consist in feelings? Other problems concern the kinds and objects of feelings, and how far they relate to things like attending and noticing. How do we use feelings in acquiring knowledge of the world? How do we know they exist, if we do, in ourselves and others? (Pain has been a prime example in the PRIVATE LANGUAGE dispute.)

G. Ryle, 'Feelings', *Philosophical Quarterly*, 1951, reprinted in his *Collected Papers*, 1971, vol. 2. (Various uses of the verb 'feel' and relations between them. Cf. also his *Concept of Mind*, 1949.)

A. R. White, *Attention*, 1964. (Includes discussion of how feeling relates to attending, noticing, desiring, etc. Cf. also his *The Philosophy of Mind*, 1967, chapter 5.)

W. P. Alston, 'Feelings', *Philosophical Review*, 1969. (What are feelings, and how is feeling angry, etc. related to being angry? Cf. Vesey (SENSATION bibliography).)

S. Hampshire, *Feeling and Expression*, 1961, pamphlet. (Emphasizes their interdependence.)

Figure. See SYLLOGISM.

Finitism. A mathematical method or system is finitist or finitary if it refuses to recognize any objects (numbers, etc.) which cannot be constructed (see INTUITIONISM) in a finite number of steps; but some variation exists about whether the construction must be possible in practice or only in principle. Finitism is thus, like intuitionism, a form of constructivism, but unlike intuitionism, appeals primarily to what can be done in a finite number of steps with a finite number of elements. It is therefore sometimes more rigorous than intuitionism, and is associated more with formalism. It is, moreover, a method rather than, like intuitionism and formalism, a theory. Extreme forms of it, which allow only constructions which can be carried out in practice and in a feasible number of steps, or insist like Wittgenstein that a mathematical statement only gets sense from the way it is proved, are sometimes called *strict finitism*.

S. Körner, *The Philosophy of Mathematics*, 1960, esp. pp. 77–9.
P. Edwards (ed.), *The Encyclopedia of Philosophy*, 1967, vol. 5, p. 65.
P. Benacerraf and H. Putnam (eds), *Philosophy of Mathematics*, part 4. (Wittgenstein. Cf. esp. p. 505.)

First cause argument. See COSMOLOGICAL.

Focal meaning

Focal meaning. See AMBIGUITY.

Form. Plato's words for his Forms or Ideas (*eidos*, *idea*, roughly synonymous) meant both visible form and nature, kind, or species. Plato's Forms (now often distinguished by a capital F) were in some sense independent objects (cf. UNIVERSALS). For Aristotle forms normally existed only in combination with matter. A horse was a lump of flesh 'in-formed' by the form or essence of horse, i.e. made into something having the essential properties and powers of a horse. Basically therefore an Aristotelian form is that which makes an object what it is. It can also be called the *formal cause* of the object. In the Middle Ages this notion was called a *substantial form*. A substantial form classified an object as what it basically is, while an *accidental form* was any set of properties of an object, whether essential to it or not. It is not always clear whether there is a different substantial form for each individual object, or only for each type or species. The Aristotelian form is itself unclear in this respect.

In logic the form of a proposition is the kind or species to which it belongs, such as the universal or the negative. It is contrasted with the content or matter (cf. 'subject-matter'), what the proposition is individually about. Form is also relative: 'All cats are black' and 'No dogs are brown' are of the same form in that both are universal, but of different forms in that only one is negative.

The distinction between form and content is often hard to make. A proposition's form seems to be an abstract pattern it exemplifies, in virtue of which formal inferences can be drawn from it. 'Every *a* is a *b*, so every non-*b* is a non-*a*' is a valid inference pattern, because an inference exemplifying it is valid irrespective of the meanings of whatever terms replace '*a*' and '*b*'. 'Smith is a bachelor, so he's unmarried' is valid, but only because of what 'bachelor' means. It is a non-formal inference. Formal inference also depends on what words like 'every' mean, and it is hard to say when a pattern is abstract enough to be called formal. Is '*x* exceeds *y* and *y* exceeds *z*, so *x* exceeds *z*' an abstract pattern, i.e. can 'exceeds' count as a formal word?

Other questions include whether form really belongs to propositions. Does it belong to sentences instead? And how is logical form related to grammatical form?

W. Sellars and R. Albritton (see bibliography to SUBSTANCE).

W. Leszl, *Logic and Metaphysics in Aristotle*, 1972, part 6. (Includes discussion, largely intelligible by itself, of form and matter. Occasional Greek.)

P. F. Strawson, *Introduction to Logical Theory*, 1952, pp. 40–56. (Logical form, including its relations to patterns.)

D. Mitchell, *An Introduction to Logic*, 1962, chapter 1. (Form and validity. Cf. also chapter 5 and pp. 151–3.)

C. H. Whiteley, 'The idea of logical form', *Mind*, 1951.

J. Bennett, *Kant's Analytic*, 1966, pp. 79–81. (Both these raise difficulties about form.)

Formalism. Any doctrine somehow emphasizing FORM against matter or content (e.g. in aesthetics; but not metaphysical doctrines emphasizing form in the way Platonists or Aristotelians do). In ethics, the doctrine that an action's value or rightness depends on what kind of act it is (e.g. one of promise-keeping), not on its consequences; cf. deontology (ETHICS). For formalism in mathematics see INTUITIONISM.

Formal mode. Sentences about words, such as 'Red is a quality-word' or 'Red is an adjective', are said to be in the *formal mode*. Sentences about objects, qualities, etc., are said to be in the material mode. Thus 'Red is a quality' is in the material mode. Philosophers have sometimes thought that 'metaphysical' notions like substance, quality, etc., could and should be dispensed with by translating sentences that seemed to involve them into sentences about language, i.e. out of the material mode and into the formal mode, as illustrated above.

R. Carnap, *The Unity of Science*, 1934, pp. 37–42.

Formation rules. See AXIOM.

Four-term fallacy. Arguing in a SYLLOGISM whose premises are true, if at all, only if the middle term has a different sense in each, e.g. 'All cats miaow; that woman is a cat; therefore that woman miaows.'

Freewill and determinism. Our natural feeling that, special circumstances apart, we always could do otherwise than we do do is often thought to conflict with the view that every event is caused and that human actions cannot be excepted. Resolutions of this conflict have naturally been viewed mainly in the light of how they affect moral responsibility.

Fatalism holds that the future is fixed irrespective of our attempts to affect it. Seldom held as a philosophical doctrine this view often appears in literature (e.g. the Oedipus legend). A similar view, more discussed than actually held, is *logical determinism*, which argues that a given future event must either occur or not occur. Whichever happens, the prediction that it would happen will turn out to be correct, and therefore was correct all along, whether or not we knew it. Therefore since one statement about the apparent future alternatives is already true, nothing we can do will alter matters. This puzzle affects the nature of TRUTH: can a statement (one about the future) be true at one time (when the future comes) and not at another (before the future comes), or is it senseless to talk of a statement as true 'at a time'?

Other forms of determinism allow that our choices and actions are effective as links in the causal chain, but insist that they are themselves caused. Determinists are sometimes divided into hard and soft. *Hard determinists* say that our actions are caused in a way that makes us not as free as we might have thought, so that responsibility, if it implies freewill, is an illusion. The causes may be physical and physiological (events in the brain), or else mental (e.g. conscious or unconscious desires, and childhood

Freewill and determinism

experiences which cause such desires). *Soft determinists* or *compatibilists*, by far the largest class in recent times, say that our actions are indeed caused, but we are not therefore any less free than we might be, because the causation is not a constraint or compulsion on us. So long as our natures and choices are effective as items in the causal chain, the fact that they are themselves caused is irrelevant and does not stop them being what they are. *Indeterminists*, however, insist that determinists, of whatever complexion, can give no sense to the sentence 'He could have done otherwise', where this means something more than simply 'He *might* have done otherwise (had his nature or circumstances been different)'. Soft determinists often hold that what justifies praise and blame is solely that they can influence action. This, say indeterminists, surely misses the point of those concepts.

One difficulty with indeterminism is that mere absence of causation does not seem enough. If our actions are no more than random intrusions into the causal scheme of things, how can we be any more responsible for them than if they were caused? Indeterminists who deny this randomness are sometimes called *libertarians*. But more strictly, libertarians are those who postulate a special entity, the 'self', which uses the body to intervene from outside, as it were, in the causal chain of events, but is itself immune to causal influence. Sometimes this self is said to be immune only where moral considerations arise, with obvious difficulties about which considerations are MORAL.

Such a self must at least be open to pressure from things in the world (or why would it ever make a wrong or weak-minded choice?), and to define its actual relations to the world seems difficult. More usually now indeterminists appeal not to a separate entity but to the very nature of those things (choosing, intending, deciding, acting, etc.) which characterize persons as such, whatever may be the relation between being a person and having (or being?) a body. It may not make sense for choices or actions to be caused. Reasons offered for this include the following: physical causes can only cause physical movements, like an upward movement of a leg, but not ACTIONS, like a kick, for actions always involve things like intentions and a context, which go beyond mere movement (Peters). On the other hand, alleged mental causes like desires, intentions, motives, etc., are not separate states or events: they are features of actions which provide ways of classifying them. (Ryle says one's greed is not something causing one to act, but consists simply in one's acting in a greedy manner.) Another view is that a desire, etc. can only be specified as the desire to do a certain action, and so is not sufficiently independent of the action to be able to cause it, for a cause and its effect must be two *separate* things (Melden).

Recently these views have been attacked, and causation has somewhat returned to favour. But there are still difficulties about reason. If our beliefs are caused, why should we assume they are reliable? On the other hand we do not normally, if ever, choose our beliefs, but do not think our freedom diminished because we are 'compelled by the evidence' to believe something. Again reasoning, whether on theoretical or practical matters, and also choosing and deciding, seems to be possible only if we at least believe that their outcome is not yet determined. We cannot try, or even want (as against idly wishing), to do something we firmly believe is impossible.

A related problem concerns causation, prediction and explanation. To act freely is not to act unpredictably or inexplicably, as indeterminism in the sense of *mere* absence of causation seems to imply. On the other hand even a caused event cannot be predicted without adequate information, and it seems that we could never know enough to predict our own actions strictly, since we cannot take into account the result of the prediction itself. (Cf. how opinion polls affect elections they predict.) Therefore it seems that an action may be unpredictable even though caused, or predictable even though uncaused. This raises questions about what grounds are in fact available to us for predictions, and what sorts of explanation can be given of actions.

All these problems clearly have bearings on the mind-body problem (philosophy of MIND). See also CAUSATION, REASON, EXPLANATION.

Aristotle, *De Interpretatione*, chapter 9, transl. with notes in J. L. Ackrill, *Aristotle's Categories*, 1963. (Classic discussion of logical determinism. For modern development of Aristotle's view see also J. Lukasiewicz, 'On determinism' in S. McCall (ed.), *Polish Logic 1920–1939*, 1967, reprinted in Lukasiewicz's *Selected Works* (ed. L. Borkowski, 1970). For Aristotle on freewill generally cf. his *Nicomachean Ethics*, 3, 1–5.)

S. Morgenbesser and J. Walsh (eds), *Free Will*, 1962. (Includes medieval contributions.)

B. Berofsky (ed.), *Free Will and Determinism*, 1966. (Contains many classic discussions, including R. E. Hobart, 'Free will as involving determination and inconceivable without it', *Mind*, 1934, A. I. Melden, *Free Action*, 1961 (selection. See text above), D. Davidson, 'Actions, reasons, and causes', *Journal of Philosophy*, 1963 (often reprinted. Rehabilitation of causation), A. C. MacIntyre, 'Determinism', *Mind*, 1957 (the role of rationality), J. L. Austin's 'Ifs and cans' (criticism of soft determinist analyses of 'could have . . .' in terms of 'would have . . . . . .if . . .'; cf. also his 'A plea for excuses', *Proceedings of the Aristotelian Society*, 1956–7). For the rehabilitation cf. also D. W. Hamlyn, 'Causality and human behaviour', *Proceedings of the Aristotelian Society*, supplementary vol., 1964, reprinted in N. S. Care and C. Landesman (eds), *Readings in the Theory of Action*, 1968, and G. Madell, 'Action and causal explanation', *Mind*, 1967.)

D. F. Pears (ed.), *Freedom and the Will*, 1963. (Based on BBC series of popular talks.)

T. Honderich (ed.), *Essays on Freedom of Action*, 1973.

K. Lehrer (ed.), *Freedom and Determinism*, 1966. (Two sets of modern contributions, rather more advanced than Pears volume.)

R. S. Peters, *The Concept of Motivation*, 1958.

G. Ryle, *The Concept of Mind*, 1949. (Classic discussion of, *inter alia*, emotions, motives, the will, terms like 'voluntary' and 'involuntary'.)

Frege, Gottlob

P. Herbst, 'Freedom and prediction', *Mind*, 1957. (Action and predictability. Same volume contains MacIntyre's article, reprinted in Berofsky volume.)

K. Popper, 'Indeterminism in quantum physics and in classical physics', *British Journal for the Philosophy of Science*, 1950. (Prediction in men and machines.)

J. R. Lucas, *The Freedom of the Will*, 1970. (Uses one of GÖDEL'S THEOREMS to argue that human mind cannot work on same principles as computer.)

D. Locke and H. G. Frankfurt, 'Three concepts of free action', in *Proceedings of the Aristotelian Society*, supplementary vol., 1975.

Frege, Gottlob. 1848-1925. German mathematical logician who was born in Wismar and worked in Jena. His work on the foundations of MATHEMATICS, which he hoped to derive from pure logic, was seriously interrupted when he received Russell's paradox from RUSSELL. His greatest contributions to logic were his invention of QUANTIFICATION and his elaboration of the distinction between sense and reference (see MEANING). Also influential were his distinction between CONCEPT and OBJECT, his use of the notion of FUNCTION, and his rejection of a 'speech act' analysis of NEGATION (which was later important for ethics: see NATURALISM). *Begriffsschrift*, 1879 (quantification). *Die Grundlagen der Arithmetik* (*The Foundations of Arithmetic*), 1884. *Die Grundgesetze der Arithmetik*, 2 vols, 1893, 1903. P. T. Geach and M. Black (eds), *Translations from the Philosophical Writings of Gottlob Frege*, 1952 (contains 'Function und Begriff' ('Function and Concept'), 1891, 'Über Begriff und Gegenstand' ('Concept and Object'), 1892, 'Über Sinn und Bedeutung' ('On Sense and Reference'), 1892, and 'Die Verneinung' ('Negation'), 1919, as well as chapter 1 of the *Begriffsschrift*). See also ASSERTION, FUNCTION, IDEA, IDENTITY, INTENSIONALITY, REFERRING, SENTENCES, UNIVERSALS.

Function. (This entry is confined to logic and mathematics, except for its bibliography.) Some expressions have either numerical values or TRUTH VALUES which we can calculate once we give values to the VARIABLES in the expression. The rest of the expression is then called a function of the variables. Thus $3x + 7$ contains a variable (x) and a function $(3\ (\ ) + 7)$. But 'function' is often applied to the whole expression, including the variables. The function is then called a function of x. Its value in either case depends on the value given to x. Again if p and q are propositions, p *and* q (but not p *because* q) is a *truth function* of p and of q. We can know the truth value of p *and* q (but not that of p *because* q) once we know the truth values of p and of q.

A value assigned to a variable in a function is called an *argument* of the function. $3x + 7$ has the value 19 for the argument 4.

Functions are closely related to predicates. . . . *is red* can be thought of as a function, because we can assign a truth value to x *is red* by assigning a value to x (i.e. replacing x by the name of something; x *is red* becomes true if we replace x by 'blood'), or alternatively by quantifying over x

74

(see QUANTIFICATION). In fact predicates stand to functions rather as SENTENCES stand to propositions. A predicate is a linguistic or notational representation of a function. *x is red* can be called a *propositional, statemental* (rare) or *sentential function*, according as *blood is red* is regarded as a proposition, statement or sentence. Sentential functions are often called *open sentences*. The term *closed sentential function* is occasionally used of ordinary sentences.

P. T. Geach and M. Black, *Translations from the Philosophical Writings of Gottlob Frege*, 1952. (Contains Frege's 'Function and concept' (cf. CONCEPT). Frege's symbolism is awkward and outdated.)

R. Carnap, *Introduction to Semantics*, 1942, § 37. (Ambiguities, here ignored, of 'function' and 'propositional function'.)

R. Sorabji, 'Function', *Philosophical Quarterly*, 1964. (Non-logical senses.)

G

Gambler's fallacy. Assumption that if, for example, an unbiased coin has come down heads many times in succession, it is more likely to come down tails next time to 'restore the balance'. If the coin and its throwing *are* unbiased the tosses will be independent of each other and the coin is equally likely to come down heads next time. No finite run of heads, however long, violates the 'laws of chance'. (A long run of heads might suggest the coin is biased, so that the laws of chance do not apply, or not in the same way, and further heads should be expected. The 'gambler' assumes that the laws of chance do apply, and that therefore tails are to be expected. His mistake lies in the 'therefore'.) Cf. von Mises's 'principle of the impossibility of a gambling system', and the frequency theory of PROBABILITY.

R. von Mises, *Probability, Statistics and Truth*, 1928, transl. 1939, chapter 1.

Game theory. See DECISION THEORY.

General. See SENTENCES.

Genetic fallacy. Assumption that because the origins of something can be traced, the thing in question is somehow illegitimate or only apparent; e.g. that conscience is illusory if it develops from childhood fear of authority.

Given. See PERCEPTION.

Gnoseology. See EPISTEMOLOGY.

Gödel's theorems. In 1931 K. Gödel showed that for any AXIOM SYSTEM adequate to axiomatize arithmetic there will always exist at least one well-formed formula (see AXIOM SYSTEM) which is not DECIDABLE in the system, even though we can see on other grounds that it is true. He also showed that a system's CONSISTENCY cannot be proved within the system itself. These are respectively his *first* and *second incompleteness theorems*;

either or both are known as *Gödel's theorem*. *Gödel's completeness theorem* (1930) says that the first-order predicate CALCULUS is weakly COMPLETE.

E. Nagel and J. R. Newman, *Gödel's Proof*, 1959. (Remarkably clear exposition for layman.)

J. R. Lucas, *The Freedom of the Will*, 1970. (Uses Gödel to distinguish men from machines.)

Good. Very roughly, the property or characterization of a thing giving rise to commendation. Ever since Aristotle and his medieval followers failed to include 'good' in the scheme of CATEGORIES except by making it apply in all of them (see BEING on transcendentals) 'good' has caused bewilderment by its many uses. What have the following cases in common? 'Good thing', 'good man' (said by preachers and by politicians), 'good citizen', 'good thief', 'good knife', 'good painting', 'good cricketer', 'good at cricket', 'good idea', 'good argument', 'good student', 'holds good', 'very good of you', 'good with children', 'beer is good for you', 'good to eat', 'good often comes from evil', 'pleasure is the good', 'pleasure and friendship are good', 'goods train', 'I've a good mind to give you a good hiding'. Evidently the noun as well as the adjective raises problems. Some help can be got from studying the most natural opposites, if any, in each case, like 'bad', 'evil', 'poor', 'weak', 'faulty', and also the relations between 'good' and similar positive terms like 'valuable' and 'great'.

Traditionally various kinds of goodness have been distinguished. Some things are good as ends, or in themselves and for their own sakes (*intrinsic goods*). Other things are good as means to ends (*instrumental goods*). Others again are good as being part of a whole and contributing to its goodness, as a colour-patch, valueless in itself, may enhance a painting (*contributory goods*). Instrumental and perhaps contributory goods are among *extrinsic goods*. They owe their goodness to something outside themselves. But many of the above examples are not obviously either extrinsic or intrinsic. C. I. Lewis, holding that only experiences can be intrinsically good, calls *inherently good* those things the experience of which is intrinsically good. Features of things, as well as things themselves, may be called good. One can apply 'good' to pleasant experiences, or to the pleasure which is a feature of them and which could not of course exist on its own. The highest good, *summum bonum*, may be either that thing or feature which taken by itself is better than anything else, or that total situation which contains more good than any other. (Kant used *supremum bonum* for the former and summum bonum for the latter.) Both of these are distinct from what is merely *good on the whole*, where other things may be better. A further kind of goodness is *moral goodness*, which is limited mainly to men, actions, intentions, and perhaps emotions, desires, and institutions (cf. MORAL).

One reason why goodness is complex is that it is usually a CONSEQUENTIAL CHARACTERISTIC. 'Good' is also sometimes said to be logically ATTRIBUTIVE. A good thief need not be a good man, and a knife good for cutting butter need not be good for cutting leather. But is 'good' attributive in 'Pleasure, friendship and loyalty are all good'? These considerations suggest we should distinguish between the meaning of 'good' and the CRITERIA (loose sense) for applying it (i.e. the features which make a thing good). A good car satisfies very different criteria from a good apple, but does 'good' mean different things when applied to each of them? A difficulty arises here about whether certain kinds of things have, as it were, inbuilt criteria for goodness, so that it would be contradictory to say an object did not satisfy the criteria but was good, or satisfied them but was not good. Some things have functions, e.g. razors are for shaving. Suppose only sharp razors shave. Is it then contradictory to say 'This razor is irremediably blunt, but it's a good razor'? (A blunt razor might be a good razor to give a homicidal maniac, but is it therefore a good razor?) Again take 'This razor is sharp, safe, etc., but it's not a good razor'. Can we so fill in the 'etc.' that this statement becomes contradictory? What happens where the function is not so obvious (apples), or there are many functions (legs may be judged for running, dancing, beauty, etc.)? Can we make any sense of phrases like 'good molecule', 'good drop of water'? Can just anything be good? (Perhaps anything can be a 'good example of a ...'?)

Properties like sharpness are sometimes called *good-making* properties. But these properties may be logically or causally good-making. If sharpness is logically relevant to being a good razor, so that it is contradictory to call a blunt razor good, sharpness is logically good-making here. But if it is (say) smooth-cuttingness that is logically relevant, and it is simply a matter of fact (not of logical necessity) that sharp razors cut more smoothly than others, then sharpness is causally good-making here (von Wright, p. 26 note).

Some theories of the meaning of 'good' have held that goodness is a quality (perhaps indefinable and discerned by intuition), or a relational property, e.g. that of causing certain feelings or reactions in humans. Definitions of 'good' have been offered in terms of notions like causing pleasure, or satisfying certain desires of interests.

An alternative view of the meaning of 'good' bases it on the idea that 'good' is primarily used to commend or express approval, or to perform similar SPEECH ACTS. A difficulty for this view is that very often no relevant speech act seems to be involved. When I say 'Were it good, it would be expensive' I am not commending it, nor even saying 'Were I to commend it, ...'.

Recent attention has been given to the linguistic behaviour of 'good', e.g. whether any significance can be drawn from such facts as that 'good heavy brown table' is more natural than 'heavy good brown table'. It is hoped that this will throw light on questions about the meaning of 'good'.

As well as these questions about the meaning of 'good' and the nature of goodness, there are other questions about what things are good, and in particular whether the good is one or many. These questions, however, are likely to be affected by answers given to the former kinds of question (though this connexion between the kinds of question would be denied by various recent schools like logical POSITIVISM and much of linguistic PHILOSOPHY; cf. NATURALISM, ETHICS). See also NATURALISM, BETTER.

G. H. von Wright, *The Varieties of Goodness*, 1963. (Full discussion of the different uses of 'good'.)

Aristotle, *Nicomachean Ethics*, book 1. (The good for man.)

G. E. Moore, *Principia Ethica*, 1903. (Good as a simple indefinable quality. Last chapter discusses what things are good.)

P. Ziff, *Semantic Analysis*, 1960. (Last chapter defends analysis of 'good' in terms of interests.)

P. T. Geach, 'Good and evil', *Analysis*, vol. 17, 1956, reprinted in P. Foot (ed.), *Theories of Ethics*, 1967. (Claims that 'good' is attributive and descriptive (see NATURALISM.) See short bibliography added in reprint for examinations of linguistic behaviour of 'good'.)

R. M. Hare, *The Language of Morals*, 1952. (Speech act analysis. Meaning and criteria. Can just anything be good? On this last cf. P. Foot, 'Moral beliefs', *Proceedings of the Aristotelian Society*, 1958–9, reprinted in P. Foot (ed.), *Theories of Ethics*, 1967.)

J. R. Searle, 'Meaning and speech acts', *Philosophical Review*, 1962, reprinted with discussions and additions in C. D. Rollins (ed.), *Knowledge and Experience*, 1962. (Attacks speech act analyses of 'good'.)

A. Montefiore, 'The meaning of "good" and the act of commendation', *Philosophical Quarterly*, 1967. (Fairly complex discussion of replies speech act analysis might make to Searle.)

A. Gewirth, 'Meanings and criteria in ethics', *Philosophy*, 1963. (Further discussion of speech act analyses.)

Grammar (depth, surface). See STRUCTURE (DEEP AND SURFACE).

Grammars (generative etc.). A generative grammar is a set of elements and rules from which the grammatically acceptable sentences of a language can be generated, in a way that reveals their grammatical structure. (Cf. the way the rules of chess generate possible situations on a chessboard.) N. Chomsky in his early work distinguishes three types of generative grammar, in order of increasing adequacy: *finite state grammars, phrase-structure grammars, transformational grammars*. Generating something involves rules whereby one set of symbols is replaced by another. Sometimes the rules of a phrase-structure grammar specify that the relevant symbols are replaceable only if they are preceded or followed by certain other symbols. Such more powerful rules, and grammars containing at least one of them, are *context-dependent* (*context-sensitive*). The remaining replacement rules, and grammars limited to them, are *context-free*. See also STRUCTURE.

J. Lyons, *Chomsky*, 1970. (Elementary. For more elaborate treatment see J. Lyons, *Introduction to Theoretical Linguistics*, 1968.)

Greatest happiness principle. See UTILITARIANISM.

Grelling's paradox. See HETEROLOGICAL.

H

Hare, Richard M. 1919– . British philosopher, working in Oxford, whose main contribution has been to ETHICS, where his approach is inspired by 'linguistic philosophy'. He opposes NATURALISM, advocates a 'prescriptivist' analysis of moral judgments, and treats moral judgments and philosophical analyses as distinct and independent of each other. He combines all this with an emphasis, derived from KANT, on UNIVERSALIZABILITY as what distinguishes moral from other evaluative judgments. *The Language of Morals*, 1952. *Freedom and Reason*, 1963 (develops his earlier book). See also CRITERION, GOOD, IMPERATIVE, OUGHT, PHRASTIC.

Hedonism. *Psychological hedonism* has three main forms: That everyone desires only his own PLEASURE or happiness. That everyone necessarily aims only to maximize his own pleasure. That everyone always acts on his strongest desire. The term also sometimes applies to the theory that only pleasant thoughts can motivate actions.

Ethical hedonism has two main forms: That only pleasure is ultimately good. That every action should aim for pleasure (not necessarily the agent's).

For *qualitative hedonism* see PLEASURE.

The *paradox of hedonism* says that pleasure is often best attained by not seeking it. See also UTILITARIANISM.

Hegel, Georg W. F. 1770–1831. Born in Stuttgart, he worked at various German universities, especially Berlin. He is usually classified as an objective IDEALIST. His system is characterized by the use of a DIALECTIC of thesis, antithesis and synthesis (though some scholars warn against reading too much of this into Hegel), and could perhaps be described as an attempt to trace the development or emergence of 'spirit' or 'Geist', both systematically in a logical doctrine of categories and historically in the process of world history. He influenced such widely diverse thinkers as MARX, BRADLEY and CROCE, and stimulated vigorous hostility in KIERKEGAARD and SCHOPENHAUER. *Phänomenologie des Geistes*, 1807. *Wissenschaft der Logik*, 3 vols, 1812, 1813, 1816. *Die Encyclopädie der philosophischen Wissenschaften im Grundrisse*, 1817 (first part is often known as the 'Lesser Logic', second part concerns philosophy of nature, third part covers same ground as the *Phänomenologie*). *Grundlinien der Philosophie des Rechts*, 1820 (or 1821). See also IDEA, METAPHYSICS.

Heidegger, Martin. 1889– . Born in Baden, he has lived and taught in Germany, especially in Freiburg. He is a leading EXISTENTIALIST and his work centres round an investigation of 'being', both that which is proper to human beings, '*Dasein*', and that which belongs to things in general. In his early days he was much influenced by HUSSERL. *Sein und Zeit* (*Being and Time*), 1927. *Kant und das Problem der Metaphysik* (*Kant and the Problem of Metaphysics*), 1929. *Holzwege* (*Woodpaths*), 1950. *Einführung in die Metaphysik* (*Introduction to Metaphysics*), 1953. *Die Frage nach dem Ding; zu Kants Lehre von den transzendentalen Grundsätzen*, 1962. See also JASPERS, MARCEL.

Hereditary property. If an object *a* stands in relation R to any object *b*, any property of *a* which must belong to *b* is R-hereditary. If R is the relation *greater by two than*, then the property of being even is R-hereditary among numbers.

Heterological. Not applying to itself. 'German' (which is not a German word) and 'monosyllabic' (which is not a monosyllabic word) are heterological adjectives. *Homological* (or *autological*) means 'applying to itself'. 'English' (which is an English word) and 'polysyllabic' (which is a polysyllabic word) which do apply to themselves, are homological adjectives.

The heterological paradox, attributed to K. Grelling (1886–) and H. Weyl (1885–1955), asks whether 'heterological' is itself a heterological adjective. If it is, it does not apply to itself, and so is not heterological. If it is not, it does apply to itself, and so is heterological. A related, but different, paradox asks whether the attribute (not adjective) *not-possessing-itself* possesses itself. Both paradoxes are of the kind sometimes called semantic (see PARADOX, and also RUSSELL'S PARADOX, TYPES).

G. Ryle, 'Heterologicality', *Analysis*, vol. 11, 1951, reprinted in M. Macdonald (ed.), *Philosophy and Analysis*, 1954, and in Ryle's *Collected Papers*. 1971, vol. 2.

Heuristic. Concerning discovery, as against proof. *Heuristics* is the study of methods of discovery.

G. Polya, *How to Solve It*, 1945.

Historicism. Originally, any of several views emphasizing the importance of history, especially the view that things should always be seen in terms of their historical development. But for Popper, who uses *historism* for the above, historicism is the view that historical events are determined by inevitable laws, which history aims to predict, and that corporate wholes cannot be reduced to the individuals composing them.

D. E. Lee and R. N. Beck, 'The meaning of "historicism" ', *American Historical Review*, 1953–4. (Cf. also G. D. Mitchell (ed.), *A Dictionary of Sociology*, 1968.)

Historism

K. R. Popper, *The Poverty of Historicism*, 1957, written earlier. (Cf. his *The Open Society*, 1945.)

Historism. See HISTORICISM.

History (philosophy of). History proper seems limited to the sphere of human action—things like the 'history of the universe' seem rather secondary. Problems in the philosophy of mind, about action, freewill, causation, rationality, are therefore especially relevant to the philosophy of history, and are connected to the question what is the aim of history: is this to describe the course of events or to explain it, and what sorts of EXPLANATION can be given? Are general laws to be sought, and if so, of what kinds? Is history a science?

Another set of problems concerns how history is possible and how historical claims can be justified. The reality of the past and the justifiability of using memory are subjects for metaphysics and epistemology, but the philosopher of history asks how statements about the past can be verified, and what is their meaning. Are they really, as some logical positivists held, about the extant evidence? On what principles are facts and topics to be selected, and how far can or should the historian be objective and neutral? Should he 'stick to the facts'? What counts as doing this?

The purpose *of* history must be distinguished from purpose *in* history. Can purposes or patterns be discerned in history either as a whole or in parts? Is history in any way cyclic? What can we learn from it? *Critical philosophy of history*, as well as covering the questions mentioned previously, asks what kind of answers these latter questions can have and what count as answers. The answers themselves are the province of *speculative philosophy of history*. Some questions, e.g. the elucidating of concepts like *progress, historical event, historical period*, may fall between these provinces.

Metahistory properly means philosophy of history, but is often limited to the speculative branch. See also HISTORICISM, EXPLANATION.

W. H. Walsh, *An Introduction to Philosophy of History*, 1951.
W. H. Dray, *Philosophy of History*, 1964. (Two introductions to both critical and speculative sides.)
A. Bullock, 'The historian's purpose', C. Dawson, 'The problem of metahistory', *History Today*, 1951 (February, June). (Both on metahistory.)
S. Hook (ed.), *Philosophy and History*, 1963. (Discussions between philosophers and historians.)

Hobbes, Thomas. 1588–1679. Born at Malmesbury he lived in England and France. He is now best known for his political philosophy, defending an absolute sovereignty as the only way to ensure social security and prevent life from being 'solitary, poor, nasty, brutish and short', as it was in the 'state of nature'. This sovereignty he based on a social contract among men, but the sovereign had duties only to God. As usually interpreted, he based the duty of political obedience on self-interest. (Cf. also ROUSSEAU.) He also developed a nominalist view of universals, and a philosophy of nature which analysed everything, including man, in terms of matter and motion. He was also much influenced by his study of geometry. At one point he engaged in controversy with Descartes. *De Cive*, 1642 (political). *Leviathan*, 1651 (main political work, including also treatment of man). *De Corpore*, 1655, transl. 1656 as *Elements of Philosophy, The First Section, Concerning Body* (metaphysics and treatment of inanimate nature). See also COLLINGWOOD, MODALITIES.

Homological. see HETEROLOGICAL.

Hume, David. 1711–76. Scottish, generally regarded as the greatest of 'British empiricists', Hume was an historian and a man of letters as well as a philosopher. His opinions stood in the way of his having an academic post but he was for a short time Chargé d'Affaires in Paris where he was much celebrated and he later came to hold the post of Under-Secretary of State in England from which he resigned in 1769. He examined meticulously our modes of thinking, both deductive and inductive, and claimed that they were far less powerful than we assumed. This led him to generally sceptical conclusions about such notions as REASON, CAUSATION and necessity (see MODALITIES), and about how far we are justified in postulating a world outside ourselves, or indeed a self for it to be outside (as against a mere set of experiences). He developed a philosophy based on 'impressions', and drew out its implications also for psychology and ethics. KANT claimed that it was Hume who 'aroused him from his dogmatic slumbers'. *A Treatise of Human Nature*, 1739–40. *An Enquiry concerning Human Understanding*, 1748. *An Enquiry concerning the Principles of Morals*, 1751. (The two *Enquiries* are shorter and later versions of parts of the *Treatise*.) *Dialogues concerning Natural Religion*, 1779. See also ANALYTIC, HUTCHESON, IDENTITY, MORAL SENSE, NATURALISM, PERCEPTION, POSITIVISM, REID, ROUSSEAU, RUSSELL, SCEPTICISM.

Husserl, Edmund. 1859–1938. Born in Moravia, he spent his life teaching in German universities. He is usually regarded as the leading figure in PHENOMENOLOGY, which took two successive forms in his own work, descriptive and transcendental. His early work (1891) was still under the influence of psychologism, which in his mature and phenomenological stages he vigorously rejected. His early phenomenology (1900–1) has some affinities with linguistic philosophy. He was influenced especially by BRENTANO and in turn influenced EXISTENTIALISM. *Philosophie der Arithmetik*, 1891. *Logische Untersuchungen*, 1900–1. *Ideen zu einer reinen Phänomenologie und phänomenologischen Philosophie*, 1913. *Meditations Cartésiennes*, 1931. *Die Krisis der europäischen Wissenschaften und die transzendentale Phänomenologie*, 1936 (in part); full edition 1954). See also CATEGORIES, HEIDEGGER, MERLEAU-PONTY.

Hutcheson, Francis. 1694–1746 (or 1747). Born in Ulster, he worked in Dublin and at Glasgow university. Though he also wrote on metaphysics and logic, he is important mainly as a theorist of the MORAL SENSE school

Hypothesis

who also anticipated some features of utilitarianism. He developed and systematized the work of SHAFTESBURY, and influenced HUME. *Inquiry into the Original of Our Ideas of Beauty and Virtue*, 1725. *An Essay on the Nature and Conduct of the Passions and Affections with Illustrations on the Moral Sense*, 1728. See also PRICE, SMITH.

Hypothesis. See LAWS.

Hypothetical. See CONDITIONALS.

Hypothetical constructs. See LOGICAL CONSTRUCTIONS.

Hypothetico-deductive method. See INDUCTION.

I

Icons. See SIGN.

Idea. The Greek words 'idea' and 'eidos', virtually synonymous, and etymologically linked with 'vision', may originally have meant 'visible form' but by Plato's time could mean 'nature', 'essence' or 'kind'. Plato's Ideas were non-material objects outside the mind, though the mind could know them. The translation 'Form' is therefore often preferred as less misleading. (Cf. FORM, UNIVERSALS.) Plato considered but rejected the view that 'ideas' were something in our minds. Some stoics adopted it, but in later Greek and medieval writings ideas tended to be in the mind of God.

For many modern philosophers 'idea' has been a technical term important for their systems, used in many senses, often in the same philosopher (notably Locke), but almost always for something in or having reference to the mind.

Its meanings include: what is immediately present to the mind in an experience (SENSE DATUM, feeling); what is before the mind when it reflects, remembers, introspects, imagines (images, etc.); what the mind preserves from its experiences, or finds within itself, or constructs in various ways out of simpler ideas (one's idea of red, colour, gratitude, number); things like these latter but common to different people ('the' idea of red); a quality in an object which causes experiences (Locke, but rare); the meaning of a word; the subjective associations of a word, contrasted with its meaning (Frege); a representation of something that cannot be experienced (Kant, based on Plato). For Hegel 'idea' means something like the overall pattern or purpose in the universe or is a term whose use centres on this. In aesthetics 'idea' is sometimes used in a Platonic sense, for what a work of art aims to embody or copy.

Because it is so ambiguous, particularly between uses for datable existents (sense datum, image, etc.) and logical uses (meaning of a word, 'the' idea of . . ., etc.), 'idea' has been replaced for technical purposes by more specific terms like 'sense datum', 'image', CONCEPT.

On innate ideas see A PRIORI.

I. Hacking, *Why Does Language Matter to Philosophy?*, 1975. (Discusses seventeenth-century usage of 'idea'.)

Ideal

F. H. Bradley, *Principles of Logic*, 1883, 2nd (revised) edition 1922. (Opening chapter, based on idealist standpoint, criticizes confusion due to ambiguity of 'idea'.)

Ideal. Entity or attribute of a kind suggested by 'IDEA'. 'Ideal' suggests freedom from the imperfections of the material world, together with unattainability (cf. Platonic 'Ideas'), but also the unreality of what depends simply on the mind. There is also the neutral sense, 'connected with ideas, or the mind'. The 'unreality' and 'neutral' strands are rather commoner in philosophy, especially before this century, than in popular usage.

Idealism. A doctrine, or set of doctrines, to the effect that reality is in some way mental. Idealism is contrasted primarily with REALISM, though also with materialism. Rarely, it means simply that the universe is spiritual in the sense of depending on God. Sometimes, however, views are called idealist which hold that reality is outside the mind, but can only be described from some point of view—there are different ways of looking at reality, none of which is more correct than the others, rather as whether Oxford is to the right of Cambridge depends on where one is looking from. In this wide sense, such outlooks as PRAGMATISM and CONVENTIONALISM are idealist. Kant, similarly, held that reality existed independently, but that how it appeared to us was determined by the structure of the human mind. Public empirical knowledge was therefore possible, but only of appearances ('phenomena'). He called himself an empirical realist but a transcendental idealist. Idealism is concerned with 'IDEA' more closely than with IDEAL. It is not primarily concerned with ethics or conduct, though certain ethical views have sometimes been associated with it.

Full-blooded idealism holds that reality is mental. 'To be is to be perceived', as Berkeley said. Matter does not exist except in the form of ideas in the mind, or as a manifestation of mental activity. The 'mind' in question may be one's own mind (solipsism: see SCEPTICISM), minds in general, or the mind of God (Berkeley).

Absolute idealism developed after Kant, notably with Hegel, and was popular in Britain from about 1865 to 1925. It takes many forms, but its central point is that there is only one ultimately real thing, the Absolute, which is spiritual in nature. Other things are partial aspects of this, or illusory appearances generated by it. Here idealism becomes a form of MONISM.

A distinction is sometimes made between *subjective* and *objective idealism*. 'Subjective idealism' is used mainly of views that the only reality is ideas in the mind, especially the human mind. The term is often, however, applied to Berkeley, though he himself used *immaterialism*. 'Objective idealism', like absolute idealism, applies mainly to forms of idealism which place reality outside the human mind. It is used especially when the arguments in favour of idealism say that appearances are contradictory, and therefore are *mere* appearances of a reality lying behind them; subjective idealism, by contrast, says that appearances and minds are the only reality (cf. also PHENOMENALISM).

Identity

Plato's theory of IDEAS, or FORMS, is not usually called idealism now, since these Ideas, though not material, are not mental or mind-dependent. See also BEING.

A. C. Ewing (ed.), *The Idealist Tradition*, 1957. (Selections from leading idealists.)
A. C. Ewing, *Idealism: A Critical Survey*, 1934. (Sympathetic, though not himself an idealist.)
J. Hospers, *Introduction to Philosophical Analysis*, 1956, chapter 8. (Discusses subjective idealism in relation to other theories.)

Identically true, false. See IDENTITY.

Identity. Attribute of being a single thing or single kind. In ordinary speech two things may be called numerically identical (or one in number: 'Persia and Iran are identical'), or identical (or one) in type or species (exactly similar, as with 'identical twins'). Philosophers keep 'identical' for the first sense, using 'indiscernible' for the second (see LEIBNIZ'S LAW). But what is identity, in this first sense? Is it a relation between a thing and itself? If so, every true statement of identity should be trivial, or else senseless. Hume used time to solve the problem, saying that identity statements state that an object existing at one time is the same as itself existing at another, e.g. 'This chair is the same as the one here yesterday.' But this covers only some cases. Suppose Smith is mayor of a certain town. Then 'Smith is Smith' is trivial but 'Smith is the mayor' is not, even though the words 'the mayor' refer to Smith. It was this that made Frege distinguish between sense and reference (see MEANING), saying that what gave content to an identity statement was the different ways in which the object was described.

A distinction exists between two approaches to identity statements. On a *conceptualist* approach one can only say '*a* is the same so-and-so as *b*' where 'so-and-so' is a SORTAL term. On a *realist* approach 'so-and-so' can be replaced by a non-sortal term like 'thing' or 'object'. The identity is here given, as it were, in the world itself and does not depend on the concepts we apply. It is a further question, however, whether identity is relative, in the sense that *a* might be the same so-and-so, but not the same such-and-such, as *b*, e.g. was Nixon the same official (namely the American president), though not the same man, as Eisenhower?

This distinction between two approaches may be relevant to various problems which arise because things persist in time, for they may persist for different periods if described in different ways. Suppose a gold coin melts. Then it seems that the coin is destroyed but the piece of gold is not. If the coin *is* the piece of gold, then the same thing seems to be destroyed and not destroyed. If the coin is not the piece of gold, then we seem to have two things in the same place at the same time (though not *throughout* the same time). Perhaps the gold is not identical with, but 'constitutes', the coin (Wiggins, cf. BEING).

Furthermore, a coin which melts is presumably destroyed, but a baby

87

Identity

which grows up is not destroyed, though it stops being a baby. But *what* stops being a baby and lives to be eighty? And how long does the baby last? Eighty years? (Terms like 'baby' are called *phase terms* or *phase universals*.)

Also can identity statements be contingent? 'Smith is the mayor' seems contingent. Yet 'Smith is Smith' seems to be necessary. See MODALITIES.

Sometimes *a* is called *strictly identical* with *b* if whatever can be said of one can be said of the other (INTENSIONALITY apart). On this view a man is identical, but not strictly identical, with the baby he once was, because the man but not the baby could be called, for example, married. One can say, 'The baby you knew is now married.' But there are no married babies.

Further problems concern the criteria of identity, both for objects and for events, properties, propositions, etc. Is the property red identical with that of reflecting or emitting light of certain wave-lengths? Spatiotemporal continuity is an obvious criterion to use for objects, but a suit need not possess it (if trousers and coat are separated), and a sound or toothache can be intermittent. We must also ask, continuity of what? Not of matter, since a body, and still more a flame, are constantly changing their matter; and perhaps they change their shape and other properties too. Furthermore we must be able to individuate places and times themselves, i.e. tell when we have one and when another, if we are to use them to individuate objects. Particular attention has been given to the question of *personal identity*. What is a PERSON? How are persons, minds and bodies related? What role do things like memory and traits of character play?

Questions of identity are also important in aesthetics. How is Olivier related to Hamlet when it is true to say both that Olivier is now alone on the stage and that Hamlet is now alone on the stage?

To identify *a* with *b* is simply to claim, or assume, that *a* and *b* are identical. To identify *a as b* (or as a *b*) is to pick out *a* by either taking it to be identical with *b* or attributing *b*-type characteristics to it. I can identify Smith *with* a spy only if I already have some spy in mind, but I can identify him *as* a spy without this.

The *law of identity*, one of the traditional 'laws of thought', says that everything is what it is, or that if something is true, it is true. A proposition that is an instance of this law (e.g. 'A cat is a cat'), or one that can be transformed into such an instance by applying to it the rules of logic (e.g. 'If Tiddles is a cat, Tiddles does not fail to be a cat'), can be called *identically true*, and its negation identically false. See also LEIBNIZ'S LAW, IDENTITY THEORY OF MIND.

D. Hume, *Treatise*, 1739, book 1, part 4, § 2 (pp. 200–1 in L. A. Selby-Bigge's edition.)

D. Wiggins, *Identity and Spatio-Temporal Continuity*, 1967. (Discussion of identity, substance, and personal identity. Conceptualist but claims identity never relative. Cf. his 'On being in the same place at the same time', *Philosophical Review*, 1968 (rather easier), and symposium with M. J. Woods, 'The individuation of things and places', *Proceedings of the Aristotelian Society*, supplementary vol., 1963.)

A. Flew, 'Locke and the problem of personal identity', *Philosophy*, 1951. (Personal identity and memory.)

B. A. O. Williams, 'Personal identity and individuation', *Proceedings of the Aristotelian Society*, 1956–7. (Bases personal identity on bodily continuity.)

M. K. Munitz (ed.), *'Identity and Individuation'*, 1971. (Essays.)

S. Shoemaker, *Self-Knowledge and Self-Identity*, 1963. (Extended discussion of personal identity. See pp. 36–8 for further sense of 'strict' or 'perfect' identity.)

S. Kripke, 'Naming and Necessity', in G. Harman and D. Davidson (eds), *Semantics of Natural Language*, 1972. (Discusses, among other things, identity across possible worlds and identity theory.)

Identity of indiscernibles. See LEIBNIZ'S LAW.

Identity theory of mind. Theory that various conscious phenomena are identical with states or processes in the brain or central nervous system. *Brain process theory, physicalism* (see POSITIVISM) and *central state materialism* are alternative names for the theory (the third for the version using the central nervous system). The conscious phenomena concerned may be limited to sensations and pains, or may include also thoughts, beliefs, desires, emotions. In the former case a BEHAVIOURIST explanation of emotions, etc. may be given. Standard versions of the theory insist that the identity is contingent (see MODALITIES); a commonly used example is the identity of a lightning flash with an electric discharge. Criticisms of the theory include asking how it could be verified, and whether the IDENTITY could be strict. The theory stems largely from Australia in the mid-1950s, though akin to Spinoza's DOUBLE ASPECT THEORY and to neutral MONISM.

C. V. Borst (ed.), *The Mind/Brain Identity Theory*, 1970. (Expository and critical essays, including several main original sources.)

C. F. Presley (ed.), *The Identity of Mind*, 1967. (Papers from a symposium on the theory, with some extra items. Much less full than Borst.).

J. O'Connor (ed.), *Modern Materialism*, 1969. (Further essays, overlapping with Borst.)

K. Campbell, *Body and Mind*, 1970, chapters 5, 6. (Elementary discussion.)

Identity theory of predication. Theory that apparent subject/predicate statements, like 'X is red', are properly to be analysed as identity statements of the form 'X is identical with some red thing'.

If. See CONDITIONALS.

Iff. If and only if.

Illocutions. See SPEECH ACTS.

Illusion (argument from). See PERCEPTION.

Immaterialism

Immaterialism. See IDEALISM.

Imperative. Kant divided imperatives into *categorical* (or *apodictic*) and *hypothetical*. The former were unconditional ('Do X') and the latter conditional on some end ('If (or since) you want Y do X'). Since he was concerned only with imperatives, of each kind, valid for all rational agents he recognized only one categorical imperative, which formed the basis of morality. He formulated it variously, but the general point was, roughly, that one should act only in ways that are UNIVERSALIZABLE. The problems of the categorical imperative are largely those of universalizability. But is the hypothetical imperative really an imperative at all, and not just a statement that fully willing the end involves willing the means? Recently imperatives have been important in prescriptivist views of ethics (see NATURALISM), and there has also been discussion of what logical relations they can stand in.

H. J. Paton, *The Moral Law*, 1948. (Best translation of Kant's *Grundlegung*. Cf. also Paton's commentary, *The Categorical Imperative*, 1947.)

R. Edgley, *Reason in Theory and Practice*, 1969, chapter 4, § 11. (Hypothetical imperatives.)

R. M. Hare, *The Language of Morals*, 1952, part 1. (Logic of imperatives. Also prescriptivism.)

B. A. O. Williams and P. T. Geach, 'Imperative inference', *Analysis*, 1963 (supplement). (Can one infer one imperative from another?)

Implication and entailment. 'Implication' is the most general name for those relations between propositions or statements in virtue of which we can infer the truth of a proposition or statement from something else. A minimum condition for such a relation to hold (except contextual implication: see below) is that if one proposition, p, implies another, q, it is not the case that p is true and q is false. Whenever this condition is fulfilled, and provided p and q are each either true or false, we say that p *materially implies* q. Hence a false proposition materially implies any proposition (for if p is false it is not the case that p is true and q false), and any proposition materially implies a true proposition; these facts are called the 'paradoxes' of material implication, though they are only paradoxical in the sense of sounding odd because 'implies' in ordinary speech suggests a stronger relation. Material implication is usually symbolized by '⊃', which is specific to it, or '→', which can also stand for other relations, including entailment.

Strict implication (C. I. Lewis; usually symbolized by '⊰') holds from p to q when it is logically impossible (see MODALITIES) for p to be true and q false. Hence it too has 'paradoxes', that an impossible (i.e. necessarily false) proposition strictly implies any proposition, and any proposition strictly implies a necessary proposition. Occasionally the impossibility and necessity involved may be general, not just logical.

Entailment is a special relation introduced by Moore, who said it held from p to q when and only when q can be logically deduced from p.

Implication and entailment

Entailment in this sense, as against the looser popular sense, can be called *logical entailment* (whether or not it is strictly a logical relation: see below). Entailment is often thought to differ from strict implication, by requiring that the propositions that it links have some relevance to each other, or connexion of meaning, so that the paradoxes of strict implication do not apply to it. On this view entailment is not always simply a logical relation. Many writers have tried to formalize this relevance requirement and show that it avoids the paradoxes, but these attempts remain controversial.

Logical implication is implication that holds as a matter of logic, or is logically necessary. Though often equated with strict implication, logical implication is more general. It need not be limited to a relation whereby a contradiction implies any proposition and any proposition implies a necessary proposition. If entailment is a logical relation different from strict implication, 'logical implication' can cover both. 'Logical implication' is also used as a general contrast to 'contextual implication' (see below).

Presuppositions are carried by certain statements, questions, etc. 'Have you stopped beating your wife?' presupposes that you have one and have beaten her. Strawson and others distinguish presuppositions from entailments because when p entails q, if q is false p is false, but when p presupposes q, so does not-p, and if q is false p is neither true nor false (if you have no wife you have neither stopped nor not stopped beating her). It is disputed, however, whether presupposition and entailment in fact exclude each other (Linsky, Strawson). *Absolute presuppositions* is Collingwood's term for statements which are not (as most statements are, he thought) answers to questions. They are neither true nor false, but underlie the thought of persons or epochs.

Contextual or *pragmatic implication* is related to, and not always easily distinguishable from, presupposition. *Implicature* is also used for much the same notion. Perhaps the main difference is that presupposition affects the truth of what is said, while contextual implication affects the rationality or correctness of saying it. Normally if one says something one contextually implies that one believes it. If I say 'It's raining' I contextually imply that I believe it is; but it could be raining even if I do not believe it is. 'A speaker in making a statement contextually implies whatever one is entitled to infer on the basis of the presumption that his act of stating is normal' (Hungerland). For both presupposition and contextual implication it is disputable what does the presupposing, etc. Is it what is said, the saying of it, or the sayer? Saying (which here includes asking, etc.) may even be replaced by something non-linguistic: 'By (deliberately) frowning he implied he was angry.' A non-deliberate frown could only 'imply' anger causally, rather as clouds imply rain. Contextual implication lies between such a causal sense and logical implication. See also CONDITIONALS, INFERENCE.

G. E. Moore, *Philosophical Studies*, 1923, p. 291. (Entailment introduced.)
C. I. Lewis and C. H. Langford, *Symbolic Logic*, 1932, chapter 8. (Equates entailment with strict implication.)

Implicature

E. J. Nelson, 'Intensional relations', *Mind*, 1930.

C. Lewy, J. L. Watling, P. T. Geach, 'Entailment', *Proceedings of the Aristotelian Society*, supplementary vol. 1958.

T. J. Smiley, 'Entailment and deducibility', *Proceedings of the Aristotelian Society*, 1958–9. (All these try to separate entailment from strict implication.)

G. H. von Wright, 'A note on entailment', *Philosophical Quarterly*, 1959. (Comments on Geach above.)

J. Bennett, 'Entailment', *Philosophical Review*, 1969. (General survey, defending Lewis.)

B. Mates, *Stoic Logic*, 1961, chapter 4. (Philonian, Diodorean and Chrysippean implication.)

N. Wolterstorff, 'Referring and existing', *Philosophical Quarterly*, 1961.

L. Linsky, *Referring*, 1967, chapter 6.

W. Sellars, 'Presupposing', P. F. Strawson, 'A reply to Mr Sellars', *Philosophical Review*, 1954. (These, with Wolterstorff and Linsky, discuss Strawson's earlier views on presupposition, and its relation to entailment.)

A. R. Anderson and N. Belnap, 'Tautological entailments', *Philosophical Studies*, 1962.

R. G. Collingwood, *An Essay on Metaphysics*, 1940, esp. part 1. (Absolute presuppositions.)

I. Hungerland, 'Contextual implication', *Inquiry*, 1960. (Contextual implication and presupposition. For quotation see p. 255.)

H. P. Grice, 'The causal theory of perception', *Proceedings of the Aristotelian Society*, supplementary vol., 1961, reprinted in G. J. Warnock (ed.), *The Philosophy of Perception*, 1967, esp. § 3. (Some kinds of implication.)

P. H. Nowell Smith, 'Contextual implication and ethical theory', *Proceedings of the Aristotelian Society*, supplementary vol., 1962.

Implicature. See IMPLICATION.

Incomplete symbol. See LOGICAL CONSTRUCTIONS.

Incongruent or incongruous counterparts. Pairs of things differing only as an object and its mirror-image do, or a pair of hands, or opposite spirals. The precise characterization of this difference (probably first attempted by Kant) is difficult, and may be important for studying the nature of space. Also called *enantiomorphs*.

J. Bennett, 'The difference between right and left', *American Philosophical Quarterly*, 1970.

Inconsistent triad. See ANTILOGISM.

Incontinence. Also called *acrasia* (*akrasia*), *weakness of will*. The Socratic paradox that no one errs willingly (for a willing error is not an error) raises the problem whether one can act against one's better judgment, be the judgment moral or prudential, etc. Similarly, can one assent to something against the evidence, or deceive oneself (cf. BAD FAITH)?

G. W. Mortimore (ed.), *Weakness of Will*, 1971. (Selections ancient and modern.)

Incorrigible. A statement is incorrigible for someone if he cannot be in error in believing or disbelieving it. Whether such statements exist is disputed, but typical candidates are reports of immediate experience like, 'I now seem to see something red.' Incorrigible statements are not the same as necessarily true or false statements. The above example, if true, is only contingently true, and we can make mistakes about necessary statements (e.g. in mathematics). In a weaker sense a statement is incorrigible if we can be mistaken about it but there is no way of correcting us, e.g. perhaps statements reporting our dreams.

A statement is *indubitable* for someone if he cannot rationally doubt or reject it. I can reject the statement that I seem to see something red, but not, according to Descartes, the statement that I exist. 'Incorrigible' and 'indubitable' are often used more loosely, and even interchangeably.

J. L. Mackie, 'Are there any incorrigible empirical statements?', *Australasian Journal of Philosophy*, 1963. (Uses 'incorrigible' in weak sense, and 'indubitable' for strong sense.)

Independent. See AXIOM.

Indeterminism. See FREEWILL.

Indexicals. See TOKEN-REFLEXIVES.

Indicator terms. See TOKEN-REFLEXIVES.

Indifference (principle of). Also called *principle of insufficient reason* (different from Leibniz's principle of SUFFICIENT REASON). Principle that if we have no reason to expect one rather than another of n mutually exclusive and collectively exhaustive possibilities to be realized, we should assign a probability of $1/n$ to each of them. The principle's validity is disputed. See also PROBABILITY.

W. C. Kneale, *Probability and Induction*, 1949, §§ 31, 34. (Criticizes principle, but defends variant of it. Cf. S. Blackburn, *Reason and Prediction*, 1973, chapter 6.)

Indiscernibility of identicals. See LEIBNIZ'S LAW.

Individuals. There seem to be three main senses: (i) whatever can be counted, one by one ('individuated'), or can be talked of or referred to (logical subjects: see MEANING). In this sense all particulars (see UNIVERSALS) are individuals, but not vice-versa. Beauty is an individual. We can talk about

Indubitable

it and distinguish it from other things, but it is a universal and not a particular (it seems not to exist 'all at once' in a spatiotemporal or quasi-spatiotemporal way). Tennis is an individual, though not a particular, nor perhaps a universal ('tennis' does not seem to behave like words in '-ity', '-ness', '-hood', etc.) 'Individual' in this first main sense resembles 'OBJECT' when the 'existence' strand of that word is dominant.

(ii) In logic individuals are contrasted with predicates or functions (i.e. universals). They are what 'individual VARIABLES' range over, and so they are whatever the subject of a logical expression can refer to—but the expression must belong to the first-order (or 'restricted') predicate CALCULUS, and must not appear only in the 'extended' predicate calculus (where predicates can be referred to).

(iii) Same as 'particular'.

(ii) has affinities with both (i) and (iii). (iii) is the oldest sense.

P. F. Strawson, *Individuals*, 1959. (See esp. pp. 226–7, and his 'Categories' in O. P. Wood and G. Pitcher (eds), *Ryle*. 1970, pp. 196, 199. Cf. also Strawson's *Introduction to Logical Theory*, 1952, p. 144.)

J. Valberg, 'Improper singular terms', *Proceedings of the Aristotelian Society*, 1970–1, esp. pp. 136–41. (Some difficulties in defining 'individual'.)

F. Sommers, 'Predicability', in M. Black (ed.), *Philosophy in America*, 1965, esp. pp. 277 ff. (Defines individuals, in sense perhaps nearest to (iii), in terms of what can be predicated of them.)

Indubitable. See INCORRIGIBLE.

Induction. In its widest sense, any rational process where from premises about some things of a certain kind a conclusion is drawn about some or all of the remaining things of that kind. An argument is inductive in a narrow or strict sense (called *simple* or *enumerative induction*) if it claims to draw such a conclusion from such premises directly in a single step. Those who accept that simple induction is, given certain conditions, a rational process are often called *inductivists*.

The traditional form of simple induction, 'All observed a's are b's, so all a's are b's', can be regarded as a special case (where n = 100) of the form 'n per cent, of observed a's are b's so about n per cent of all a's are b's'. Some writers, notably J. S. Mill, think that inductive inference goes from particulars to particulars, i.e. to further instances, not to a generalization. Others think a conclusion about particulars can be reached only through a generalization, i.e. that one can only argue from 'All (or n per cent of) observed ravens have been black' to 'The next raven will be black' by using the intermediate conclusion 'All (or n per cent of all) ravens are black'. Of course the smaller n is, the weaker the argument will be.

Anti-inductivists say that simple induction is not a rational process, and that inductive arguments in fact work in other ways. They may claim that inductive arguments are really DEDUCTIVE arguments some of whose premises have been suppressed; if these premises were made explicit the deductive nature of the argument would become clear. Alternatively they may claim that inductive arguments really work by the *hypothetico-deductive method*, whereby a hypothesis is set up and conclusions are deduced from it and tested against experience: if the conclusions turn out false the hypothesis is rejected. Inductivists can also use this method, but anti-inductivists, notably Whewell and Popper, believe that the hypothesis cannot be directly supported: all we can do is try to falsify it.

Inductivists and anti-inductivists agree nowadays that no formal rules can be given for reaching the right hypothesis (cf. PSYCHOLOGISM), which does not imply that ways of reaching it cannot be assessed as rational. What distinguishes inductivists is that they think the hypothesis, however acquired, may be supported directly by evidence (not merely indirectly, by its surviving attempts to falsify it). Anti-inductivists tend to think that an INFERENCE, or a step in argument, is 'deductive or defective' (A. C. MacIntyre).

Hypotheses about objects not directly observable such as electrons or magnetic fields are sometimes called *transcendent hypotheses*. They cannot be reached or directly confirmed by simple induction. The process by which they are reached or confirmed is sometimes called *secondary induction* (Kneale), especially when it is regarded as rationally assessable and not merely a matter of psychology. 'Secondary induction' can also refer to any induction whose premises themselves result from induction. We might conclude inductively that all ravens have feathers, and that all swans do, and then conclude by a further induction from ravens and swans that all birds do.

Much of inductive logic consists in asking whether simple induction has any place in scientific enquiry, and, if so, what rules can be elaborated to govern its use as a method of CONFIRMATION. The *problem of induction* has traditionally been the problem of justifying not so much particular rules as simple induction in general (sometimes by the back-handed method of reducing it to disguised deduction; cf. the first type of anti-inductivist above, and (ii) below). Most justifications of induction refer to simple induction. The main attempts to justify simple induction are as follows.

(i) Mathematical facts about the relations between samples and their parent populations are used.

(ii) Some grand overall premise is sought which can turn inductive arguments into deductive ones: that the future resembles the past, that nature is uniform, that every event has a cause, and that the variety in the universe is finite in amount, have been favourite candidates. The difficulties have concerned formulating these premises (how closely must the future resemble the past?) and then justifying them. (ii) is now unpopular.

(iii) Perhaps induction can be used to justify itself. This seems circular, but is the circularity only apparent?

(iv) The *pragmatic* or *practicalist* approach has it that induction cannot indeed be validated, in the sense of being shown to be likely to work, but it can be rationally justified as a practical policy because every alternative is less rational; the claim is now that induction is likely to work *if any method is*. *Vindicated* is sometimes used here. We do not know what the actual

Induction

universe is like. In some possible universes induction would work better than other methods, while in some (notably, chaotic ones) no method would work. But in no possible universe, it is claimed, would any method work better than induction. Here we must distinguish alternatives which deliberately predict results conflicting with inductive predictions (*negative induction* or *counter-induction*) from those which are merely indifferent to induction (e.g. appeal to soothsayers). The former are easier to deal with. The 'long-term' problem of whether a certain method is rational if given an indefinitely long time to work in differs from the 'short-term', and more interesting, problem of whether it is rational when we are only interested in a finite time ahead.

(v) Induction may not need justification because it is a going concern. There are generally acknowledged criteria of inductive soundness. We may well study in detail what they are, but it is senseless to reject them because they are our touchstone for rejecting any inductive arguments, and so we should be appealing to them even in rejecting them (cf. PARADIGM CASE ARGUMENT).

Various processes called 'induction' must be distinguished from induction proper. *Intuitive induction* is a process where particular cases serve as psychological causes rather than rational justifications for generalizations whose justification is a priori. If we notice that something coloured is extended, this may make us *realize* rather than infer that all coloured things are extended. Proof by *mathematical, recursive* or *course-of-values induction* is the process whereby we prove that something holds for every term in a series (e.g. for every natural number) by proving that it holds for the first term, and that it holds for any later term x whenever it holds for all terms before x. Cf. also DEFINITION by induction. 'Mathematical induction' is different from the use of simple induction as a preliminary move in mathematics. A mathematician might argue, 'All examined even numbers are the sum of two primes, so (perhaps) all even numbers are', and then try to prove this conclusion. *Perfect induction* or *induction by complete enumeration* (not by simple enumeration, which is simple induction) consists in asserting, e.g. 'All the chairs in this room are wooden' after checking them one by one. The 'inductive leap' consists simply in assuming that the chairs checked are all there in the room. See also CONFIRMATION, PROBABILITY, CAUSATION.

S. F. Barker, 'Must every inference be either deductive or inductive?', in M. Black (ed.), *Philosophy in America*, 1965.

A. C. MacIntyre, 'Hume on "is" and "ought"', *Philosophical Review*, 1959. (See p. 453 for 'deductive or defective'.)

W. Whewell, *Novum Organum Renovatum*, 3rd (revised) edn 1858.

K. Popper, *The Logic of Scientific Discovery*, 1959 (German original 1934). (These two works advocate hypothetico-deductive method as self-sufficient. Cf. Popper's 'personal report' in C. A. Mace (ed.), *British Philosophy in the Mid-Century*, 1957, reprinted in Popper's *Conjectures and Refutations*, 1963, chapter 1; and cf. his *Objective Knowledge*, 1972, chapter 1.)

W. Kneale, *Probability and Induction*, 1949. (Part 2 discusses various kinds of induction and pseudo-induction (intuitive etc.).)

N. Goodman, 'Seven strictures on similarity', in L. Foster and J. W. Swanson (eds), *Experience and Theory*, 1970. (Induction and resemblance.)

B. Russell, *Problems of Philosophy*, chapter 6. (Classic statement of problem of induction.)

M. Black, 'Self-supporting inductive arguments', *Journal of Philosophy*, 1958.

P. Achinstein, 'The circularity of a self-supporting inductive argument', *Analysis*, vol. 22, 1962. (Both reprinted in P. H. Nidditch (ed.), *The Philosophy of Science*, 1968. Cf. further debate between Black and Achinstein in *Analysis*, vol. 23, 1962–3, and cf. also R. B. Braithwaite, *Scientific Explanation*, 1953, chapter 8.)

H. Reichenbach, *The Theory of Probability*, 1949 (German original 1935), final section. (Vindication of induction from point of view of frequency theory of PROBABILITY; cf. also his *Experience and Prediction*, 1938, §§ 38–40.)

J. O. Wisdom, *Foundations of Inference in Natural Science*. (Follows Popper in general. Chapter 24 offers vindication. Chapter 23 criticizes mathematical justification of simple induction.)

S. Blackburn, *Reason and Prediction*, 1973. (Attempts vindication by version of principle of indifference.)

P. Edwards, 'Bertrand Russell's doubts about induction', *Mind*, 1949, reprinted in A. Flew (ed.), *Logic and Language*, vol. 1, 1951. (Claims induction needs no defence.)

R. Swinburne (ed.), *The Justification of Induction*, 1974. (Includes several of above items.)

Inference. Assertion on the basis of something else. 'All cats are black, so this cat is black' represents an inference, though 'inference' can refer to the conclusion, 'This cat is black', as well as to the process. 'If all cats are black then this cat is black', where neither antecedent nor consequent is actually asserted, represents an IMPLICATION. Inferences need not necessarily be DEDUCTIVE.

In *immediate inference* a conclusion is drawn from a single premise, especially by OBVERSION, CONVERSION, CONTRAPOSITION and INVERSION. In *mediate inference* two or more independent premises are involved, as in a syllogism. This distinction is not exact. See also INDUCTION.

G. Ryle, ' "If", "so", and "because" ', in M. Black (ed.), *Philosophical Analysis*, 1950. (Inference and implication.)

J. S. Mill, *A System of Logic*, 1843, book 2, chapter 1. (Nature of inference.)

M. Deutscher, 'A causal account of inferring', in R. Brown and C. D. Rollins (eds), *Contemporary Philosophy in Australia*, 1969.

Infinity. See METAPHYSICS.

Inscription. A written token (see UNIVERSALS). *Inscriptivism* (*inscriptionism*) is any view making significant use of inscriptions, e.g. the *inscriptional*

Instrumentalism

theory of intentionality explains intentionality (see INTENSIONALITY) in terms of relations between utterers and token sentences (considered as written, for convenience).

W. V. Quine, *Word and Object*, 1960, pp. 214–15.

Instrumentalism. Theory that scientific laws and theories are instruments for predicting observable phenomena, and are therefore to be judged by their usefulness and not classified as propositions which can be true or false. Somewhat similar to CONVENTIONALISM. Also a development of PRAGMATISM by Dewey. Also the view that values (generally, or in some sphere, e.g. aesthetics) are instrumental (e.g. in promoting satisfaction); see GOOD.

S. E. Toulmin, *The Philosophy of Science*, 1953. (Example of instrumentalist outlook.)

K. R. Popper, *The Logic of Scientific Discovery*, 1934, transl. 1959, p. 423. (Critical, with references.)

Insufficient reason (principle of). See INDIFFERENCE.

Intensionality. Roughly, that set of features which concerns the meaning of a term as against the things to which it applies. *Intension* and *extension* are related in the same way as what a term means and what it applies to are related, but both are complex and ambiguous. Notions like *connotation* and Frege's 'sense' are called intensions. *Denotation* and Frege's 'reference', and also classes, can all be called extensions. (For these notions see MEANING.) Usually the context determines just what is meant. The *comprehension* of 'man' is the whole set of properties shared by all men, or else the set which (logically) must be shared by them. In seventeenth-century usage it means 'connotation'.

Extensions correspond roughly to classes, and intensions to properties. A property like that of being a man determines at most one class. There is only one class of men, though it may have sub-classes. But one and the same class may correspond to more than one property. The class of ruminants, for example, is the same as the class of cloven-hoofed animals. A class itself is said to be *taken in extension* if it is specified by enumerating its members, and *taken in intension* if it is specified in the ordinary way as containing whatever things have a certain property.

So long as we are interested only in a group of objects and not in how they are viewed, we can substitute for our first description of them any other description that picks out the same class (e.g. 'cloven-hoofed things' for 'ruminants'), and what we say will remain true, if it was true with the first description. If all ruminants are mammals, then all cloven-hoofed things are mammals. This is expressed by saying we can substitute the second description *salva veritate*. Similarly if we study propositions only in respect of their TRUTH-VALUES (as logicians often do. Cf. truth-FUNCTIONS), then for any proposition another with the same truth-value can be substituted salva veritate. Therefore truth-values count among extensions.

Propositions themselves, which cannot be substituted like this when our interests are less restricted, count among intensions, which are sometimes called *intensional objects*.

Extensions are simpler than intensions, and in one loose but intelligible sense they are more objective, in that they concern the world rather than how we look at it. Logicians therefore prefer extensions, and would like to dispense with intensions, by showing that statements containing intensional notions can always be translated into statements free from them. The view that this can be done is called the *extensionality thesis* (cf. LEIBNIZ'S LAW) and defended by LOGICAL ATOMISTS, logical POSITIVISTS, nominalists, and in general those who prefer a sparse and austere universe. It is attacked by those who accept the richness and complexity of the universe at its face value. Its defenders, notably Quine, also argue that if it is not accepted no coherent system of logic can be elaborated, i.e. they claim that there is no intensional logic. This view can itself be called a version of the extensionality thesis.

If in a certain context a referring phrase cannot, salva veritate, be replaced by another phrase referring to the same object or objects, the context is called *referentially opaque*. Otherwise it is *referentially transparent*. 'Opaque' and 'transparent' are also used of other contexts to distinguish whether replacements cannot, or can, be made, e.g. 'was hanged' occurs opaquely in 'Smith believes that Hitler was hanged', because we cannot replace it by 'suffered the same fate as Goebbels', even if Goebbels was hanged, since Smith may not know this (and so may not believe that Hitler suffered the same fate as Goebbels). Opacity is thus in effect the same as intensionality, though applied more narrowly. Contexts can be opaque. Properties, etc. can be called intensional, but not opaque. Perhaps opacity should be called an effect of intensionality.

Intentionality, though historically different from intensionality, is often confused or equated with it. It is controversial whether they are really the same notion. *Non-extensional* is often used for 'intensional', presumably to avoid this confusion. 'Extension' and its derivatives are always spelt with 's'.

Intentional situations may perhaps be thought of as those where a relation appears to exist but does not really (but there are difficulties: see next paragraph). This happens primarily in certain psychological contexts, and the basic problem concerning intentionality has been to define it so that it picks out and explains the peculiarities of just these psychological contexts. Sometimes the truth of statements about an object depends on how the object is described. This is especially so with psychological notions like believing, thinking, wanting. Cicero and Tully are one man, but Smith may believe that Cicero is an orator without believing that Tully is one (though he believes *of* Tully that he is one, since his belief concerns that man (Cicero) who in fact is also Tully). Also the object may not exist. Smith may believe that Apollo is an orator, or that unicorns live in Africa. Since Brentano, who brought these issues to light and revived some medieval terminology, objects like Cicero, Apollo and unicorns, in these contexts, are called *intentional objects*, and are sometimes said to have *intentional*

Intensionality

inexistence (existence in the mind, or as an object of the mind's activity). One can perhaps think of them as what the mind is intent upon, though this may be historically inaccurate (Kneale). Sometimes, as with Cicero but not Apollo, the intentional object corresponds to a real object. The relations between the two are then not clear. If they are identical, the intentional object of Smith's belief should also be Tully. If they are not identical, the intentional object seems to be merely in the mind, but this is unsatisfactory, since the belief, in both the Apollo and Cicero cases, claims to be about something outside the mind. The whole notion of intentional objects is thus difficult (cf. THINKING), and various theories exist about their nature and reality.

It is tempting to pick out the psychological contexts as those in which no assumptions are made about the existence or non-existence of the things mentioned. Two sorts of difficulty arise here. First it is not clear how far the 'psychological' extends. 'John is shooting at unicorns' mentions a physical activity, though with a psychological aspect. Since, on one interpretation, it does not imply that there are any unicorns it is on that interpretation presumably intentional. On the other hand 'John knows (realizes, admits) there are unicorns' is presumably psychological and yet does imply there are unicorns. Moreover, perception and feeling pain are surely psychological but do not seem always to involve ways of looking at things, or assumptions about existence, i.e. they do not seem to be psychological in the way required.

The second difficulty is that whatever features are picked out to mark off the psychological contexts as intentional seem to apply also to many clearly non-psychological contexts, e.g. modal ones (see MODALITIES): 'Possibly unicorns are vegetarian' need not imply that there are unicorns or that there are not, and so seems to be intentional. It is this that raises doubts about the distinction between intentionality and intensionality (since modal contexts are agreed to be intensional).

Intentions in the ordinary sense form just one kind of intentional context, and have no special privilege in their connexion with the intentionality here at issue. See also MEANING, THINKING.

L. S. Stebbing, *A Modern Elementary Logic*, 1943. (Chapter 6 discusses relevant terminology in traditional logic.)

W. V. Quine, 'Reference and modality' in *From a Logical Point of View*, 2nd (revised) edn 1961, reprinted with some (difficult) discussions following from it in L. Linsky (ed.), *Reference and Modality*, 1971. (Referential opacity and its effects on modal logic and intensional logic in general.)

Proceedings of the Aristotelian Society, supplementary vol., 1968. (Includes two relevant symposia: J. O. Urmson (easiest) and L. J. Cohen, 'Criteria of intensionality', equate intentionality with intensionality and discuss criteria stemming from R. Chisholm. W. C. Kneale and A. N. Prior, 'Intentionality and intensionality', distinguish these notions and discuss various problems, including the relations of these notions to nominalism. Kneale includes historical material.)

A. Kenny, *Action, Emotion and Will*, 1963. (Chapters 9 ff. discuss 'objects' of emotions, etc., referring to Chisholm, etc. Spells with 's'.)

R. Scruton, 'Intensional and intentional objects', *Proceedings of the Aristotelian Society*, 1970–1. (Separates them and makes further distinctions within intentionality.)

Intentionality. See INTENSIONALITY.

Intersubjective. Something is intersubjective if there are ways of reaching agreement about it, even though it may not be independent of the human mind (and hence not objective), e.g. the hypothesis that a certain chemical tastes like pineapple might be intersubjectively testable. Intersubjectivity is usually contrasted with subjectivity rather than with objectivity, which it may include.

Intervening variables. See LOGICAL CONSTRUCTIONS.

Intuition. Generally a direct relation between the mind and some object, analogous to what common sense thinks is the relation between us and something we see unambiguously in a clear light.

What we are said to intuit may be objects not accessible to the senses (numbers, universals, God, etc.), or truths. The emphasis is on the directness of the relation, free from any influence of the environment or interpretation. Hence Kant used 'intuition' for our relation to sensible objects too, so far as this was considered as abstracted from anything contributed by the mind. Intuition thus considered has something in common with Russell's 'acquaintance' (cf. EPISTEMOLOGY).

Intuition of truths may take the form of knowledge which we cannot account for, simply because we are unconscious of the reasons which led us to it (the intuition attributed to women and bank managers). In the case of such 'hunches' investigation will often uncover the reasons. More philosophically important are cases where, allegedly, there are no reasons to be uncovered, and no means of checking the truth of apparent intuitions, except perhaps by their coherence with further intuitions.

Intuitions of this kind have been important especially in philosophy of mathematics (see INTUITIONISM) and ethics, and also in logic and metaphysics. Whether such intuitions can be accepted, and whether ultimately they are unavoidable, are disputed questions. Cf. also RATIONALISM.

D. Pole, *Conditions of Rational Inquiry*, 1961, chapter 1. (General discussion of intuition.)

H. L. A. Hart, G. E. Hughes, J. N. Findlay, 'Is there knowledge by acquaintance?', *Proceedings of the Aristotelian Society*, supplementary vol., 1949.

W. Hudson, *Ethical Intuitionism*, 1967. (Brief introduction.)

H. Sidgwick, *Methods of Ethics*, 1874, esp. book 1, chapter 8. (Types of ethical intuitionism. The book reached its final version in the sixth edition.)

Intuitionism

Intuitionism. Any doctrine emphasizing the role of INTUITION. Mathematical intuitionism, associated especially with L. E. J. Brouwer (1881–1966) and A. Heyting (1898–   ), confines the subject-matter of mathematics to what is given in intuition. In particular it refuses to assume that infinite sets actually exist, though it allows rules which generate ever larger finite sets. It is a form of *constructivism*, which insists that we should postulate entities (numbers, etc.) only if we know how to construct them, i.e. how to specify them systematically in terms of things we already accept. But intuitionism insists further that in mathematics we should call something true or false only if we either know it intuitively or know how to prove or disprove it, using steps known by intuition. (Hence an acceptable proof of something's existence involves constructing it.) Intuitionism therefore introduces a special kind of negation for use in mathematics, which has the consequence that we can deny a (non-counter-intuitive) proposition only if we can disprove it. Since intuitionists think that some (non-intuitive) mathematical propositions cannot be proved or disproved, they insist that the law of EXCLUDED MIDDLE does not apply to this kind of negation. On negation outside mathematics they have no united view.

Formalists too limit mathematics to what is in a sense within our control. Some of them (e.g. H. B. Curry) make mathematics consist of formal systems whose elements are mere symbols or meaningless marks, to be operated on by fixed rules. Mathematics is not about abstract objects like numbers or classes that these marks might be thought to stand for. D. Hilbert (1862–1943), the most famous formalist, thought the logical paradoxes showed that non-finitary mathematics (see FINITISM) needed justifying. He therefore interpreted it as a formal system and used finitary means to prove the consistency of this system (cf. METAMATHEMATICS). See also INTUITION (for bibliography on ethical intuitionism).

P. Benacerraf and H. Putnam (eds), *Philosophy of Mathematics*, 1964, esp. pp. 66–77 (Brouwer), 134–51 (Hilbert).

G. T. Kneebone, *Mathematical Logic and the Foundations of Mathematics*, 1963. (Pp. 243–50 gives elementary account of intuitionism, showing link with Kant.)

S. Körner, *The Philosophy of Mathematics*, 1960. (Includes full treatment of intuitionism and formalism.)

W. and M. Kneale, *The Development of Logic*, 1962. (See index.)

W. V. Quine, *Philosophy of Logic*, 1970, pp. 87–8. (Intuitionism and constructivism.)

Inversion. In traditional formal logic, replacement of a proposition by a logically equivalent one, its *inverse*, having as subject the negation of the original subject, e.g. 'Some non-cats are non-black' is the inverse of 'All cats are black'.

Isomorphic. Sharing the same structure. Two or more sentences are *intensionally isomorphic* (Carnap) if they are logically equivalent, and have the same number of component sentences, and any component sentence in one is logically equivalent to the correspondingly placed component sentence in each of the others. The definition can be extended to certain other expressions. *Isomorphism* is the property or state of being isomorphic.

R. Carnap, *Meaning and Necessity*, 1947, pp. 56–9.

J

James-Lange theory. Sometimes called the *peripheric theory*. Theory that emotions are consequences, not causes, of bodily disturbances, that 'the bodily changes follow directly the perception of the exciting fact, and that our feeling of the same changes as they occur *is* the emotion'. 'A purely disembodied human emotion is a nonentity' (though not a contradiction).

W. James, *The Principles of Psychology*, 1901, vol. 2, chapter 25. (Quotations on pp. 449, 452.)

James, William. 1842–1910. Psychologist and philosopher, and brother of novelist Henry James, he was born in New York and spent his life partly travelling and partly working at Harvard. Philosophically he is best known as a leading PRAGMATIST, though also in connexion with the JAMES-LANGE THEORY of the emotions and with neutral MONISM. *The Principles of Psychology*, 1890 (includes much philosophy too). *The Varieties of Religious Experience*, 1902. *Pragmatism*, 1907. *The Nature of Truth*, 1909 (supplement to *Pragmatism*). *Essays in Radical Empiricism*, 1912 (neutral monism). See also EMPIRICISM.

Jaspers, Karl. 1883–1969. Born in Oldenburg in Germany, he worked mainly at Heidelberg and Basel. He was a leading EXISTENTIALIST philosopher, whose work was much influenced by his early training in medicine and psychiatry, and has greater connexions with contemporary social and political problems than does that of HEIDEGGER. He treats human existence in terms of various notions, including *Dasein*, which he uses in a sense different from Heidegger's sense. *Philosophie*, 1932. *Vernunft und Existenz*, 1935 (5 lectures). *Existenzphilosophie*, 1938 (3 lectures). *Die Schuldfrage*, 1946 (on German war guilt). *Von der Wahrheit*, 1947. *Vernunft und Widervernunft in Unserer Zeit*, 1950 (3 lectures). See also MARCEL.

Judgment. Act of judging, or, less commonly, proposition, or content of an act of judging. Acts of judging by different people or at different times, but with the same content, may, however, count as a single judgment (e.g. if you and I both judge that grass is green). Whether it is acts or contents that logic is primarily concerned with has been disputed. Idealists and pragmatists have tended to prefer acts, and formal logicians contents. Judgment is closely connected to (and often equated with) BELIEF, which, however, is a state or disposition rather than an act.

Judgments are sometimes limited, in both 'act' and 'content' senses, to cases where an element of assessment or evaluation is concerned, e.g. moral *judgments* may be contrasted with *statements* of fact. See also SENTENCES, THINKING.

P. T. Geach, *Mental Acts*, 1957. (One view of judgments. Fairly difficult.)

K

Kant, Immanuel. 1724–1804. German philosopher who spent all his life in Königsberg (now Kaliningrad). He is often regarded as synthesizing the 'British EMPIRICIST' and 'Continental RATIONALIST' schools by standing back from the questions they asked ('What is the nature of the world?', 'How do we know about the world?') and saying we must first give a critique of our faculties; he asks what it is *possible* for any mind like the human mind to know. Hence his philosophy after 1781 is often called the 'critical' philosophy. Much of his philosophy centres round his defence of synthetic a priori propositions. He also tried to derive morality from reason alone, and to elaborate a notion of the self compatible with our possession of freewill. *Kritik der reinen Vernunft* (*Critique of Pure Reason*), 1781 (2nd edn 1787). *Grundlegung der Metaphysik der Sitten* (*Fundamental Principles* (or *Groundwork*) *of the Metaphysic of Morals*), 1785. *Kritik der praktischen Vernunft* (*Critique of Practical Reason*), 1788. *Kritik der Urteilskraft* (*Critique of Judgment*), 1790. See also ANALYTIC, APPERCEPTION, A PRIORI, BEAUTIFUL, BEING, CATEGORIES, COSMOLOGICAL, DESIGN, EPISTEMOLOGY, ETHICS, FORM, GOOD, HARE, HEIDEGGER, HUME, IDEA, IDEALISM, IMPERATIVE, INCONGRUENT, INTUITION, MANIFOLD, MODALITIES, NOUMENON, OUGHT, PHENOMENOLOGY, REASON, REID, SCHOPENHAUER, SPACE, STRAWSON, TRANSCENDENTAL ARGUMENTS, UNIVERSALIZABILITY.

Kierkegaard, Søren A. 1813–55. Danish philosopher who spent his life as a pastor in Copenhagen and is normally considered the first EXISTENTIALIST. His principal interest was in ethics, where he emphasized the importance of pure choice, but, more than many later existentialists, developed his philosophy in a Christian framework. He also, like SCHOPENHAUER, reacted against the then prevalent philosophy of HEGEL. *Either/Or*, 1843. *Philosophical Fragments*, 1844. *The Concept of Dread*, 1844. *Concluding Unscientific Postscript to the Philosophical Fragments*, 1846.

Knowledge. See EPISTEMOLOGY.

L

Language (philosophy of). Not the same as linguistic PHILOSOPHY, nor as *linguistics*, which studies the general features of natural languages structurally (*synchronic*) or historically (*diachronic*, also called *philology*).

As a separate study, philosophy of language is a recent offshoot of logic, connected also to epistemology, metaphysics and philosophy of mind. It asks general questions about language as such, not (like linguistics) about particular languages. The latter, of course, provide examples.

The primary end of language is communication. Other ends, like getting people to do things, depend on this. Many things can be communicated—information, requests, commands, ideas, innuendoes, etc. (cf. SPEECH ACTS). Whether the primary function of language is to inform, or assert, may be disputed, but this function in fact receives most attention. Two concepts which are therefore of central importance are TRUTH and FACTS. The question of how communication is possible, or how language works, involves us in studying the notion of MEANING. CONCEPTS, propositions and statements (see SENTENCES) have been thought necessary to account for meaning, and they raise problems about what they are and what properties they have (e.g. the ANALYTIC/synthetic distinction).

A study of language in general will naturally ask whether there are any features every language must share. Such features might be ones without which a language could not exist. It might be claimed, for example, that every language must include ways of referring to particular objects, or ways of negating; or the features might be needed because human nature is what it is. (N. Chomsky claims that certain features of deep structure (see GRAMMARS) are universal and throw light on how the mind works. Cf. CATEGORIES.)

Further general questions about language include how far animals can have language, whether there can be a PRIVATE LANGUAGE, and whether ideal languages are possible, of which natural languages are defective versions (as, for example, Russell and perhaps Plato thought). Artificial languages, whether used in science or constructed for theoretical interest, can also be studied.

After the Second World War, naming and verificationist theories of MEANING were rejected, and there followed the piecemeal approach of

107

Language game

linguistic PHILOSOPHY. METAPHYSICS has also used philosophy of language on topics like SUBSTANCE. Currently, there is some return to large-scale theorizing under Chomsky, whose contribution involves applying mathematical techniques to problems connected with the attempt to specify all the sentences constructable in a given language.

W. Alston, *Philosophy of Language*, 1964. (General introduction.)
J. L. Austin, *How to Do Things with Words*, 1962. (Functions of language.)
J. F. Bennett, *Rationality*, 1964. (Can animals have language?)
P. F. Strawson, *Individuals*, 1959. (Part 2 discusses role of referring. Cf.
  R. Stoothoff, 'Elimination theses', *Mind*, 1968, for more general discussion of what can be eliminated from language. Both fairly difficult.)
J. Lyons, *Chomsky*, 1970. (Elementary introduction.)

Language game. Wittgenstein discussed the way language works by inventing small-scale languages for special spheres, such as house-building, and asking how they might work and what they must be like. Comparing them to certain children's games he called them language games. He then compared them to the complexities of actual language, and used them to emphasize the role of words in certain human practices like doing science and play-acting. He originally thought of them as primitive or autonomous, i.e. as not presupposing the rest of language. But 'language game' came to be applied also to certain parts or spheres of already existing languages, e.g. religious language, or language as used in connexion with promising, can be called language games, though they could hardly exist except as parts of a language used more generally.

L. Wittgenstein, *Philosophical Investigations*, 1953, esp. part 1, §§ 7, 23.
R. Rhees, *Discussions of Wittgenstein*, 1970, chapter 6. (Discussion of some difficulties by sympathizer.)

Law (philosophy of). The study of problems concerning prescriptive laws (as against laws of nature, often called descriptive, which are studied by philosophy of science. On 'natural law' see LAWS.)

There are widely different views about what a law is. Is it a command of the sovereign? Or a prediction of what judges will decide? Or a prediction that certain actions will be followed by sanctions? Or a statement of an intention to impose sanctions? Or something else? Are there formal conditions (as against conditions affecting its content) that a law must satisfy, like being initiated in certain ways by a body with special authority, or not being inconsistent with itself or with other laws in the same system? Are there restrictions on content, e.g. is an alleged law not a law at all if it prescribes what is impossible, or violates divine, natural, or moral law? And are these kinds of law, if they exist, all law in the same sense? Also is a law still a law if there is either no prescribed sanction or no power of enforcement?

Some of these questions raise issues of justification. To justify a law or to justify a legal system may be either to show that it really is one, or to show that it is good, fair, proper, impartial, etc. How closely these tasks are related is disputable. Other things that need justifying are judgments within a legal system, e.g. those of lawyers or of judges, and the duty of obedience. Closely related are questions about the justification of punishment, be it of punishment in general, of particular penalties for particular types of case, or of individual cases. The notions of intention and strict liability are relevant here.

Certain problems concern the different branches of law (constitutional, civil, commercial, criminal) and how they relate to each other and to equity. Constitutional law in particular raises questions about how it can change. In other branches the role of judges in making law is relevant. Questions of sovereignty and sanctions lead to problems about the possibility and nature of international law.

R. S. Summers (ed.), *Essays in Legal Philosophy*, 1968, *More Essays in Legal Philosophy*, 1971. (First volume covers questions of analysis and justification. Second discusses historical figures. See Summers's introductions for survey of issues.)

H. L. A. Hart, *The Concept of Law*, 1961. (Full discussion of many problems.)

H. L. A. Hart, *The Morality of the Criminal Law*, 1965. (Hart's side in famous debate with Lord Devlin. Cf. P. Devlin, *The Enforcement of Morals*, 1959, reprinted with other relevant items in book of same title, 1965.)

T. Honderich, *Punishment: The Supposed Justifications*, 1969.

Laws. The traditional distinction between 'prescriptive' laws (legal, moral, divine) and 'descriptive' laws (scientific) is convenient, but not necessarily accurate. 'Prescriptive' laws (see philosophy of LAW) may not be prescriptions, and 'descriptive' laws may not describe the world. The laws of logic and mathematics are simply accepted, and usually important, statements in those subjects. The *laws of thought* are the logical laws of IDENTITY, CONTRADICTION and EXCLUDED MIDDLE. Whether they are more important than other logical laws is disputed. The rest of this entry mainly concerns scientific laws.

Generalizations may be closed (limited in space and time: 'All the coins now in my pocket are silver') or open ('All ravens, at all times and places, are black'). But on another interpretation open generalizations have the form, 'Anything whatever, if it is so-and-so, is such-and-such', where 'so-and-so' may or may not contain spatiotemporal restrictions like 'now in my pocket'. On this interpretation both the first two examples would be closed, because they each have a limited subject-matter (coins and ravens).

In so far as scientific laws are generalizations, they are usually regarded as open on the first interpretation (though this excludes those of Kepler (see below) and Galileo). They also seem to imply counterfactuals (see CONDITIONALS): 'All ravens are black', if a law, seems to imply 'If there were ravens on Mars (though there aren't) they would be black'. For both these reasons laws cannot be conclusively verified. Also many laws seem to have no direct application: 'All bodies unacted on by forces move with constant velocity in a straight line'—but there are no such bodies. For these

Laws

and other reasons scientific laws are sometimes thought to be rules governing the scientist's expectations, and so prescriptive, or else idealized descriptions to which the world approximates, as triangles on a blackboard approximate to Euclidean triangles. On this last view the point of Newton's first law of motion (quoted above) is that any deviation by an object from uniform rectilinear motion must be attributed to its being acted on by forces. Some writers refuse to call laws 'true' on the grounds that they are not straightforwardly descriptive.

A *hypothesis* is a statement not yet accepted as true, or as a law, while a law is only called a law if it is accepted, whether or not we call it 'true'. (But occasionally laws are called hypotheses, e.g. 'Avogadro's hypothesis'.) A *lawlike statement* is sometimes a statement resembling a law except that it is not accepted and is perhaps rejected, and sometimes a statement not general enough to be a law because it refers to individual objects (e.g. Kepler's 'laws' about how 'the' planets go round 'the' sun, which do not mention suns and planets in general). Occasionally it is a statement attributing dispositional characteristics, e.g. 'Glass is brittle'.

Theory has various meanings: (i) One or more hypotheses or lawlike statements (either of first two senses), regarded as speculative. (ii) A law about unobservables like electrons or evolution, sometimes called a theory because evidence about unobservables is felt to be inevitably inconclusive. (iii) A unified system of laws or hypotheses, with explanatory force (not merely like a railway timetable). (iv) A field of study (e.g. in philosophy: theory of knowledge, logical theory). These senses sometimes shade into each other.

A *principle* may be a high-grade law, on which a lot depends, or it may be something like a rule. To call all scientific laws principles suggests they hover between being rules and being idealized descriptions. Legal, moral, aesthetic, etc., principles may resemble scientific laws in being descriptions of ideal worlds, set up to govern actions as scientific laws are to govern expectations. However, they are not idealized descriptions of the real world, to be rejected unless the real world approximates to them in the relevant ways. (Other uses of 'law' and 'principle' exist.)

Scientific laws are often called *laws of nature* or *natural laws*. *Natural law* (generic singular) is the moral law (i.e. set of laws) regarded as derivable from the general nature of the universe by reason alone, without appeal to revelation, feelings, interests, etc. See also EXPLANATION, MODALITIES, CONVENTIONALISM, INSTRUMENTALISM.

S. E. Toulmin, *Philosophy of Science*, 1953. (Advocates 'idealized description' view, though without so calling it, and discusses other views.)

W. Kneale, *Probability and Induction*, 1949. (Part 2 discusses various kinds of scientific law, and claims that they express objective necessities.)

R. B. Braithwaite, *Scientific Explanation*, 1953. (Pp. 300–3 analyse scientific laws in terms of their explanatory function.)

M. Singer, *Generalization in Ethics*, 1963, chapter 5. (Moral rules and principles.)

A. P. D'Entreves, *Natural Law*, 1951. (Sympathetic discussion.)

Learning paradox. See EDUCATION.

Leibniz, Gottfried W. 1646–1716. German mathematician and philosopher who was born in Leipzig and, after holding various court posts, worked as a librarian and historian in Hanover. He and Newton, independently, invented the differential calculus. He is usually included among the 'Continental RATIONALISTS', and in METAPHYSICS he claimed that all propositions are really ANALYTIC, and that reality consists of independent MONADS, which mirror but do not influence each other, and contain within themselves a sort of blue-print of their entire life-histories, which they work through according to a 'pre-established harmony' arranged by God. Leibniz is also noted for LEIBNIZ'S LAW, and although he denied the reality of relations, he defended a relational view of SPACE and time (in letters to S. Clarke, representing Newton). *Discours de Metaphysique*, written 1685–6, published 1846. *Principes de la nature et de la grace, fondés en raison*, written 1714, published 1718. *La Monadologie*, written 1714, first published in German 1720. *Nouveaux Essaies sur l'entendement humain*, written 1704, published 1765 (critique of LOCKE'S *Essay*). See also APPERCEPTION, A PRIORI, CONCEPT, ENTELECHY, INTENSIONALITY, OCCASIONALISM, PSYCHOPHYSICAL, SUBSTANCE, SUFFICIENT REASON.

Leibniz's law. There are two principles which together form what is now called Leibniz's law, though Leibniz himself seems only to have held the first of them. The *identity of indiscernibles* is the principle that if a group of things have all their properties in common, or belong to exactly the same classes, they are identical in the sense of being really only one thing. The *indiscernibility of identicals* (Quine) is the principle that if a group of things are identical (i.e. are really one thing, though perhaps described in different ways), they have all their properties in common. Sometimes the term 'Leibniz's law' is limited to the second principle.

The identity of indiscernibles can be held in various forms, which differ in strength according to what sort of properties are considered relevant. In a weak, and thereby more plausible, form spatiotemporal properties are included. The principle then says only that things sharing the same place at the same time are identical. But a stronger form says that things will be identical if they have all their non-relational properties in common (i.e. properties which do not, like spatiotemporal ones, involve a relation to something else). This would mean there cannot be two or more things exactly similar. In the weaker form, but not in stronger ones, the identity of indiscernibles is the converse of the indiscernibility of identicals.

Leibniz himself often said that things are identical when they can be substituted for each other without making a true proposition false. This leads to apparent limitations of the law because of problems connected with INTENSIONALITY (see the Cicero example there). However, it is really words or descriptions, not things, that can be substituted for each other. The law therefore (since, as viewed so far, it concerns things, not words) does not apply to the Cicero case, and so need not be limited. But the law might be expressed as a principle of substitutivity, in which case its two

Liar paradox

halves will say that if whatever can be said of *a* can be said of *b*, then *a* and *b* are identical (weak form of identity of indiscernibles), and vice versa (indiscernibility of identicals). It therefore seems necessary to allow exceptions to the law. The view that these exceptions can, however, be ultimately dispensed with (or alternatively that only in so far as they can is formal logic possible) is called the *extensionality thesis*, *principle*, or (especially in formal contexts) *axiom*. See also IDENTITY, SPACE, INTENSIONALITY, SUFFICIENT REASON.

P. F. Strawson, *Individuals*, 1959. (Chapter 4 discusses a strong form of the identity of indiscernibles, partly in terms of Leibniz.)

L. Linsky, *Referring*, 1967. (Substitutivity distinguished from Leibniz's law on p. 79.)

M. J. Loux, (ed.), *Universals and Particulars*, 1970. (Includes items on identity of indiscernibles.)

Liar paradox. 'This statement is false' seems to be false if true, and true if false. Traditionally attributed to Epimenides the Cretan in the (inadequate) form, 'All Cretans are liars', this paradox is often called a semantic PARADOX. It raises difficulties especially for the correspondence theory of TRUTH, for it is hard to find a fact for 'This statement is false' to correspond to, or fail to correspond to. This paradox was also mainly responsible for the semantic theory of TRUTH taking the form that Tarski gave it. See also RUSSELL'S PARADOX, TYPES.

G. Ryle (see bibliography to HETEROLOGICAL).

R. L. Martin (ed.), *The Paradox of the Liar*, 1970. (Brief history, followed by recent discussions. Extensive bibliography.)

Libertarianism. See FREEWILL.

Likelihood. If we know how a property is distributed in a population (e.g. how many of all the swans in the world are white) we can infer the probability of any given distribution of the property in any random sample. But the converse inference from sample to population involves a simple inversion, which (unlike the inversion involved in BAYES'S THEOREM) will not work for probabilities. R. A. Fisher (1890–1962) therefore introduced *likelihood* as a notion for which this simple inversion is valid. (But outside technical contexts 'likelihood' is usually synonymous with 'probability'.)

To see how Fisher's likelihood relates to probability, consider the probability that a ball is white when randomly chosen from a bag of three balls, each white or black. Let h_n be the hypothesis that the bag contains exactly n white balls. Let w/h_n and b/h_n signify the probabilities that the chosen ball is white or black, respectively, given h_n. Then $w/h_n + b/h_n = 1$, i.e. the probabilities on a given hypothesis, add up to one. Now consider the four probabilities w/h_0, w/h_1, w/h_2, w/h_3. These, though exhaustive and non-overlapping, do not add up to one (but to two, in this case). They are therefore called likelihoods, but it is obscure what likelihoods are, unless we merely say they are probabilities grouped in a way that stops them obeying the laws of PROBABILITY theory. They can indeed usually be mathematically manipulated to add up to one. But this does not lessen the difficulty.

I. Hacking, *Logic of Statistical Inference*, 1965. (See index.)
M. G. Kendall and A. Stuart, *The Advanced Theory of Statistics*, vol. 1, 1958, chapter 8.
A. W. F. Edwards, *Likelihood*, 1972. (Full technical treatment.)

Locke, John. 1632–1704. Born in Somerset, he worked mostly in Oxford and London when not in exile because of his political activities against the Stuarts before 1688. His central work was in epistemology, where his 'new way of IDEAS' has led to his being regarded as the first main 'British EMPIRICIST'. He also wrote on political theory from a liberal point of view. *Letters concerning Toleration*, 1689 and after. *Two Treatises of Government*, 1690. *An Essay concerning Human Understanding*, 1690. See also A PRIORI, BERKELEY, BUTLER, ESSENCE, IDENTITY, MEANING, PERCEPTION, SHAFTESBURY, SORTAL, SPACE, SUBSTANCE.

Locutions. See SPEECH ACTS.

Logic. The central topic of logic is valid reasoning, its systematization and the study of notions relevant to it. This gives it two main parts, *formal logic* and *philosophical logic* (also called *logical theory*).

The main task of *formal logic* is to axiomatize (see AXIOM SYSTEM) various subject-matters. The *propositional calculus* deals with propositions joined by words like 'and', 'or', 'if . . . then', but it ignores differences between kinds of propositions. The *predicate calculus* (i.e., roughly, calculus of things one can say about something) takes things further by distinguishing between different kinds of propositions. 'All cats are black' and 'Some cats are black' are different propositions, but with similarities. The predicate calculus takes account of these similarities, which the propositional calculus ignores. Theorems are then proved in and about the resulting system to bring out their properties. The important properties include CONSISTENCY, COMPLETENESS and the possession of DECISION PROCEDURES.

Systems complex enough to axiomatize mathematics turn out to have these properties only to a severely limited extent (see GÖDEL'S THEOREMS). Also the logical PARADOXES make it harder to construct these systems. Much of modern formal logic consists in trying to avoid or minimize these limitations and difficulties. How relevant they are in the wider sphere of philosophical logic, or even outside it, is disputed. The main issues are the nature of truth, especially in view of the LIAR PARADOX, and the relations between formal systems and ordinary language. Some, especially adherents to linguistic PHILOSOPHY, have argued from these or other considerations that ordinary language has no exact logic (cf. also OPEN TEXTURE). The study of ordinary language from this point of view is sometimes called *informal logic*, though this can also refer to the study of

Logic

those inferences which depend on the content rather than form of the sentences concerned. We infer 'Smith is unmarried' from 'Smith is a bachelor' because of the meaning of 'bachelor', not because 'Smith is a bachelor' has a certain form. A formal inference from 'Smith is a bachelor' might yield 'Bachelors include Smith' (see FORM).

Formal logic also studies NATURAL DEDUCTION, and formal parts of modal and deontic logic (see below).

A topic related to formal logic is *set theory* (see CALCULUS). This and *proof theory* (see METAMATHEMATICS) are normally together called *mathematical logic*, and lead towards the philosophy of MATHEMATICS. Modern formal logic and mathematical logic are each, or together, often called *symbolic logic*, to mark the more intensive use of symbols, or *logistic*.

Deontic logic studies logical relations between propositions containing terms like 'obliged', 'commanded', 'permitted', 'forbidden', though the term tends to be confined to the construction of formal systems using deontic terms, and the problems these systems raise. A rather similar subject is the *logic of preference*, which asks, for example, what sets of preferences can consistently be held together (e.g. can one prefer *a* to *b*, and *b* to *c*, but *c* to *a*?)

Philosophical logic examines the concepts involved in formal logic and uses its results, but is not concerned with the mechanics of the various systems. However, the boundaries between these kinds of logic are not sharp. It also studies the nature of logical systems as such, and whether there can be alternative logics.

As a study devoted to valid reasoning, it naturally asks about reasoning in general and how many kinds of it there are. Is all reasoning, properly speaking, deductive, or is there also inductive reasoning (see INDUCTION, philosophy of SCIENCE), and perhaps other kinds, e.g. in morals, history, aesthetics? Are there several kinds of validity? Validity is closely connected to logical necessity, and thence to necessity in general and other modal concepts such as possibility and impossibility (see MODALITIES). Modal concepts are studied by *modal logic*, though in practice this term, like 'deontic logic', tends to be confined to the study of formal systems using modal terms. General analyses of necessity, etc. belong to philosophical logic, which also asks how these modal notions are related to the A PRIORI and the ANALYTIC.

Reasoning involves passing from premises to conclusions, and so involves a relation and the things which it relates. Both of these are subjects for philosophical logic. The relation in its most general form is IMPLICATION, which raises problems about its different kinds and its relation to INFERENCE. The things it relates are SENTENCES, propositions or statements, which again raise problems about what they are.

Logic, including philosophical logic, is thought of mainly as a formal subject, because it concentrates on the form rather than the content of its materials. But the distinction between FORM and content is itself difficult.

However, logic also studies meaning in general, of ordinary words as well as of formal words like 'all', 'and', etc., and of both words and sentences. This broadens into the study of language in general: how it does what it does and how it relates to the world. (Cf. above on relating ordinary language to formal systems.) These problems now form a subject of their own, philosophy of LANGUAGE, but they still fall broadly under logic. Two further notions important in this area are DEFINITIONS and TRUTH (see above; truth also belongs to epistemology). Logic borders on metaphysics when we ask how far various logical views commit us to asserting that certain kinds of things, like propositions, exist, and how we should analyse existential QUANTIFICATION (cf. BEING).

Formal logic effectively began with Aristotle, who systematized immediate INFERENCE and the SYLLOGISM, which remained the basis of *traditional* or *classical logic* until about a century ago. Vigorous developments in both formal and philosophical logic were made by the Stoics, and in philosophical logic in the Middle Ages, but these were forgotten and have only recently been revived. The syllogism is now seen to form a small part of the predicate calculus.

A key feature in the history of modern logic has been the development of a *logic of relations*. This comes from realizing, and taking seriously, that not all propositions consist of a subject and predicate linked by the copula, 'is' ('are'). Traditional logic had unduly restricted itself by assuming that they do, and could not formalize so simple an argument as 'Ten exceeds nine and nine exceeds eight, so ten exceeds eight', where the main verb stands for a relation. See also TOPIC-NEUTRAL.

J. N. Keynes, *Formal Logic*, 1884, 4th (revised) edn 1906. (Standard treatment of traditional logic. Introductions to modern formal logic are legion.)

J. N. Crossley *et al.*, What is Mathematical Logic?, 1972. (Brief. Fairly elementary.)

G. H. von Wright, *An Essay in Deontic Logic*, 1968. (Introduction, with bibliography.)

G. H. von Wright, *The Logic of Preference*, 1963. (Introduction.)

G. E. Hughes and M. J. Cresswell, *An Introduction to Modal Logic*, 1968. (Comprehensive.)

F. Waismann, 'Are there alternative logics?', *Proceedings of the Aristotelian Society*, 1945–6, reprinted in his *How I See Philosophy*, 1968.

S. E. Toulmin, *The Uses of Argument*, 1958. (Claims there are many kinds of reasoning, Cf. S. F. Barker (see bibliography to INDUCTION).)

P. F. Strawson, *Introduction to Logical Theory*, 1952. (Represents 'linguistic philosophy' outlook, that there is no exact logic of ordinary language.)

B. Mates, *Stoic Logic*, 1953.

Logical atomism. Theory associated mainly with Russell (middle period) and Wittgenstein (early period) which seeks to analyse thought and discourse in terms of indivisible components. *Atomic propositions* consist of a subject term and a predicate term ('John is clever'), or a set of terms linked by a relation term ('John hates Tom'), and they are true if they correspond directly to FACTS, which are all (for this theory, at least in its purest form) atomic. *Molecular propositions* are truth-FUNCTIONS of atomic ones and

Logical constructions

correspond in complex ways to those same facts. This shows, it is claimed, that the logical connectives (see CONJUNCTION) do not name or correspond to elements of facts, or anything else. They simply connect propositions. However, it was not clear on this view how atomic propositions could be false, and various kinds of propositions supposed to be molecular in the above sense created difficulties when treated as such, e.g. general (see UNIVERSAL) and negative propositions; it was difficult to make them correspond, even in complex ways, to atomic facts.

As for the constituents of atomic facts, Wittgenstein left them unspecified, calling them simply 'objects', but Russell treated them as SENSE-DATA. See also INTENSIONALITY (for the 'extensionality principle').

B. Russell, 'The philosophy of logical atomism' in his *Logic and Knowledge*, 1956, reprinted in D. Pears (ed.), *Russell's Logical Atomism*, 1972. (A popular account. The essay 'Logical atomism' in the same volume is harder.)

L. Wittgenstein, *Tractatus Logico-Philosophicus*, 1921, transl. D. F. Pears and B. F. McGuinness, 1961. (Very difficult.)

J. O. Urmson, *Philosophical Analysis*, 1956. (Fairly elementary.)

D. F. Pears, *Betrand Russell and the British Tradition in Philosophy*, 1967. (Fuller and harder than, and sometimes critical of, Urmson.)

Logical constructions. When we say 'The average man has 2·4 children' we are really saying something about Smith, Jones, etc. The sentence is analysable into a set of sentences in which the phrase 'the average man' does not appear. The average man is therefore a *logical construction*, and 'the average man' is an *incomplete symbol*. These notions were introduced by Russell.

Later writers, especially Wisdom, distinguished weak and strong senses of 'incomplete symbol'. A symbol was incomplete in a weak sense if (i) it purported to refer to something, (ii) the sentence containing it would be replaced, in a proper logical language, by sentences not containing it, but (iii) these new sentences would only be true, in simple affirmative cases, if the thing apparently referred to did indeed exist. If 'The present king of France is bald' is analysed by the theory of DESCRIPTIONS, 'the present king of France' is an incomplete symbol in a weak sense. A symbol was incomplete in a strong sense if (i), like 'the average man', it disappeared when the sentence containing it was properly reformulated, but (ii) the reformulated version could be true, in simple affirmative cases, even though what the symbol apparently referred to did not exist (no man with 2·4 children exists). 'Logical construction' (or 'construct') was thereafter kept for what incomplete symbols in a strong sense purported to refer to, i.e. the average man, but not the present King of France, would be a logical construction. There is, however, a complication: Moore held that if 'the average man' is an incomplete symbol, then so is 'has 2·4 children'; but this latter does not seem, straightforwardly, to involve a logical construction.

Logical constructions, therefore, lost the role they had in the theory of descriptions, but they remained a powerful tool for reductive analysis (see PHILOSOPHY, PHENOMENALISM). Although Russell sometimes used the phrase *logical fictions*, logical constructions are not hypothetical, inferred, fictitious or imaginary entities. The average man is none of these. They are often contrasted with inferred entities (i.e. entities we infer to exist, but cannot observe). In scientific contexts those logical constructions which purport to be properties (as the average man purports to be an object), e.g. density, which can vary in degree, are sometimes called *intervening variables*, while inferred entities are called *hypothetical constructs* (but usage varies).

J. Wisdom, 'Logical constructions', *Mind*, 1931–3. (Series of articles forming locus classicus for strong sense logical constructions. Cf. esp. 1931, pp. 188–95.)

J. O. Urmson, *Philosophical Analysis*, 1956, pp. 27–41. (Traces how strong sense incomplete symbols grew out of weak sense ones.)

L. W. Beck, 'Constructions and inferred entities', *Philosophy of Science*, 1950, reprinted in H. Feigl and M. Brodbeck (eds), *Readings in the Philosophy of Science*, 1953. (Compares treatment of things like electrons as logical constructions and as inferred entities.)

N. MacCorquodale and P. E. Meehl, 'Hypothetical constructs and intervening variables', *Psychological Review*, 1948, reprinted in H. Feigl and M. Brodbeck (above). (Discussed in succeeding volumes of *Psychological Review*.)

Logical fictions. See LOGICAL CONSTRUCTIONS.

Logical geography. See SPACE.

Logically proper names. See MEANING, DESCRIPTIONS.

Logical subject. See MEANING.

Logicism. See MATHEMATICS.

Logics (many-valued). See TRUTH-VALUE.

Logistic. See LOGIC.

Logos. The Greek concept has two basic and interconnected strands: (i) the result of speaking, i.e. speech, discourse, theory (as against practice), sentence, story. (ii) The result of picking out or counting, i.e. account, formula, rationale, definition, proportion, reason (both as 'a reason' and as 'the power of reason'). For the connexion between the strands cf. English 'recount', 'all told'.

W. K. C. Guthrie, *A History of Greek Philosophy*, vol. 1, 1967, pp. 419 ff.

Lottery paradox. In a fair lottery with 100 tickets the chance that any given ticket will lose is 99 per cent. It therefore seems reasonable, for any given

Lottery paradox

ticket, to believe, or *accept* as a basis for action, the statement, 'This ticket will lose.' Yet the conjunction of such statements for all the tickets must be false, since some ticket will win, so we can hardly accept the conjunction. We seem to have to accept each statement separately, but not the conjunction of them. The paradox raises difficulties especially for the notion of the *acceptance* of inductive conclusions (cf. CONFIRMATION).

H. E. Kyburg, *Probability and Inductive Logic*, 1970, pp. 176–7, 179.

M

Mach, Ernst W. J. W. 1838–1916. Born in Moravia, he worked mainly in Prague and Vienna; in 1901 he became a member of the Austrian house of peers. He contributed significantly to physics as well as to philosophy of science, and his name is applied to various phenomena connected with shock waves. 'Mach's principle' defends the relational view of SPACE by saying that inertia depends on the existence of bodies like the fixed stars. In philosophy of science Mach developed a form of POSITIVISM. *Die Mechanik in ihrer Entwicklung historisch-kritisch dargestellt* (*The Science of Mechanics*), 1883. *Beiträge zur Analyse der Empfindungen*, 1886 (5th ed. enlarged as *Die Analyse der Empfindungen und das Verhältnis des Physischen zum Psychischen*, 1906). *Populärwissenschaftliche Vorlesungen* (*Popular Scientic Lectures*), 1894 (or 1896). *Erkenntnis und Irrtum: Skizzen zur Psychologie der Forschung* (*Knowledge and Error: Sketches on the Psychology of Enquiry*), 1905.

McTaggart, John McT. E. 1866–1925. Cambridge metaphysician who developed an idealist (and atheistic) system centring on the notions of substance and the part/whole relation (and also involving human reincarnation). He denied the reality of many things, such as material objects and space, but is now best known for his argument against the reality of time (see SPACE). *The Nature of Existence*, 1921 (vol. 1), 1927 (vol. 2).

C. D. Broad, *An Examination of McTaggart's Philosophy*, 1933 (vol. 1), 1938 (vol. 2). (Standard commentary.)

Magnitudes (extensive and intensive). A magnitude is extensive if (a) things can be ordered in accordance with it, and (b) there are units of it such that, for any number n, things with n such units can be constructed out of n things with one unit each. A magnitude is intensive if only the ordering is possible. Roughly, M is an intensive magnitude if 'more M than' makes sence but 'twice as M as' does not. It is extensive if both make sense. *Long* is clearly extensive, and *beautiful* clearly intensive, but examples are often hard to classify.

Major premise, term

J. J. C. Smart, 'Measurement', *Australasian Journal of Philosophy*, 1959. (Measurement in general. Confines 'magnitude' to extensive magnitudes.)

B. Ellis, *Basic Concepts of Measurement*, 1966. (More extended and technical. See p. 85.)

J. C. Hall, 'Quantity of Pleasure', *Proceedings of the Aristotelian Society*, 1966–7. (Measuring pleasure. See p. 40.)

Major premise, term. See SYLLOGISM.

Malebranche, Nicolas. 1638–1715. Born in Paris, he became a member of the religious society called the Oratoire de France. Starting largely under the influence of DESCARTES he elaborated a system which is now known chiefly for his OCCASIONALISM and his doctrine that we 'see all things in God', i.e. that the objects of almost all our knowledge are ideas, which exist independently of us and in God; we know external objects only as represented by ideas. Malebranche also wrote on science and morality. *De la Recherche de la vérité*, 1674–5. *Traité de la nature et de la grace*, 1680. *Traité de morale*, 1684. *Entretiens sur la métaphysique et sur la religion*, 1688.

Manifold. A variegated complex of elements considered as it is before being organized. For Kant especially, the sensory manifold is the as-yet unstructured variety of material presented to the senses, which the mind then organizes through concepts, so that perception results.

Many-sorted logic. A logical system is *many-sorted* if different groups of individual VARIABLES in it are restricted to ranging over different kinds of things. Where all the individual variables have the same range the system is *one-sorted*.

Marcel, Gabriel. 1889–1973. French philosopher and dramatist born in Paris. He is usually classed as an EXISTENTIALIST, though of a theistic kind as opposed to SARTRE, HEIDEGGER or JASPERS (he joined the Catholic church in 1929), but the aptness of this classification has been disputed. *Journal métaphysique*, 1927. *Être et avoir*, 1935. *Présence et immortalité*, 1959. (These three volumes form a philosophical diary.) *The Philosophy of Existence*, 1949 (republished as *Philosophy of Existentialism*, 1961; translated essays). *The Mystery of Being* (*Le Mystère de l'être*), 2 vols, 1950–1.

Maritain, Jacques. 1882–1973. French Catholic philosopher born in Paris, who worked mainly there and in North America. After being influenced by BERGSON in his youth he became interested in Thomism (see AQUINAS), developing a system which specially emphasized different kinds of knowledge (scientific, metaphysical, mystical). He also wrote on metaphysics, ethics, political philosophy and aesthetics. *Art et scholastique*, 1920. *Distinguer pour unir, ou les degrés du savoir*, 1932 (on the types of knowledge). *Humanisme intégral* (*True Humanism*), 1936.

Mathematics

Marx, Karl H. 1818–83. Born in Trier, Germany, he worked in various cities of north-west Europe, and eventually in London. He was primarily a sociologist and economist, but his views have had considerable philosophical influence. He started from HEGEL's dialectic and, in collaboration with Engels, founded the doctrine of *dialectical materialism*, and developed a system of economic determinism which was supposed to govern human activities in every sphere. *Ökonomisch-philosophische Manuskripte aus dem Jahre 1844. Die deutsche Ideologie*, written 1845–6 (with Engels). *Misère de la philosophy (The Poverty of Philosophy)*, 1847. (Criticism of P.-J. Proudhon (1809–65)). *Manifest der kommunistischen Partei*, 1848 (with Engels). *Grundrisse der Kritik der politischen Ökonomie*, written 1857–8. *Zur Kritik der politischen Ökonomie*, 1859. *Das Kapital*, 3 vols, 1867, 1885, 1893 (this follows on from the two works last mentioned, and is itself followed by a historical fourth volume called *Theorien über den Mehrwert (Theories of Surplus Value)*, written 1862–3).

Mass noun. See COUNT.

Material mode. See FORMAL MODE.

Mathematics (philosophy of). The study of concepts and systems appearing in mathematics, and of the justification of mathematical statements.

The basic objects of mathematics are numbers, of which there are various kinds (natural, real, etc., see Russell). Whether numbers are abstract entities, and how we decide this, are questions shared with metaphysics (cf. BEING). *Platonists*, or *realists*, think that numbers are abstract entities, and that mathematical truths, including those about infinite numbers, exist independently of our researches. *Formalists* deny this, and *constructivists* in general emphasize the dependence of mathematics on the activity of mathematicians (see INTUITIONISM, FINITISM). Numbers have been defined in terms of classes or sets which are themselves studied by *set theory* (cf. CALCULUS). In fact the definition of 'equinumerous class' helped G. Cantor (1845–1918) to elaborate the study of infinite numbers. One class is equinumerous to another if for each member of one there is exactly one corresponding member of the other. These definitions enable the calculus of classes, and set theory, to be used to axiomatize mathematics (cf. AXIOM SYSTEM, LOGIC). One difficulty about classes stems from RUSSELL'S PARADOX. *Logicists*, however (notably Frege and Russell), who claim to reduce mathematics entirely to logic, have used classes for this purpose. They claim that mathematical objects can be defined in logical terms, via classes, and also that mathematical proofs can be reduced to logical proofs. But there are difficulties in proving the existence of classes in general from axioms which can be reasonably regarded as purely logical.

Geometry was originally regarded as fundamentally different from arithmetic, and as dealing with space. Kant's views on space provoked questions about how different geometries relate to each other and to real SPACE. Arithmetic suggests the question how different algebras relate to each other and to the world (cf. AXIOM SYSTEM). These questions are connected with the questions whether our knowledge of mathematical concepts and propositions is empirical as, in particular, J. S. Mill thought, or A PRIORI. Modern developments on all these questions have tended to unite arithmetic and geometry.

Other questions include: what is truth in mathematics, and how is it related to provability? Is every mathematical truth provable (cf. GÖDEL'S THEOREMS), and can we know mathematical truths by direct insight as well as by proof?

B. Russell, *Introduction to Mathematical Philosophy*, 1919. (General.)

S. F. Barker, *Philosophy of Mathematics*, 1964. (Elementary.)

S. Körner, *Philosophy of Mathematics*, 1960. (Rather more advanced.)

P. Benacerraf and H. Putman (eds), *Philosophy of Mathematics*, 1964. (Important collection of readings, of varying difficulty.)

G. Frege, *Foundations of Arithmetic*, 1884, transl. by J. L. Austin, 1950. (Fairly elementary discussion of numbers, etc. from Platonist and logicist viewpoint by a pioneer of modern logic. Includes more technical appendix on Russell's paradox.)

H. Wang, 'Process and existence in mathematics', in Y. Bar-Hillel, *et al.* (eds), *Essays on the Foundations of Mathematics*, 1962. (Brings out some of the issues in mainly simple language.)

G. Ryle, C. Lewy, K. R. Popper, 'Why are the calculuses of logic and arithmetic applicable to reality?', *Proceedings of the Aristotelian Society*, supplementary vol., 1946.

I. Lakatos, 'Proofs and refutations', *British Journal for the Philosophy of Science*, 1963–4. (Elaborate discussion, in dialogue form with historical notes, of genesis of some problems about proof.)

L. Goddard, ' "True" and "provable" ', *Mind*, 1958. (Cf. discussions in *Mind*, 1960, 1962.)

Meaning. Problems about meaning fall into three main and interrelated groups: What things can be subjects of the verb 'mean'? What is meaning, in the sense in which words and sentences have meaning? What different kinds of meaning are there, and how are they related to various other notions?

The verb 'mean' can have as its subject words and other symbols, sentences, propositions if interpreted as indicative sentences, people, actions, works of art, and natural events, states and processes. 'Mean' can have natural objects or events as its subject when these are symptoms ('Those spots mean measles') or causes ('Clouds mean rain') or things having value or importance ('That locket means a lot to me'). 'His life has no meaning' seems to come between this last sense and the sense of pattern, order, idea in which works of art have meaning. Actions have meaning either in these ways or in the way sentences have it. People are not said to 'have meaning', but they 'mean something' when they speak, etc. They intend to convey some idea, to refer to something ('I mean you'), or simply to do something ('I meant to come yesterday'). They may also 'mean' something in the sense of suggesting something beyond what they mean in

Meaning

the direct sense ('In saying "Time's getting on" he meant it was late, and he also meant it was time for you to go'). An interesting question, discussed by Wittgenstein, concerns what it is to mean what one says.

Of words and sentences one can ask what they mean, or what meaning they have, in general, and what they mean, what the speaker means by them, on a given occasion. Words and sentences differ from each other: We *construct* sentences, and can understand ones we have not seen before. Sentences have meaning because of the words in them, while words only have meaning because they are fitted to play a role in sentences. Different words may have meaning in different ways, but whether all words have meaning is disputed. Do proper names (see below)? Does 'to' in 'I want to go'?

Grice divides the various kinds of meaning into two main groups, *natural*, the group applying to natural events etc., and *nonnatural*, the group applying to people and symbols, words and sentences etc.

Discussions of what meaning is have mainly concerned words and sentences, and until recently notions like naming, referring to, or standing for have dominated them. *Naming* (*denotative, referential*) *theories* of meaning say that a word's meaning is what it names or stands for, or else its relation to that. Cf. the slogan *unum nomen unum nominatum*: 'For every name there is exactly one thing named'. Proper names are taken as the primary case. Hence the nickname '*Fido*'-*Fido theory*. The word 'Fido' has as its meaning the dog Fido which it names. On this theory a general word like 'dog' could stand for the UNIVERSAL, doghood (Russell), or the class of dogs, or different dogs on different occasions (also Russell). 'Red' could stand for the colour red, 'runs' and 'running' for the action of running, even perhaps 'if' for the notion of doubt or conditionality.

Ideational theories make words stand for ideas or thoughts etc. (Aristotle, Locke). They provide a single kind of thing (ideas) for very different kinds of words to stand for, though usually without explaining the notion of *standing for*.

All these are *relational* or *correspondence theories*. They say that a word's meaning is or involves a thing (physical, mental or abstract) to which it is related. They have recently been much attacked.

This attack on relational theories implied that meanings are not 'things', and led to the slogan 'Don't ask for the meaning, ask for the use'. *Use theories* explain meaning in terms of use. They provoke questions about whether the connexion between meaning and use is the same for words and for sentences, whether meaning is as wide a notion as use (see below on speech acts), and whether what matters most is actual use or rules for use. This last distinction is one version of that between *de facto* and *de jure theories*. De facto theories explain meaning in terms of what happens or is the case, e.g. how people actually do use words. De jure theories explain it in terms of norms, rules, conventions, standards, or in general what ought to be the case, e.g. they might claim that 'I didn't do nothing' cannot properly mean 'I didn't do anything', despite Cockney usage.

Causal or *stimulus/response theories* explain the meaning of a word or sentence in terms of its effect on the hearer or the cause of the speaker's

Meaning

uttering it. They are examples of de facto theories, stemming from BEHA-VIOURISM, and they claim the advantages of a scientific approach. They become naming theories too, if they say that the object named is the meaning while the object's effects are what make it the meaning. A theory of sentence-meaning also stimulated by science is the *verification theory*, whereby a sentence's meaning is the method of verifying it; cf. logical POSITIVISM for this, and for the operationalist theory of word meaning. *Picture theories* are analogues for sentences of naming theories for words and like naming theories they are correspondence theories. They are especially associated with LOGICAL ATOMISM, and with the correspondence theory of TRUTH. On picture theories sentences, whether true or false, have meaning because they picture possibilities; true sentences picture those possibilities which are facts. But can picture theories cater for the *stating* involved in stating facts? A common modern theory says that to give the meaning of a standard indicative sentence is to give its TRUTH-CONDITIONS.

With the general question of what meaning is belongs also the question of *synonymy*, i.e. when words or sentences have the same meaning.

Turning to the third of the original questions, about kinds of meaning, and related notions, we can for suitable words distinguish between *intension* (roughly: what a word means) and *extension* (roughly: what it applies to). Cf. INTENSIONALITY. Thus Mill distinguishes *connotation* from *denotation*. A word denotes the things it applies to, and connotes the attributes it implies that those things have. 'Man' connotes, perhaps, the attribute *being a rational animal*, and denotes all men. 'Connotation' can refer to the relation or to what is connoted, and 'denotation' similarly.

Frege distinguishes *Sinn* and *Bedeutung*, standardly translated *sense* and *reference* respectively. (Other translations exist, and some writers prefer 'denotation' to 'reference' here, e.g. Russell, for whose views on denoting see DESCRIPTIONS.) The phrases 'the evening star' and 'the morning star' have the same reference, Venus, but different senses. Frege uses this to explain why 'The evening star is the morning star' is not trivial, like 'Venus is Venus'.

The relations between these terms are complex. Roughly, a term denotes, independently of occasion, all those things we can refer to on a given occasion by using certain phrases containing the term. 'Cats' denotes cats in general, and we can use a phrase like 'that cat' to refer to, say, Tiddles on some occasion. Strictly it is we who refer to Tiddles by saying 'that cat', but the phrase 'that cat' can itself be said to refer to Tiddles on this occasion. ('Denote', especially, is often used loosely.) A term has *divided reference* (Quine) if, like 'shoe' or 'red' but unlike 'water', it can be used, without additions like 'piece of', to refer to different objects.

The connotation/sense distinction is difficult, but an example may help. Is it contradictory to say, 'The queen of England is not queen at all but illegitimate'? Yes, if 'the queen of England' is interpreted as having connotation, since the statement then implies that the person referred to by the phrase has the property of reigning. But the sense of the phrase can be used to pick out the person, without this implication, for a hearer, for example, who believes that Elizabeth II is legitimate. If the phrase is thus

124

interpreted as still having sense, but not connotation, the statement is not contradictory. If Elizabeth II were not legitimate, the sentence could be used to say so without contradiction, and might be useful for ensuring that the supposed hearer knew who was being talked about. Sense and reference apply to subject expressions and sometimes to sentences (Frege thought the reference of a sentence was its TRUTH-VALUE), but not (for Frege) to predicate expressions. Connotation and denotation can apply to subject expressions and predicate expressions, but not to sentences. Sense is close to the non-technical notion of sense.

Proper names, which provide the model of meaning for naming theories, raise problems about whether they have connotation or sense or both. 'That man there' picks someone out as being a man and being in a certain place, but 'John' makes no obvious reference to any of its bearer's properties. In what sense are proper names words? Do they form part of a language? They are hardly meaningless, but they do not appear in dictionaries. Russell followed Mill in thinking they lack connotation. However, he thought this only of *logically proper names*, i.e. those names which were not abbreviated descriptions, as he thought ordinary proper names in fact were. He thought 'Socrates' was not really a name at all, but an abbreviation for, for example, 'the philosopher who drank hemlock'. A *logical subject* is either the subject of a sentence in a logically ideal language, i.e. a language where a sentence's real and apparent subjects coincide, or it is what such a subject refers to.

Under the influence of logical positivism, cognitive, descriptive or factual meaning has been distinguished from other kinds, notably emotive, evaluative, and prescriptive: see NATURALISM. Arising out of these distinctions and generalizing from them is Austin's theory of SPEECH ACTS, which distinguishes between the meaning of what is said and what he calls the 'illocutionary force' of saying it. Attempts have been made to analyse the meanings of some words, including 'good', 'true', 'probable', in terms of speech acts they are used in making, and to ground meaning itself in illocutionary force (a kind of use theory).

A further question concerns meaninglessness: how many kinds of it are there, and how are they related to contradiction and falsity? (cf. CATEGORIES). See also REFERRING, AMBIGUOUS, DEFINITION, OPEN TEXTURE.

H. P. Grice, 'Meaning', *Philosophical Review*, 1957, reprinted in P. F. Strawson (ed.), *Philosophical Logic*, 1967. (Criticizes causal theory and develops theory using intention (which might, however, itself be called a causal theory).)

B. Russell, *An Inquiry into Meaning and Truth*, 1940, esp. chapters 1–7, 13–15. (Complex theory of meaning of words and significance (as he calls it) of sentences. Cf. his *My Philosophical Development*, 1959, chapters 13, 14.)

Plato, *Cratylus*. (Earliest surviving connected discussion of meaning.)

Aristotle, *De Interpretatione*, esp. chapters 1–4, transl. with commentary in J. L. Ackrill, *Aristotle's Categories and De Interpretatione*, 1963. (Basis of Aristotle's theory of meaning, though only elementary.)

Meaning postulates

J. Locke, *An Essay on the Human Understanding*, 1689, book 3.

L. Wittgenstein, *Philosophical Investigations*, 1953, esp. §§ 1–43. (Classic criticism of naming theories in favour of use theory.)

L. J. Cohen, *The Diversity of Meaning*, 1962 (revised 1966). (Chapter 2 introduces de facto/de jure distinction.)

E. Daitz, 'The picture theory of meaning', *Mind*, 1953, reprinted in A. Flew (ed.), *Essays in Conceptual Analysis*, 1956.

J. L. Keynes, *Formal Logic*, 1884, 4th (revised) edn 1906. (Full details of traditional terminology of intension and extension. For later terms cf. also R. Carnap, *Meaning and Necessity*, 1947, chapter 3.)

N. Goodman, 'On likeness of meaning', *Analysis*, vol. 10, 1949, reprinted in M. Macdonald (ed.), *Philosophy and Analysis*, 1954. (Difficulties over synonymy.)

J. S. Mill, *A System of Logic*, 1843, book 1, chapter 2. (Connotation/denotation distinction. Classic discussion of names.)

G. Frege, 'Sinn und Bedeutung', 1892, transl. in P. Geach and M. Black, *Translations from the Philosophical Writings of Gottlob Frege*, 1952, and also in H. Feigl and W. Sellars (eds), *Readings in Philosophical Analysis*, 1949.

C. Kirwan, 'On the connotation and sense of proper names', *Mind*, 1968. (Clear on connotation. Brief on sense. Leaves distinction unexplained)

L. J. Cohen, 'Do illocutionary forces exist?', *Philosophical Quarterly*, 1964, reprinted in K. T. Fann (ed.), *Symposium on J. L. Austin*, 1969. (Attacks Austin's distinction between meaning and illocutionary force.)

J. R. Searle, (see bibliography to GOOD.)

W. P. Alston, 'Meaning and use', *Philosophical Quarterly*, 1963, reprinted in G. H. R. Parkinson (ed.), *The Theory of Meaning*, 1968. (Develops a use theory in terms of illocutionary acts.)

A. C. Ewing, 'Meaninglessness', *Mind*, 1937.

C. Coope *et al.* (eds), *A Wittgenstein Workbook*, 1970, chapter 5. (Nonsense and senselessness in Wittgenstein.)

S. Kripke, 'Naming and necessity', in G. Harman and D. Davidson (eds), *Semantics of Natural Language*, 1972. (Discusses meaning, particularly in connexion with names and reference.)

Meaning postulates. A device whereby implicitly ANALYTIC sentences, like 'Bachelors are male', are introduced into a formal language (one whose terms are rigorously defined) by postulates like 'Anything, if it is a bachelor, is (to count as) male'. More interestingly, 'Anything, if it is a raven, is (to count as) black' could be used as a meaning postulate to fix a sense of 'raven'. Anything we refuse to call black we will then refuse to call a raven.

R. Carnap, 'Meaning postulates', *Philosophical Studies*, 1952, reprinted in his *Meaning and Necessity*, 2nd edn 1956.

Meinong, Alexius. 1853–1920. Austrian, born in Lemberg (Lwow), he worked mainly in Graz. He developed BRENTANO's view by insisting on a distinction between the content and the object ('Gegenstand') of a thought, and his philosophy largely concerns the various kinds of such objects. These include chairs and tables, which exist, 'objectives' like the *being* of chairs and the *difference* between red and green, which subsist, dragons and the golden mountain and the round square, which neither exist nor subsist but still have 'Sosein' ('being so'). He also supplemented Brentano's distinction between ideas and judgments by introducing 'supposals' or 'assumptions' ('Annahmen'), and he elaborated a theory of value. *Zur erkenntnistheoretischen Würdigung des Gedächtnisses*, 1886. *Über Annahmen*, 1902. *'Über Gegenstandstheorie'*, in A. Meinong (ed.), *Untersuchungen zur Gegenstandstheorie und Psychologie*, 1904. *Über Möglichkeit und Wahrscheinlichkeit*, 1915. *Zur Grundegung der allgemeinen Werttheorie*, 1923. See also BEING, OBJECT, REFERRING.

Mentioning. See REFERRING.

Merleau-Ponty, Maurice. 1908–61. Born in Rochefort in France, he worked mainly in Lyon and Paris. He is best known for his work on the PHENOMENOLOGICAL description of the phenomena of consciousness, emphasizing particularly the role of the body. He disagrees in some respects with Husserl, and has affinities with existentialism. He also had ethical and political interests, and was a friend and associate of SARTRE, though differing in his attitude to Marxism. *La Structure du comportement*, 1942. *La Phénoménologie de la perception*, 1945. *Sens et non-sens* (*Sense and Nonsense*), 1948 (collected essays).

Metahistory. See HISTORY.

Metalanguage. A language lacking devices for talking about languages (i.e. lacking terms like 'word', 'true', 'say', or quotation marks) is an *object language*. A language rich enough for talking about some language (which may or may not be itself, or part of itself, and may or may not be an object language) is a *metalanguage* for the language which can be talked about. 'Metalanguage' is thus usually a relative term, though a language rich enough for talking about a metalanguage is sometimes called a *metametalanguage*. Like 'metalanguage', however, 'object language' too can be relative, so that, for example, a language L_2 could be a metalanguage for L_1 while being an object language for L_3. In the first sense mentioned, the absolute sense, 'object language' means 'language for talking about objects'. In the second sense mentioned, the relative sense, it means 'language which is the object of investigation'.

Metamathematics. Also called *proof theory*. Study of the concepts used in mathematics, especially of the properties of formal systems (see AXIOM). Often now confined to analyses springing from that of D. Hilbert (1862–1943), who insisted on FINITIST restrictions for metamathematics which he relaxed for mathematics itself. Cf. INTUITIONISM (for formalism).

D. Hilbert, 'On the infinite', in P. Benacerraf and H. Putnam (eds), *Philosophy of Mathematics*, 1964.

Metaphysics

Metaphysics. That which comes after 'physics', the latter being the study of nature in general. Thus the questions of metaphysics arise out of, but go beyond, factual or scientific questions about the world.

A central part of metaphysics is *ontology*. This studies BEING, and in particular, nowadays, what there is, e.g. material objects, minds, PERSONS, UNIVERSALS, numbers, FACTS, etc. There is the question of whether these all 'are' in the same sense and to the same degree. One can also ask whether particular views on logic commit one to particular views on what exists (e.g. propositions, numbers). A particular theory about what exists, or a list of existents, can be called an ontology. Another question involving logic is whether existence is a predicate (or property). Ontology borders on philosophy of religion with questions like: Does anything exist necessarily (cf. ONTOLOGICAL and COSMOLOGICAL ARGUMENTS)? Is it necessary that something, no matter what, should exist? Can any answer be given to the question, 'Why is there something rather than nothing?'? 'Ontology' is also a technical name for part of the system of S. Lesniewski (1886–1939).

Metaphysics is distinguished by its questions being general. As well as seeking an inventory of kinds of things that exist it asks what can be said about anything that exists, just in so far as it exists. Can we classify all that exists into different fundamental kinds, in one or more ways (see CATE-GORIES)? Is there any hierarchy among kinds of things? Do some depend on others for their existence? These questions involve the relations between very general notions like thing, entity, OBJECT, INDIVIDUAL, UNIVERSAL, particular, SUBSTANCE, and also EVENT, process, state. Here three main, though overlapping, metaphysical outlooks may be distinguished. One outlook (e.g. Plato, the rationalists), takes one or more substances as the basis of the universe. A second takes act and potency (e.g. Aquinas), and a third takes events and processes (e.g. Heraclitus, the Stoics, Hegel, Bergson, Whitehead). These outlooks, especially the first and third, are connected with attitudes towards change. Adherents of the first outlook have often held either that change is not fully real, or that the most basic things in the universe do not change except in secondary or unimportant ways. The third outlook puts change at the heart of things. It does not deny all unity and constancy, which would result in unintelligible chaos, but makes these depend essentially upon change.

The distinction of act from potency, or actuality from potentiality, derives from Aristotle, as does that of FORM from matter and 'privation' (i.e. the absence of form where it could be present). These distinctions are both needed when we examine the nature and kinds of change, and they lead us to examine matter itself and its relations to space and substance. SPACE AND TIME in fact provide a whole range of problems about their reality, nature, absoluteness and uniqueness. Change is also closely related to IDENTITY and CAUSATION, both of which also raise special problems in philosophy of mind, concerning personal IDENTITY and FREEWILL.

These notions of change, identity and causation lead to further questions about the general pattern of change in the universe. Is it, in the long run random or does it lead in a certain direction? Or is it cyclic or repetitive, a view commoner among the Greeks than today though revived in modern cosmology? Is there even, as was believed by some Pythagoreans and Stoics, followed by Nietzsche, an *eternal recurrence* of the same cycle, an endless repetition of exactly the same world-history? Here we must distinguish between repetitions of the same participants, including ourselves, and repetitions of the same pattern with different participants, our 'doubles'. The same problems arise over 'mirror universes' (cf. SPACE, LEIBNIZ'S LAW, SUFFICIENT REASON).

Questions about space and time suggest further questions about infinity. Is the universe finite or infinite? Here, as in the last paragraph, philosophy and science may overlap. And which is 'higher' or more real, the finite or the infinite? There is a distinction here between Christianity, emphasizing the limitations of finite things, and the Greeks, especially the Pythagoreans and Aristotle, who regarded the infinite as essentially incomplete.

All these enquiries about the overall nature of the universe lead to the question whether a necessary being, or God, must be postulated to explain the universe. What sort of EXPLANATIONS can be given? In particular, are teleological EXPLANATIONS needed or possible?

A further general question about the universe is whether in some relevant sense we should regard it as one (MONISM) or many (pluralism). Since monists must presumably admit that plurality is at least apparent, the real/apparent distinction becomes relevant, and with it questions about how far SCEPTICISM with regard to the reality of things can be consistently taken: How different can the world be from what it seems, and how far can we know things as they are? (cf. EPISTEMOLOGY). Another view which relies heavily on the real/apparent contrast, because it differs widely from common sense, is IDEALISM, which regards reality as basically mental or dependent on the mind. But idealism need not be sceptical.

A recently influential source of scepticism, however, is interest in the influence of language. Some have thought, especially logical POSITIVISTS like Carnap, that the distinction between substance and attribute is simply a reflexion of the grammatical distinction between noun and adjective, so that instead of talking of things and qualities we should talk of *thing-words* and *quality-words*. We will then see, it is claimed, that we need not regard (say) beauty as a metaphysical entity merely because we have the thing-word 'beauty' (cf. FORMAL MODE). How far does 'ontology recapitulate philology'? Philosophers like the logical positivists, who emphasize language, often react against *speculative metaphysics* (the construction of all-embracing systems that cannot be tested by observation). Many empiricists, notably Hume, do so too. *Descriptive metaphysics* claims to avoid the vices of speculative metaphysics, without abandoning metaphysics altogether. It confines itself to analysing various concepts, like SUBSTANCE, which it claims to show are basic and unavoidable.

Metaphysics also borders on ethics and aesthetics. It asks where values are grounded in the nature of things, or contribute to the cosmic process, and what kind of reality is possessed by works of art and the things that make them up (e.g. the figures in a painting).

Taken as the name of a subject 'metaphysics' is no longer a 'bad word', but the current mood, though far less restrictive than logical positivism,

Methodology

remains hostile to anti-common-sense speculations, including idealist or sceptical systems. At the same time it regards most forms of DUALISM as over-simplifying.

D. F. Pears (ed.), *The Nature of Metaphysics*, 1957. (Elementary broadcast talks reflecting the then prevailing outlook. 'Sins' catalogued in last twelve lines are less prominent now.)

W. H. Walsh, *Metaphysics*, 1963. (General introduction from fairly traditional viewpoint.)

Aristotle, *Metaphysics*. (See esp. books 4 (or Γ) and 6 (or E), transl. with notes by C. Kirwan in Clarendon Aristotle series, 1971, for Aristotle's conception of metaphysics. His *Physics* also contains much now regarded as metaphysics, including discussion of infinity in book 3.)

G. J. Warnock, 'Metaphysics in logic', in A. Flew (ed.), *Essays in Conceptual Analysis*, 1956. (Does logic commit one to certain metaphysical views?)

R. Carnap, *Meaning and Necessity*, 2nd edn 1956, supplement A, reprinted in C. Landesman (ed.), *The Problem of Universals*, 1971. (Holds that much metaphysics depends on language.)

P. F. Strawson, *Individuals*, 1959. (Defends descriptive metaphysics. Fairly difficult.)

Methodology. See SCIENCE.

Metric. A set of rules, with suitable units, for measuring extensive MAGNITUDES. As an adjective 'metric' or 'metrical' means 'measurable' ('metric SPACE') or 'involving measurement' ('metric geometry').

Middle term. See SYLLOGISM.

Mill, John Stuart. 1806–73. The son of *James Mill* (1773–1836), who was a philosopher of somewhat similar tendencies, Mill was born in London where he worked in the India office. He is noted as an EMPIRICIST and early PHENOMENALIST, and in ethics as a (somewhat wayward) UTILITARIAN and defender of liberty. He also wrote on political philosophy. His logic is largely remembered for his distinction between connotation and denotation (see MEANING), his criticism of the SYLLOGISM, his elaboration of a philosophy of science along the lines of Bacon's and his empiricist treatment of basic MATHEMATICAL propositions. His approach was of the general type now called extensionalist. *A System of Logic, Ratiocinative and Inductive*, 1843. *On Liberty*, 1859. *On Representative Government*, 1861. *Utilitarianism*, 1863. *An Examination of Sir William Hamilton's Philosophy*, 1865 (contains his phenomenalist views). See also BRADLEY, DEFINITION, INDUCTION, INFERENCE, PLEASURE, RUSSELL, SELF-REGARDING.

Millet paradox. See ZENO'S PARADOXES.

Mind (philosophy of). Also called *philosophical psychology*. Psychology deals with questions that can be settled by observation, experiment and measurement, while philosophy of mind settles its different questions by reflection. It currently gives special attention to our ways of thinking and speaking about the topics concerned. It analyses concepts connected with mentality in general, considering their relations to each other and to other concepts, like cause and substance.

Traditionally, the central problem has concerned what mind is and how it relates to body, with soul or spirit sometimes replacing, sometimes being additional to, mind. Answers to this *mind-body* or *body-mind problem* range between idealist views that only the mind is real and materialist views that either the body alone is real (cf. BEHAVIOURISM) or mental phenomena are identical with certain physical ones (IDENTITY THEORY OF MIND). These views, along with the DOUBLE ASPECT THEORY, neutral MONISM, and Aristotle's view that mind is to body as FORM to matter, are all MONIST views. They deny that mind or mental phenomena and body or bodily phenomena are quite distinct things. DUALIST views assert this distinctness and include interactionism, EPIPHENOMENALISM, PSYCHO-PHYSICAL PARALLELISM and OCCASIONALISM.

Idealist and most dualist views are currently unfashionable, while the identity theory is still being vigorously discussed. A variant dualist view is Strawson's which distinguishes bodies from PERSONS. The related topic of personal IDENTITY is important for questions like: Can a mind animate several bodies, successively, as in reincarnation, or at once? Can several minds animate the same body (one view of 'multiple personality' cases)? Can a mind exist without a body at all, whether or not originally joined to one? Clearly much depends on what counts as a mind. This is one of the few areas where philosophy may affect our predictions of the future. Discussion has been stimulated by the possibility of brain transplants. Early work in psychical research has been relevant here and in connexion with extrasensory perception, precognition, telepathy, etc.

Consciousness is something akin to mind. What is it, and what role does it play in thoughts and activities? How far can these be duplicated or imitated without it, whether in conscious beings (the 'unconscious') or in artefacts, and when ought we to say consciousness is present? Interest in these questions has been stimulated by Freud's use of the unconscious, the scientific advantages of studying man in terms of observable behaviour, and recent advances in cybernetics.

A topic linking philosophy of mind closely to ethics is *philosophy of action*. The FREEWILL question makes us ask whether actions can be caused, e.g. by reasons or intentions, and calls for a general analysis of concepts like motive, intention, volition, wanting, trying, Are they the sort of things that could be causes? Are they mental states? Can they be identified or described independently of actions? Are there limitations on our irrationality (cf. INCONTINENCE)? Ethics as well as philosophy of mind can ask whether there are logical limits to what we can approve of or feel obliged to do. Are there things such that nothing would *count* as our approving of them?

Cognition raises questions about pleasure and pain (cf. psychological HEDONISM), and about FEELINGS and emotions. In what sense, for example, are feelings 'in' the body or mind, and how are emotions to be analysed and distinguished from feelings and from each other? Many such questions, like many on perceiving and imagining, border on aesthetics.

This brings us to the more centrally cognitive notions like perception, sensation, judgment, together with more specific ones like attending, noticing, observing, and the more purely intellectual ones like thinking, understanding, believing, doubting, feeling sure, reasoning, inferring. Epistemology concentrates primarily on questions of justification, while philosophy of mind analyses these concepts rather from the point of view of what logical conditions someone must satisfy if he is to be said to be perceiving, thinking, etc. Knowledge is not in the above list, because knowing involves being correct or justified; its analysis therefore belongs to epistemology. Again, the question whether believing is being disposed to act in certain ways belongs primarily to philosophy of mind, but the question whether one can properly be said to believe something where one could not be wrong, such as believe one is in pain, belongs to epistemology. But the distinction is not rigid.

G. N. A. Vesey (ed.), *Body and Mind*, 1964. (Selections from Descartes onwards.)

J. W. Reeves, *Body and Mind in Western Thought*, 1958. (History plus anthology.)

K. Campbell, *Body and Mind*, 1970. (Introductory.)

A. R. White, *The Philosophy of Mind*, 1967. (Combines general survey with detailed analyses.)

G. Ryle, *The Concept of Mind*, 1949. (Classic attack on some dualist ('ghost in the machine') mind/body views, with discussions of feelings, emotions, etc.)

A. C. MacIntyre, *The Unconscious*, 1958.

A. R. Anderson (ed.), *Minds and Machines*, 1964. (Can machines think? and similar questions.)

A. Kenny, *Action, Emotion and Will*, 1963. (Discussion of these concepts.)

A. P. Griffiths (ed.), *Knowledge and Belief*, 1967. (Discussions in both epistemology and philosophy of mind.)

A. Kenny, 'Philosophy of mind in the Anglo-American tradition', in R. Klibansky (ed.), *Contemporary Philosophy*, vol. 3, 1969. (Short survey of some recent developments.)

Minor premise, term. See SYLLOGISM.

Modalities. Ways in which something can exist or occur or be presented, or stand. *Sense modalities* are ways in which we perceive, namely seeing, hearing, etc. *Alethic modalities* are the necessity, contingency, possibility, or impossibility of something being true. Alethic means 'concerned with truth'. *Deontic modalities* include being obligatory, being permitted and being forbidden. Among *epistemic modalities* are being known to be true, and being not known to be false. This last notion is potentially ambiguous: it is unclear whether it covers both being probable, certain, etc., and being believed, doubted, etc. Tenses are sometimes called modalities; cf. *moods* of a verb. 'Modality' is also used for the property of being or having a modality.

Unless otherwise specified, 'modal' and 'modality' normally refer to the alethic modalities, of which the most important are necessity, possibility and impossibility. Terms like 'necessary', 'possible', 'must', 'may' are called *modal terms*.

The relations between these modal terms are rather ambiguous. In particular the *possible* may include everything not impossible, including the necessary; or it may be limited to what is neither necessary nor impossible; or it may be further limited to the merely possible as against the actual. The *contingent* is normally what is neither necessary nor impossible. 'Factual', like 'actual' in one sense, may denote what is neither necessary nor impossible nor merely possible; but it can also be opposed to 'logical', and so apply to a kind of necessity (see below). 'Actual', in this sense, is not used of statements, but 'factual' in both senses, 'possible' in all the above senses and 'contingent' can apply to false statements as well as to true ones, (cf. FACTS). The logical relations between modal terms, e.g. whether being necessary entails being possible, clearly depend on the senses in which the terms are taken.

A statement is necessary if it must be true. A statement which claims that something is necessary, one containing modal terms like 'necessary' or 'must', is called *apodictic*. A statement containing modal terms like 'possible' or 'may' is called *problematic*. A statement containing no modal terms is called *assertoric*. A necessary statement need not be apodictic. 'Twice two is four' is necessary in standard arithmetic, but not apodictic: it contains no word like 'necessary'. Nor need an apodictic statement be necessary. 'Necessarily all cats are black' is apodictic, but not necessary nor even true. In fact whether a statement is apodictic, problematic or assertoric is independent of whether it is necessary or possible, etc. A statement containing 'impossible' or its equivalents counts as apodictic. 'Apodictic' can also mean 'connected with demonstration', as often in 'apodictic necessity', and is sometimes synonymous with 'necessary'. (Kant uses 'apodictic', etc. slightly differently, to indicate how judgments are thought, not expressed; cf. also IMPERATIVE.) 'N', 'L', '□' are among symbols for 'necessarily' or 'it is necessary that' ('L' is limited to logical necessity (see below); in Polish notation 'N' means 'not'). 'M', '◇' are among symbols for 'possibly' or 'it is possible that'. Statements containing modal terms are the subject matter of *modal logic* (see LOGIC), which is not always limited to the alethic modalities.

When a modal term is applied to a statement itself containing one, as in 'It is *possible* that that statement is *necessary*', we have *nested* or *iterated* *modalities*.

A difficult and controversial distinction, of medieval origin, is that between *de re* and *de dicto* modality. Roughly, cases where modal terms apply to the possession of an attribute by a subject are de re and cases where they apply to a proposition are de dicto. Consider the sentence, 'The number of the gospels necessarily exceeds three.' On a de dicto interpretation this means, 'It is necessary that the number of the gospels exceeds

Modalities

three', which is ambiguous. It may mean it is necessary that the number in question, the number four, exceeds three, which is true; or it may mean that necessarily there are more than three gospels, which is false. On a de re interpretation, however, the term 'necessarily' remains inside the original sentence, whose subject is the number of the gospels, the number four. The sentence therefore says that the number four necessarily has the property of exceeding three, which, if it makes sense at all, is true. The difficulty concerns whether a thing's possession of its properties can be called necessary. On the de dicto interpretation only propositions are necessary. The view that de re modality is intelligible and that there are cases of it, even if ultimately they must be analysed in terms of de dicto modality, is the form usually taken in modern discussions by *essentialism*, when this means the doctrine that at least some objects have essences. Rejection of this is one form, or perhaps one aspect, of *nominalism* (cf. DEFINITION).

Properly speaking, necessity and possibility are *absolute*. But in a secondary sense they may be *relative* to (*conditional* on) some expressed or tacit condition or premise. In particular the conclusion of an argument may have *necessitas consequentis*, which is absolute, if it is necessary independently of the argument, or *necessitas consequentiae*, which is relative, if it merely follows necessarily from the premises: 'No spaniels have visited the moon' follows necessarily from 'All spaniels are dogs' and 'No dogs have visited the moon', but is not itself necessary, even though the premises are true. It therefore has only necessitas consequentiae. A conclusion in itself impossible may be possible relative to (i.e. may be consistent with) certain premises: 'Man can live without air' is possible relative to 'Man can do whatever fish can do'. If the impossibility is logical the situation is more complex: Is 'Twice two is five' consistent with 'Half five is two'? (cf. IMPLICATION, CONSISTENT). Similarly a conclusion possible in itself may be impossible relative to certain premises.

Epistemic possibility and *necessity* are relative to what we, or some given set of people, know, or to what we believe. Something possible given what we know may not be possible given everything that is the case, and something necessary given everything that is the case may not be necessary given only what we know. In ancient times it was epistemically possible that Mars was inhabited, and epistemically necessary that the earth was flat. Its flatness *followed* from other beliefs then current.

Necessity and possibility may also be *logical*, or *physical* (*causal*, *scientific*, *natural*, *factual*), or of various other kinds such as moral, legal, aesthetic. Logical necessity and possibility may be *formal* or *non-formal* (see ANALYTIC. 'Logically necessary' normally amounts to the same as 'logically true').

The nature of physical necessity and possibility has been disputed for centuries, especially since Hume. Are they independent of logical necessity and possibility, or ultimately reducible to them, or merely illusory? Are the logical/physical and absolute/relative distinctions related? Perhaps a physically necessary statement is simply one that follows logically from (i.e. is necessary relative to) the laws of an accepted scientific system. But are not the laws themselves necessary in some sense, and if so, in what sense?

It is hard to define modal terms without begging the question. The logically or physically necessary is sometimes defined as what happens in all logically or physically possible worlds, but what are these? Perhaps all conceivable worlds, or all worlds compatible with certain laws; but 'conceivable' and 'compatible' have modal endings ('-ble'), and are not the laws themselves necessary?

Is a logically necessary statement one which nothing would count as contradicting, so that 'All cats are animals' is necessary because nothing would count as a cat that was not an animal? But how do we know that nothing would so count? Is it because 'cat' and 'animal' mean what they do, so that 'All cats are animals' says nothing about cats but exhibits a rule of language, and language depends on us? This is the CONVENTION-ALIST or *linguistic theory* of logical necessity. But to apply a convention (in this case, the convention to use words in certain ways) involves following a rule, and if the rule is itself a convention we shall be led into an infinite regress. It seems that we cannot avoid logical necessity as a constraining force, and at most may hope to decide where it shall constrain us. We may alter our language but we shall always be committed to something. We can make 'Twice two is five' true by redefining 'five', but then we must accept 'Five is half eight'—unless we redefine 'eight', but we must stop somewhere.

Conceptually necessary is often loosely used as synonymous with 'logically necessary'. But if 'logically necessary' is confined to that whose denial is contradictory, 'conceptually necessary' can cover also that whose denial is unintelligible but not strictly contradictory. 'Nothing can be red and green all over' is perhaps an example (cf. ANALYTIC). But there is a problem about when something *is* contradictory.

Non-contingent is often used for 'logically necessary', but properly it denotes a looser relation: e.g. one might say that intention was non-contingently related to action. Any given intention need not be followed by the relevant action, and so the relation is not strictly a necessary one, but the concept of intention could hardly have arisen unless intentions were usually followed by the relevant actions.

Sometimes one can arrange different kinds of necessity in order of degree of stringency, and treat formally the resulting relations between them.

Further questions concern absolute possibility and actuality. Can there be possibilities which remain possibilities throughout all time but are never actualized? Aristotle and Hobbes, among others, said no.

A logical possibility is anything not self-contradictory, but a *real possibility* may be either simply a physical possibility or something having at least some probability that it will occur. See also ANALYTIC, CAUSATION.

I. Kant, *Critique of Pure Reason*, 1781 (revised 1787), B 101. (His use of 'apodictic', etc.)

R. Cartwright, 'Some remarks on essentialism', *Journal of Philosophy*, 1968. (Defends intelligibility of de re modality, while doubting if it is analysable in terms of de dicto modality.)

Mode

A. Plantinga, 'De re et de dicto', *Nous*, 1969. Explains de re in terms of de dicto modality. W. Kneale in E. Nagel, P. Suppes, A. Tarski (eds), *Logic, Methodology and Philosophy of Science*, 1962, rejects the distinction.

K. Britton, J. O. Urmson, W. C. Kneale (see bibliography to CONVENTIONALISM).

N. Malcolm, 'Are necessary propositions really verbal?', *Mind*, 1940, pp. 189 ff. (Defends linguistic view of logical necessity.)

W. V. Quine, 'Truth by convention', in H. Feigl and W. Sellars (eds), *Readings in Philosophical Analysis*, 1949. (Stresses limitations of conventionalist theory of logical necessity.)

S. E. Toulmin, *The Philosophy of Science*, 1953. (Discusses various views of physical necessity.)

L. J. Cohen, *The Diversity of Meaning*, 1962 (revised 1966), chapter 7. (Formal treatment of degrees of necessity. Technical.)

Aristotle, *De Caelo* (*On the Heavens*), book 1, chapter 12.

T. Hobbes, *Elements of Philosophy: Concerning Body*, 1655, chapter 10, § 4. (Aristotle and Hobbes reject eternal unrealized possibilities. Cf. Hintikka (bibliography to PLENITUDE).)

Mode. See SUBSTANCE.

Models. A logical or mathematical model of an AXIOM SYSTEM, or of a sentence in an axiom system, is a set of entities, which may be numbers or classes and hence abstract, whose relations can be represented by that system or sentence. A structure of such entities is a model of a sentence S if S is true in the structure. The natural numbers, taken as related in the way they are by the relation *successor of*, are a model of Peano's axioms, since these are true of the natural numbers, so taken. ('So taken', because the axioms would not necessarily be true of the natural numbers if e.g., these were taken in a different order.) Important problems concern what is true of *all* models of a given system. In some earlier literature a theory can be called a model of another theory, or can contain an interpretation of it, if the sets of objects they study are models of the same axiom system, when they are taken in the way in which they are studied. The force of this last clause can be seen by remembering that, in the above example, the natural numbers are a model of Peano's axioms only if they are taken in their proper order and related by the relation *successor of*. A scientific model is normally a theory intended to explain a given realm of phenomena, or a sort of picture intended to explain a theory by replacing its terms with more perspicuous ones (Braithwaite).

Model theory concerns logical and mathematical models. It studies relations between formal languages and interpretations of them, i.e. problems connected with saying that a sentence of a formal language (e.g. the restricted predicate CALCULUS) is true in an interpretation. This interpretation may be an abstract structure or a world, e.g. the real world as it was in 1970. The starting-point for all forms of model theory is A. Tarski's semantic definition of TRUTH.

A. Tarski, *Introduction to Logic*, 1941, § 37. (Models in logic.)

M. Brodbeck, 'Models, meaning and theories', in L. Gross (ed.), *Symposium on Sociological Theory*, 1959. (Discusses many different uses of 'model'. On scientific models see also R. B. Braithwaite, *Scientific Explanation*, 1953, chapter 4.)

J. L. Bell and A. B. Slomson, *Models and Ultraproducts*, 1969. (Technical introduction to model theory, presupposing some mathematical logic. For brief fairly elementary account see J. N. Crossley *et al.*, *What is Mathematical Logic?*, 1972.)

Modus ponens. Argument that if a conditional statement and its antecedent are true, so is its consequent, e.g., 'If this, then that. This. Therefore that.' (Some refinements are omitted.)

Modus tollens. Argument that if a conditional statement is true but its consequent is false, then its antecedent if false, e.g., 'If this, then that. But not that. Therefore not this.' (Some refinements are omitted.)

Monad. Literally, group of one. Either a numerical unit or an object which is essentially unitary and indivisible. For Leibniz, simple substances, which are what is ultimately real. *Monadic* means either 'concerning monads' or 'having only one term'. Predicates like '(is) red' are monadic (occasionally called monadic relations), since only one term needs adding to make a sentence. Relations proper are *dyadic* or *two-term* relations, or dyadic predicates, if two terms are needed (as with *bigger than*: '*a* is bigger than *b*'). They are *polyadic* or *many-term* if more than two are needed (*between* needs three: '*b* is between *a* and *c*').

G. W. Leibniz, *Principles of Nature and of Grace*, 1714, *Monadology*, 1714.

Monism. Any view which claims that where there appear to be many things or kinds of things there is really only one or only one kind. Weaker forms of monism may claim simply that the things in question are related together, or unified, in some significant way. What is said to be one in any of these ways may be the whole universe, or some lesser subject-matter. *Neutral monism* is a particular doctrine claiming that physical and mental phenomena can both be analysed in terms of a common underlying reality, sometimes called *neutral stuff*. Among major philosophers it is associated with James and Russell.

B. Russell, *The Analysis of Mind*, 1921. (Neutral monism.)

Mood. See SYLLOGISM.

Moore, George E. 1873–1958. Born in Upper Norwood, he worked in Cambridge. He led the revolt against IDEALISM at the start of this century, and was one of the fathers of analytical PHILOSOPHY. He criticized the extravagances, as he saw them, of philosophers who flouted common sense with such doctrines as that time is unreal and that all relations are

Moral

internal. He held influential, if somewhat idiosyncratic, views in ETHICS, and was particularly noted for his criticism of the 'naturalistic fallacy' (see NATURALISM). 'The Refutation of Idealism', *Mind*, 1903. *Principia Ethica*, 1903. *Some Main Problems in Philosophy*, 1953 (lectures given in 1910). 'External and Internal Relations', *Proceedings of the Aristotelian Society*, 1919–20. See also BEING, BRADLEY, GOOD, IMPLICATION, PHENOMENALISM, SCEPTICISM, SENTENCES, TRUTH, UTILITARIANISM.

Moral. Concerning habits, customs, ways of life, especially when these are assessed as good or bad, right or wrong. Etymologically the Latin 'moral' corresponds to the Greek 'ethical'. They both mean 'concerning habits, etc.' Among things we call moral are theories, arguments, outlooks, rules, reasons, men, books, actions, intentions, and perhaps desires and feelings. There is an important ambiguity between 'moral' as against 'immoral' and 'moral' as against 'non-moral'. Men are normally called moral only in the first sense, problems can be moral only in the second. An immoral principle is still a moral principle in the second sense, as against, say, a legal or aesthetic principle. 'Morality' is similarly ambiguous.

Amoral (which properly means 'non-moral', not 'immoral') is seldom used in philosophy.

The main problem for ethics here is to distinguish the moral from the non-moral and various ways of doing this have been tried. (The moral/immoral distinction is dealt with under other headings.) A moral principle might be defined as one concerning things in our power and for which we can be held responsible. This would contrast moral principles with, for example, intellectual and aesthetic ones, which it might not be in our power to apply. Or a moral principle might concern the ultimate ends of human action, e.g. human welfare. Other views have it that a moral principle is one which people in fact prefer over competing principles, or else one which they should prefer. Others again make principles moral if a certain kind of sanction is applied when they are violated. UNIVERSALIZABILITY has also been used to define moral principles.

A view may offer a necessary condition of morality, or a sufficient condition, or both (see NECESSARY AND SUFFICIENT CONDITIONS). A further distinction is that in defining morality one may be saying what counts as moral for a given person or society, or giving one's own view of what counts as moral.

G. Wallace and A. D. M. Walker (eds), *The Definition of Morality*, 1970. (Selected essays.)

G. H. von Wright, *The Varieties of Goodness*, 1963, esp. chapter 1 (last paragraph), chapter 6, §§ 5 ff. (Moral goodness and goodness generally. Acts and intentions. Assumes UTILITARIANISM.)

Morals. See ETHICS.

Moral sense. An alleged sixth sense, whose existence was hotly disputed in the eighteenth century. Its proponents held that our own and others' actions arouse agreeable or disagreeable 'sentiments', or feelings, in us according as the actions are, in conventional terms, virtuous or vicious. It is not always clear, however, what is the role of the sense, on this view, i.e. whether we perceive qualities by it, and if so, of what sort, or whether it simply arouses sentiments in us, or gives us a desire to act, when we perceive certain qualities in the ordinary way.

L. A. Selby-Bigge (ed.), *British Moralists*, 1897. (Vol. 1 contains selections from moral sense theorists, vol. 2 selections from their opponents. Cf. also the ethical writings of D. Hume (1711–76).)

D. D. Raphael, *The Moral Sense*, 1947. (Discussion, mainly historical.)

Moving rows paradox. See ZENO'S PARADOXES.

N

Natural deduction. A system which systematizes those DEDUCTIONS which involve contingent propositions (see MODALITIES), not merely TAUTOLOGIES. It therefore systematizes the 'natural' arguments of everyday life. Associated especially with G. Gentzen (1909–45) and S. Jaśkowski (1906–1965).

E. Lemmon, *Beginning Logic*, 1965. (Uses it to introduce formal logic.)

Naturalism. Originally, a general philosophical view akin to PRAGMATISM and POSITIVISM and at one time common in America, centring on the belief that the universe is all one, in the sense that all objects in it, and all aspects of it, are equally accessible to study by scientific method. 'Naturalism' has various other senses, e.g. in art, but nowadays mainly denotes a related ethical doctrine, to the general effect that there is no unbridgeable gulf between ethics and other studies. It takes two main forms, that ethical terms can be analysed into non-ethical terms, and that ethical conclusions can be logically derived from non-ethical premises.

Modern discussions start from two famous attacks on these two forms respectively, by Moore and Hume. Moore insisted that 'good' is indefinable, and that the questions what 'good' means and what things are good must be sharply distinguished, e.g. pleasure may be good, and even possibly the only good thing, but 'good' does not *mean* 'pleasant' or 'producing pleasure', etc. He called the neglect of this distinction the *naturalistic fallacy*, and said goodness is a nonnatural quality. (He never successfully explained 'nonnatural', which is now not used of qualities. For nonnatural see MEANING.) One of Moore's arguments was the *open question argument*: whatever definition of 'good' was offered, it would always be an open question whether what satisfies the definition *is* good. It is not clear, however, whether the naturalistic fallacy lies in defining 'good', defining 'good' in non-ethical terms, defining any ethical notion in non-ethical terms, defining any notion in terms of notions in a different sphere, or indeed simply confusing one notion with another. In this last form the fallacy is sometimes called the *definist fallacy*. It is difficult, however, to mark off different spheres or notions, and the errors, if any, are not strictly fallacies—no fallacious inference is involved.

Naturalism

Hume, as usually interpreted, attacked naturalism by denying that conclusions whose main verb is an 'ought', or an equivalent, can be logically derived from premises not containing such a notion. Hume was primarily concerned with the moral OUGHT, but the question also arises of whether other 'oughts' (e.g. 'doctor's orders'), receive the same answer.

The alleged distinction underlying both these attacks is often, if loosely, called the *fact/value distinction*, though 'ought' is not strictly a value term.

Moore made his distinction between different qualities, all of which objectively belonged to their possessors: whether a thing is good no more depends on the observer than whether it is, say, spherical. Various later writers, however, have tried to make the same distinction in other ways, asking how words have meaning, and what the speaker's own attitudes contribute. Thus a distinction grew up between straightforward descriptions which claim to state facts and impart knowledge, and utterances whose purpose is to express or evince emotions or attitudes, to issue prescriptions or recommendations, or to evaluate. Utterances of the former kind, and the words used in them, had *descriptive*, *factual* or *cognitive meaning;* those of the latter kind had *emotive*, *evaluative*, *prescriptive* or in general *non-cognitive meaning*. The terms in the former list in general coincide (but for ambiguities in 'factual' see FACTS). Those in the latter list do not all coincide—to express emotion is not the same as to prescribe action or attitudes—but they share the property of being contrasted with the former list. Many utterances, however, especially ethical ones, had both kinds of meaning. 'He is courageous' might mean 'He knowingly takes great risks' (factual), 'and I hereby express approval of his doing so' (emotive), or 'I hereby recommend you to follow suit' (prescriptive). 'He is rash' might have the same factual meaning but the opposite non-cognitive meaning, i.e., as above, but with 'disapproval' for 'approval' and 'forbid' for 'recommend'. *Emotivists* and *prescriptivists* analyse ethical utterances in this way, emphasizing emotive and prescriptive meaning respectively, but *descriptivists* think that ethical utterances have meaning in the same way as factual ones do, i.e. they state facts, even if of an ethical kind. Descriptivism and naturalism are in practice closely similar. Moore was a descriptivist but not a naturalist.

Understandably, the naturalist controversy is associated with another, concerning whether there are objective and agreed procedures for arriving at conclusions in matters of value or duty. Descriptivists and most naturalists claim that they are, even if they are hard to elaborate. They take the utterances in question to be saying something true or false about objective reality, and so to be stating facts. Their opponents may deny that there are such procedures. Hence the attempt common among POSITIVISTS and linguistic PHILOSOPHERS to confine ethics to certain questions only: see ETHICS. Alternatively they allow that there are such procedures, but have special difficulty in elaborating them, since special kinds of reasoning seem needed to support conclusions claiming to do something other than state facts.

Recently the fact/value distinction has come under fire. There seems to be little unity on the value side, which has to cover expressions of emotion,

Naturalism

commendations, prescriptions, etc., in each case sometimes moral and sometimes non-moral. Where a similar distinction seems viable it may still be relative (Anscombe). Emotivists and prescriptivists face objections connected with UNIVERSALIZABILITY. The theory that words like 'good' or 'ought' get their meaning by commending or prescribing, i.e. by their use in SPEECH ACTS, also faces difficulties (see GOOD).

The view that moral conclusions cannot be logically derived from non-moral premises may be called a weak non-naturalism or weak anti-naturalism if it admits that there are limits to the possible contents of ethical statements, i.e. to what we can *intelligibly* be said to commend or prescribe as a duty. Would we, for example, understand anyone who seriously thought it his duty to blink every five seconds, regardless of circumstances? It is a strong non-naturalism if it denies that there are such limits. (Cf. the question whether just anything can be GOOD.) The phrase *autonomy of morals* or *of ethics* can apply to both these versions of non-naturalism, and also to the view that practical moral questions can be separated from theoretical ethical analysis because any position on the former can be combined with any position on the latter. This last view too has been attacked because of universalizability, among other things.

Perhaps the most central question is whether there is any way of *establishing* ethical or other valuational conclusions. If there is, there seems little objection to using terms like 'true' and 'fact' in connexion with such conclusions, i.e. to adopting descriptivism. See also OUGHT, GOOD, MEANING, FACTS, ETHICS.

A. E. Murphy, review of Y. H. Krikorian (ed.), *Naturalism and the Human Spirit*, 1944, *Journal of Philosophy*, 1945, pp. 400–17. (Review of volume of essays representing naturalism in general sense.)

W. D. Hudson, (ed.) *The Is/Ought Question*, 1969. (Discussions of Hume's attack on naturalism, plus some essays on evaluation.)

P. Foot (ed.) *Theories of Ethics*, 1967. (Includes several notable discussions of naturalism.)

G. E. Moore, *Principia Ethica*, 1903, chapter 1, esp. § B. (Locus classicus for naturalistic fallacy.)

A. N. Prior, *Logic and the Basis of Ethics*, 1949. (Naturalistic fallacy in its historical setting.)

D. P. Gauthier, 'Moore's naturalistic fallacy', *American Philosophical Quarterly*, 1967. (Discusses Moore and Prior and offers own view on naturalistic fallacy.)

B. H. Baumrin, 'Is there a naturalistic fallacy?', *American Philosophical Quarterly*, 1968. (Detailed examination of Moore and different forms of the fallacy.)

G. C. Kerner, *The Revolution in Ethical Theory*, 1966. (Critical history of reactions to Moore, including discussions of leading emotivist (C. L. Stevenson) and prescriptivist (R. M. Hare).)

W. D. Hudson, *Modern Moral Philosophy*, 1970. (General introduction. Includes Hare's latest views in discussing prescriptivism, etc. Cf. also p. 171 on terminology.)

Negation

J. O. Urmson, *The Emotive Theory of Ethics*, 1968. (Extended discussion of Stevenson.)

R. F. Atkinson, 'The autonomy of morals', *Analysis*, vol. 18, 1958. (Defends fact/value distinction against some attacks of a logical nature.)

G. E. M. Anscombe 'On brute facts', *Analysis*, vol. 18, 1958. (Argues that distinction between 'brute' and 'institutional' facts is relative.)

A. K. Sen, 'Hume's law and Hare's rule', *Philosophy*, 1966. (Uses universalizability to defend naturalism.)

A. Gewirth, 'Positive "ethics" and normative "science" ', *Philosophical Review*, 1960. (Compares ethics and science as fields of enquiry.)

C. Beck, 'Utterances which incorporate a value statement', *American Philosophical Quarterly*, 1967.

R. W. Newell, 'Ethics and description', *Philosophy*, 1968. (Two attacks on fact/value distinction.)

Naturalistic fallacy. See NATURALISM.

Necessary and sufficient conditions. A necessary condition for something is one without which the thing would not exist or occur. Oxygen, or its presence, is a necessary condition for human life. A sufficient condition for something is one given which the thing does exist or occur. Prolonged absence of oxygen is a sufficient condition for human death. Necessary or sufficient conditions need not precede what they are conditions of. The existence of men is a sufficient condition for the presence of oxygen. As this last example shows, a sufficient condition may be causally connected with what it is a condition of, without being a cause of it. But necessary or sufficient conditions do not have to be causal: fine weather is a necessary condition of my going out today—because I have so decided. They can also be logical. Being an equilateral Euclidean triangle is both necessary and sufficient for being an equiangular Euclidean triangle. Conditions that are both necessary and sufficient for the same thing can be important in connexion with CAUSATION, DEFINITIONS and CRITERIA. 'Sufficient conditions' (plural) may refer to conditions jointly sufficient for something, or to conditions each of which is itself sufficient.

Negation. Denial of a proposition. A distinction is sometimes made between *external* and *internal negation*. In external negation a whole proposition is negated, in internal negation only part of one. 'It's not thought that he'll come' involves external negation if it means simply that people don't think he will come, but internal negation if it means they do think he won't. There is a similar distinction between negating a proposition and negating a predicate or term, e.g. between 'This isn't red' and 'This is non-red'. *Denial* is sometimes kept for the negation of a predicate or term. 'Positive' and 'affirmative' are generally synonymous.

The *double negation* principle says that any proposition implies and is implied by the negation of its negation. INTUITIONIST logic rejects the second half of this.

Various problems arise: Can negative and affirmative propositions be separately identified? Or can one only say that two propositions are negations of each other, neither being 'the' negative one? Is negating something a special activity? Is affirming somehow prior to negating? Can language dispense with negation?

A. J. Ayer, 'Negation', *Journal of Philosophy*, 1952, reprinted in his *Philosophical Essays*, 1954. (Definition, and dispensability, of negation.)

G. Frege, 'Negation' in P. T. Geach and M. Black (eds), *Translations from the Philosophical Writings of Gottlob Frege*, 1952. (Is negating something a special activity?)

J. D. Mabbott, G. Ryle, H. H. Price, 'Negation', *Proceedings of the Aristotelian Society*, supplementary vol. 1929. (What does negation presuppose?)

G. Buchdahl, 'The problem of negation', *Philosophy and Phenomenological Research*, 1961–2. (Are affirmative judgments prior to negative ones?)

Neoplatonists. Various groups of philosophers influenced by Plotinus (AD 205–70) and claiming Platonic inspiration. Plotinus in his *Enneads* claimed to interpret and develop PLATO, basing himself especially on certain passages suggesting that reality is somehow derived from a single thing, called the One or the Good, which transcends existence (i.e. is on too high a plane to be said to 'exist') and is unknowable. Plotinus also developed an epistemology. The Neoplatonists also tried to unify Plato and ARISTOTLE. They are now often regarded as having misinterpreted Plato. Leading Neoplatonists after Plotinus include Porphyry (c.232–c.304), Iamblichus (c.270–c.330), Proclus (c.409–c.487), Philoponus (sixth century), Simplicius (sixth century), Boethius (c.480–525). See also SEXTUS.

R. T. Wallis, *Neoplatonism*, 1972.

Neustic. See PHRASTIC.

Neutral stuff. See MONISM.

Nietzsche, Friedrich. 1844–1900. Born in Prussia, he taught classics at Basel and then lived in Switzerland and Italy, and died after eleven years of insanity. His importance lies in aesthetics, with his contrast between the Apolline and Dionysian elements in Greek tragedy, and in ethics, where he contrasted 'master' and 'slave' morality and made pungent criticisms of utilitarianism and Christian ethics. Linked with these latter views are his concepts of the 'will to power' and the 'superman'. How far his own ideal involves aggressive egoism is disputed, but self-control was an important ingredient in his ideal. He also revived the PYTHAGOREAN and STOIC notion of eternal recurrence (see METAPHYSICS). He is sometimes associated with EXISTENTIALISM. *The Birth of Tragedy*, 1872. *Beyond Good and Evil*, 1886. *Towards a Genealogy of Morals*, 1887. *Thus Spake Zarathustra*, 1883–5.

Noetic. See NOUS.

Nomic. See NOMOLOGICAL.

Nominalism. See UNIVERSALS, BEING, DEFINITION, MODALITIES, SUBSTANCE.

Nomological. Concerning or involving laws. *Nomic* means this, or sometimes 'lawlike' (see first sense of this under LAWS).

No-ownership theory. Theory that states of consciousness are not owned by anything, mental or physical.

P. F. Strawson, *Individuals*, 1959, chapter 3. (Critical, with references.)

Normative. A term or sentence, etc. is normative if its basic uses involve prescribing norms or standards, explicitly or implicitly, e.g. 'ought' is normative, and so is 'good' for anyone holding that, for example, 'Piety is good' either means or entails 'One ought to be pious'.

Noumenon. Plural: 'noumena'. Adjective: 'noumenal'. Literally, thing known by the mind as against the senses. Kant's alternative term for a *thing-in-itself*, which we could never be acquainted with, or even in any way know what it was like. But Kant thought that noumena must be postulated, to account for the appearances (*phenomena*) we are confronted with.

I. Kant, *Critique of Pure Reason*, 1781, 1787. (See index to N. Kemp Smith's translation, 1929.)

Numbers (law of large). Various related theorems about possibilities for events, among them Bernoulli's theorem and Poisson's theorem. For a rough illustration of the general idea, suppose that a tossed coin is equally likely to fall heads or tails. Then, the law says, the longer the series of tosses, the greater the probability that the frequency of heads will be within some given distance of 50 per cent (e.g. between 49 per cent and 51 per cent; it cannot be exactly 50 per cent except after an even number of tosses). The law is not itself a prediction. If we *assume*, on whatever grounds, that the coin will behave in certain ways, e.g. that it will not show any bias, then the law spells out what it is that we are assuming. To see what lies behind this illustration, consider all possible results, in terms of heads and tails, that a series of tosses could yield. Then the longer the series the greater the proportion, among the possible results for that series, of results containing between 49 per cent and 51 per cent heads. See also BAYES'S THEOREM.

J. O. Wisdom, *Foundations of Inference in Natural Science*, 1952, chapter 20. (Brief statement of some relevant theorems, with proof of one.)

O _____

Object. Anything which has independent existence (qualities, etc. have dependent existence); or, and perhaps more commonly in philosophy, what a change, a verb, or a mental attitude is 'directed at'. Here, an object need not always be real (see INTENSIONALITY). Cf. 'the object in my pocket', 'the object of my ambition'. These meanings are often intermingled. Meinong distinguished the object of an act like thinking from its content, but insisted that the object had something called 'BEING SO'. Frege treated objects as whatever can be named or talked about, and contrasted them with CONCEPTS. In this wide sense 'object' approximates to 'thing', though usually, when the 'existence' meaning is dominant, objects are limited to particulars (see UNIVERSALS). Concerning mental attitudes there are problems about distinguishing objects and causes: how are the cause and the object of an emotion related?

J. A. Passmore, *A Hundred Years of Philosophy*, 1957. (See index.)
A. Kenny, *Action, Emotion and Will*, 1963. (See index.)

Objectivism. See SUBJECTIVISM.

Object word. (i) Word standing for objects, e.g. 'cat', but not 'red' or 'snow'. (ii) Word in an object language (see METALANGUAGE).

Obligation. See OUGHT.

Obversion. Replacement of a proposition by a logically equivalent one (its *obverse*) having as predicate the negation of the original predicate, e.g. 'All cats are black' and 'No cats are non-black' are obverses of each other.

Occam. See OCKHAM.

Occasionalism. Doctrine that things or events are caused only by God, never by other things or events. Apparent causes are what God uses as occasions (hence called *occasional causes*) for creating their apparent effects. Associated especially with Malebranche and others of his time, where, however, the main emphasis is on the apparent causal relations between mind and body. Leibniz's similar view is not occasionalism, because for him God programmed minds and bodies from the creation, and did not interfere on each occasion. See also PSYCHOPHYSICAL PARALLELISM.

N. Malebranche, *Dialogues on Metaphysics and on Religion*, 1688, transl. 1923, 7th Dialogue.

Ockham, William of. c.1285–1349. English Franciscan theologian who worked mainly in Oxford, Avignon and Munich. He worked against the same general background as AQUINAS and Duns SCOTUS, but he separated philosophy further from theology by severely limiting the extent to which God's existence can be proved. He is commonly regarded as a nominalist (see UNIVERSALS), and is famous for OCKHAM'S RAZOR. He contributed substantially to logic and the theory of meaning, among other topics. His writings include the *Summa Logicae*, *Quodlibeta Septem* (seven miscellanies), and commentaries on the *Sentences* of Peter Lombard and on various works of ARISTOTLE.

Ockham's razor. Principle propounded by William of Ockham, that 'entities are not to be multiplied beyond necessity' (not his own words), i.e., it is arbitrary to postulate the existence of things, or kinds of things, unless one has to. More generally, one should choose the simplest hypothesis that will fit the facts. A stronger form claims that only what cannot be dispensed with is real and that to postulate other things is not only arbitrary but mistaken.

Omnipotence (paradox of). See RELIGION.

Omniscience (paradoxes of). See RELIGION.

One-many problem. See UNIVERSALS.

One-sorted. See MANY-SORTED.

Ontological argument. An argument for God's existence, stemming from Anselm. Very roughly: God is the most perfect being; it is more perfect to exist than not to exist; therefore God exists. More generally, any argument can be called an ontological argument which infers that something really exists because certain concepts are related in certain ways. Discussion of the topic has been closely linked with the question whether existence is a predicate (or attribute).

A. Plantinga (ed.), *The Ontological Argument*, 1968. (Versions and discussions from Anselm to present day.)
J. Barnes, *The Ontological Argument*, 1972. (Detailed examination.)

Ontology

Ontology. See METAPHYSICS.

Opaque. See INTENSIONALITY.

Open question argument. See NATURALISM.

Open texture. Loosely, a term's indeterminacy of meaning. Waismann thought that with most empirical predicates (see A PRIORI) we cannot guarantee to be able to apply or refuse to apply them in certain cases. However precise we made their meaning a borderline case could always turn up in the future. He called this feature open texture, and distinguished it from *vagueness*, which is a feature of already existing uses of predicates, not of possible future uses (see AMBIGUITY). Vagueness can be remedied by giving more accurate rules, but open texture cannot because we cannot predict future borderline cases. He compared open texture to possibility of vagueness. Open texture and vagueness are important in connexion with verifiability (see POSITIVISM) and the law of EXCLUDED MIDDLE. It is not clear that they are, as often thought, confined to empirical predicates.

F. Waismann, 'Verifiability', *Proceedings of the Aristotelian Society*, supplementary vol., 1945, reprinted in his *How I See Philosophy*, 1968, and in G. H. R. Parkinson (ed.), *The Theory of Meaning*, 1968. (Open texture and verifiability.)

L. J. Cohen, *The Diversity of Meaning*, 1962, chapter 9. (Significance of vagueness.)

I. Lakatos (see bibliography to MATHEMATICS). (Open texture of mathematical concepts.)

Operationalism. See POSITIVISM.

Operator. A logical operator is any expression whose function is to affect in a specific way the logical properties (e.g. the entailments) of an expression or expressions to which it is attached, e.g. 'and' operates on two propositions by joining them into a whole, which has entailments neither of them has separately. See also VARIABLE.

Or. See CONJUNCTION.

Order. See TYPES (THEORY OF).

Other minds problem. See SCEPTICISM.

Other-regarding. See SELF-REGARDING.

Ought, obligation, duty. Etymologically connected with 'owe', *ought* suggests a gap which requires to be filled. But the gap may not always exist: to say the kettle ought to be boiling when it clearly is boiling is normally pointless, but 'It ought to be boiling by now' does not imply that

Ought, obligation, duty

it is not; when told that it is boiling we can say 'and so it ought to be'. (But *saying* that it ought may often 'contextually imply' that it is not: see IMPLICATION.) Presumably what requires that the kettle should be boiling is the laws of science, plus statements that the gas is lighted, etc.

A term related to the closing of a gap is obviously well suited for use when guiding action. In 'You ought to take quinine' what does the requiring is presumably your state of health, the laws of medicine, and your interest in recovering. It is more difficult to explain the moral 'ought'. There may be laws of morality corresponding to those of medicine, but what corresponds to the agent's interest in recovering, without which taking quinine would be pointless? This makes us ask how morality relates to self-interest. Does it presuppose it? In fact several questions concern 'ought' and motivation. Even if 'Smith ought to X' does not imply Smith already has a motive to X, must 'ought' carry a motive with it?, i.e. can he coherently say, 'I acknowledge that I ought to X, but that gives me no motive to X'? Would this count as genuine acknowledgment? And can it be true that one ought to X, if one thinks that one ought but remains completely unmoved? Also is it the case that we ought to act from certain motives?

Furthermore, what is requirement, which of course is a metaphorical notion? And can we deduce moral conclusions (either general laws or statements about specific cases or kinds of case) from purely non-moral premises? (cf. NATURALISM).

We also use 'ought' to express what we ought to do, *all* things considered (see MORAL). How does this so-called 'final ought' relate to the moral 'ought', and in general is there really only one sense of 'ought'? Some think even the moral 'ought' is ambiguous, according as it does or does not imply that we *can* do the act in question: if we fulfil the more urgent of two competing moral claims, is there a sense in which we still ought to fulfil the other, even though now we cannot? Concerning the moral 'ought' see also IMPERATIVE.

Obligations are normally things we incur because of specific circumstances (e.g. a promise, or favours received). The basis of many obligations is a contract, which need be only implicit, if implicit contracts are possible. There may be many reasons why I *ought* to obey the law, but I only have an *obligation* to obey it if I have incurred that obligation, perhaps on some form of the social contract theory (i.e. the theory that all citizens of a state have somehow, e.g. by not emigrating, entered into a tacit contract to behave in certain ways). Obligations are primarily moral or legal. They are also always *to* some moral agent (including corporations, God, etc.). If I buy a dog I no doubt ought to feed it, but any obligation I am under must be to the seller, or perhaps to society.

Being obliged is wider than being under an obligation. It is the lack of alternatives, not the element of incurring, which is now dominant. The alternatives excluded may be physically or prudentially rather than morally or legally impossible ('I was obliged, but not under an obligation, to hand over my purse'). Also one need not, though one may, be obliged *to* someone. But one cannot be obliged to do what is not morally at least

149

Ought, obligation, duty

excusable: a soldier is not *obliged* to flee the battle, however prudent that may be.

Obligatory belongs roughly with 'obligation'. It is not confined to the moral and legal (there can be obligatory moves in a game), but it presupposes rules and does not cover cases of being physically or prudentially obliged.

Duty is primarily connected with roles, whether or not these are voluntarily undertaken. One has duties *as* a secretary, father, son, etc. Duties tend to be of longer standing and less ad hoc than obligations: one *meets* one's obligations as one incurs them, but *does* one's duty or discharges one's duties in the normal course of things.

Duties and obligations are therefore special kinds of things we morally or legally ought to do, though it does not follow that we always ought to perform them, since they may be overridden, whether by other duties, etc., or even by something non-moral: see above on the 'final ought'.

Another question introduces rights. Must there be a correlative right wherever there is a duty or obligation, and vice versa? Do animals have rights, and do we have duties to them?

Since Kant, especially, 'duty' has often been used loosely for whatever we morally ought to do. Kant, following others, distinguished *perfect duties*, which were absolute and could never be overridden, from *imperfect duties*, which could be overridden by other duties or even by inclinations (e.g. benevolence: we need not, perhaps could not, give to charity on every possible occasion, but must sometimes). This makes us ask whether the same act can be both dutiful and meritorious. *Prima facie duties* (Ross) are general duties such as benevolence and promise-keeping, which may be overridden in a given situation. The term has been objected to because it implies that when overridden they cease to be duties at all. Cf. DEFEASIBLE. *Putative* or *subjective duty* means what we think we ought to do. *Objective* or *material duty* means what we really ought to do. *Subjective* or *formal duty* means what would be our objective duty if the non-moral facts were as we suppose. It may then be argued, however, that in one sense what we 'really' ought to do is our putative, or perhaps our subjective, duty.

Finally, could there be religious, as against moral, duties?

R. M. Hare, *The Language of Morals*, 1952, part 3. (Influential analysis of 'ought' and its relation to imperatives and to 'right' and 'good'.)

H.-N. Castaneda, 'Imperatives, oughts and moral oughts', *Australasian Journal of Philosophy*, 1966. (Meaning of 'ought'. Moral and overriding ('final') 'ought'.)

F. H. Bradley, *Ethical Studies*, 1876, essay 5 ('My Station and its Duties'). (Famous idealist account of basis of moral 'ought'.)

W. K. Frankena, 'Obligation and motivation in recent moral philosophy', in A. I. Melden (ed.), *Essays in Moral Philosophy*, 1958.

D. A. Lloyd Thomas, 'Why should I be moral?', *Philosophy*, 1970.

W. J. Rees, 'Moral rules and the analysis of "ought" ', *Philosophical Review*, 1953. (Is the moral 'ought' ambiguous?)

W. K. Frankena, 'Obligation and ability', in M. Black (ed.), *Philosophical*

Analysis, 1950. (Distinguishes senses of 'ought' by using relations with ability.)

D. P. Gauthier, *Practical Reasoning*, 1963. (Includes discussion of obligation and duty.)

E. Page, 'On being obliged', *Mind*, 1973. (Senses of 'obliged'.)

J. K. Mish'alani, ' "Duty", "obligation" and "ought" ', *Analysis*, vol. 30, 1969.

H. L. A. Hart, 'Legal and moral obligation', in A. I. Melden (ed.), *Essays in Moral Philosophy*, 1958.

B. A. O. Williams and R. F. Atkinson, 'Consistency in ethics', *Proceedings of the Aristotelian Society*, supplementary vol. 1965. (Conflict of duties.)

W. D. Ross, *The Right and the Good*, 1930. (See chapter 2 for prima facie duties. Cf. also his later book, *Foundations of Ethics*, 1939 (sometimes called 'The righter and the better').)

E. F. Carritt, *Ethical and Political Thinking*, 1947, chapter 2, § 1. (Putative, etc., duties.)

Ousia. See SUBSTANCE.

P   _____

Paradigm. Basically, ways of looking at things, shared assumptions which govern the outlook of an epoch and its approach to scientific problems; or they are accepted theories, e.g. Ptolemaic or Copernican astronomy. T. S. Kuhn introduces 'paradigm' in this technical sense, or senses, into philosophy of science. In Kuhn's later work, however, *disciplinary matrix* is used for approximately the above senses, and paradigms become standard forms of solutions to problems (e.g. they become equations, formulae, etc.). These solutions are then used for solving further problems, and so govern the forms these further solutions take. Kuhn is largely concerned with how shifts of paradigms occur as science develops.

T. S. Kuhn, *The Structure of Scientific Revolutions*, 1962, 2nd edn with postscript 1970.
M. Masterman, 'The nature of a paradigm', in I. Lakatos and A. Musgrave (eds), *Criticism and the Growth of Knowledge*, 1970. (Extracts twenty-one senses of 'paradigm' from Kuhn and discusses, reducing to three groups. Cf. Kuhn's reply (ibid, § 6, and 'postscript' (above).)

Paradigm case argument. A type of argument claiming that certain things must exist or be real because certain expressions have a standard correct use in our language. It is claimed that there must be such a thing as free-will because there are standard situations, paradigm cases, where it is generally agreed to be correct to say, 'He did it of his own freewill'. Without such situations, it is argued, the word 'freewill' would have no meaning. An example seeming to support this is that only because red things exist or have existed can 'red' have the meaning it has. The argument is that certain things must exist because certain expressions have a meaning and therefore a correct use.

The argument has been attacked on various grounds. Even for 'red' to mean what it does, perhaps there need only *seem* to be red things. This assumes that there could seem to be red things though there were in fact none. If a certain expression is to have meaning, does this imply that something exists, or only that it could exist, or neither? And are there relevant differences between terms like 'red' and 'freewill'? Also how much can the argument show? Even if 'freewill' means what it does because situations exist where we are not subject to external constraint, hypnotism, etc., does this show that we have freewill in a philosophically interesting sense?

Appeal to the paradigm case argument is closely associated with linguistic PHILOSOPHY. See also TRANSCENDENTAL ARGUMENTS.

P. Edwards, 'Bertrand Russell's doubts about induction', *Mind*, 1949, reprinted in A. Flew (ed.), *Logic and Language*, 1st series, 1951. (Applies the argument to legitimize induction.)

J. W. N. Watkins, 'Farewell to the paradigm case argument', *Analysis*, vol. 18, 1957–8. (Cf. discussions in same volume.)

R. J. Richman, 'On the argument of the paradigm case', *Australasian Journal of Philosophy*, 1961. (Attacks argument. Cf. discussions by C. J. F. Williams (ibid.) and Richman (ibid., 1962).)

J. Passmore, *Philosophical Reasoning*, 1961, chapter 6. (Critical of this and related argument.)

Paradox. Etymologically, 'against belief'. Full-blooded paradoxes which affect the basis of logic exist when some statement needed for logic can apparently be both proved and disproved. Among them, paradoxes depending on purely logical or mathematical terms are called *logical paradoxes,* or *paradoxes of set theory* (e.g. RUSSELL'S PARADOX) while paradoxes depending on notions like meaning, designation, etc., are called *semantic paradoxes* (e.g. LIAR PARADOX); these are sometimes distinguished from the logical ones. In *pragmatic paradoxes* there is a contradiction not in what is said but in what is done in saying it. 'It's raining, but I don't believe it is' is not contradictory for both parts could be true. But uttering the second part frustrates the normal intentions of uttering the first.

Other paradoxes claim that apparently indispensable notions are inconsistent (e.g. ZENO'S PARADOXES), or that apparently possible situations are impossible (e.g. PREDICTION PARADOX). Loosely speaking a paradox may be little more than something odd or unexpected (e.g. material and strict IMPLICATION paradoxes). But how significant a given paradox is is often disputed. See also theory of TYPES.

A. Pap, *Semantics and Necessary Truth*, 1958, chapter 9C. (Types of paradox, especially pragmatic.)

Particulars. See UNIVERSALS, INDIVIDUALS.

Pascal's wager. If God and an afterlife exist we could face *infinite* suffering in Hell. Therefore it must be rational to act as though they do exist, however low the probability (above zero), since the resulting sacrifice of pleasure is only finite.

P. T. Landsberg, 'Gambling on God', *Mind*, 1971.

Peirce, Charles S. 1839–1914. Born in Cambridge, Mass., he worked as an astronomer, government physicist, and university teacher in America.

Perception

He is especially famous as the first main PRAGMATIST, but he also developed an elaborate system of logic. This contributed to modern mathematical logic in many ways, notably by his development of a logic of relations, including the distinction between monadic, dyadic and polyadic relations. He also developed a metaphysics based on three categories which he called firstness, secondness and thirdness. Peirce published no books in his lifetime, but apart from his *Collected Papers*, 8 vols, 1931–58, some selections exist: *Chance, Love and Logic*, 1923. *The Philosophy of Peirce*, 1940. See also UNIVERSALS.

Perception. The faculty of apprehending the world specifically through the senses, or the general exercise of it, or particular cases of its exercise, and also what is perceived. Perception raises problems which form an important branch of epistemology.

The analysis of perceiving is complicated by the variety of its objects (cf. SEEING). Does one, all in the same sense, 'perceive' that Smith is red in the face, tense, angry, an irate person, subconsciously afraid, likely to pull the trigger? And can one perceive an object without perceiving facts about it?

Usually 'perceive' is a 'success' or 'achievement' word, i.e. we can only perceive what is there or is true. But this may not always hold, if we allow that Macbeth perceived a dagger, and it does not apply to 'perceive as' (cf. SEEING). We can misperceive, i.e. make mistakes about what we perceive.

Perception is thus a complex notion, and two main and connected problems concern its relations to sensory experience on the one hand, and to intellectual notions like belief, judgment, inference on the other.

Sense-perception obviously involves the senses, but exactly how? Very often we perceive things otherwise than as they are, sometimes knowingly and sometimes not. The penny seen from one side looks elliptical, the candle seen out of focus looks double, the whistle seems to change pitch as the train passes. All this has suggested, by the *argument from illusion*, that what we 'directly' or 'immediately' perceive or are aware of (often called SENSE DATA, etc.) sometimes or always differs from what is 'out there' in the world: we perceive objects by interpreting or inferring from these sense data. More radically, the fact that we sometimes seem to perceive when we are not strictly perceiving at all, as when we dream or hallucinate, suggests SCEPTICISM about how we can know that an external world exists at all. The former position may be reinforced because we know scientifically how the physical and physiological processes involved inevitably affect the information we get through our senses.

If we do try to start from a basis limited to 'pure experience', it is difficult, as empiricists from Locke and Hume onwards have found, to get beyond it. The sense data, etc. supposed to serve as a bridge between us and the world end up as a drawbridge that keeps us from the world. This attempt has been attacked in two ways. Firstly, the arguments for it are suspect, and seem self-defeating. We can only contrast appearance with reality if we already have independent knowledge of reality, and the fact that we may be deceived on any occasion does not imply that we may, or even could, be deceived on every occasion. Secondly, it seems impossible to isolate and describe any 'pure experience' (the *given*). Not only does all describing involve language, and so memory, but experience is ineradicably affected by context and knowledge. The retinal image has two dimensions, but we see the world as having three, even with one eye closed. The penny looks round, as much as it looks elliptical (has 'looks' two senses here?), and continues to look so while being turned or moved (*object constancy*). We select part of what we see as foreground, seen against a background (the *figure/ground* theory emphasized by *Gestalt psychologists*), and there is the duck/rabbit phenomenon (see SEEING). As artists know, *perceptual reduction*, abstracting a basic 'pure experience' from our perceptions, is difficult or impossible.

Yet the facts remain that perception involves the senses, that perceptions are normally the basis for beliefs, and that illusions do occur. Any theory of perception should answer questions like these: Is there direct or immediate awareness or pure experience, and if so, has it special objects? If it has, how are these related to physical objects or parts of them, including their surfaces? Do words like 'looks', 'seems', 'appears', imply doubt, and are they ambiguous? Is perception something unitary, or has it two parts, a sensory part involving this 'direct' awareness and some process of interpretation or judgment based on this? If two parts, are they successive or simultaneous? Does a single account hold for different modes of perception such as seeing, hearing, etc.? Do we in fact perceive physical objects at all? Or do we only infer their existence? Or do we treat them as LOGICAL CONSTRUCTIONS (cf. PHENOMENALISM)? If we do perceive physical objects (and shadows, etc.), under what conditions do we do so? Must we know we are doing so? Must we notice or pick out the object? Are there really such things as unconscious and subliminal perception? What features of an object can we perceive? Its colour? Shape? Nature? Behaviour? Causal properties? Beauty? Suitability for this or that? Does the object play a causal role, and if so, what does it cause, our having an experience or our perceiving the object? And does this role enter the analysis of what we *mean* by saying we perceive the object, so that to say we perceive something is to say, among other things, that it causes us to do something? Or is it merely that our perceptions of it, or our accompanying experiences, are always in fact caused partly by it?

Views giving causation a role in one of the these ways are among *causal theories of perception*. *Representative* (*representational*) *theories* say either that what we perceive is not the object but something else (sense data, etc.) representing it, or that we do perceive the object but only by being directly aware (etc.) of such representatives which may or may not be *parts* of the object. Causal and representative theories often go together. *Realist theories* say that whatever it is that is perceived exists independently of being perceived. *Naïve realism* is properly the view, attributed to the 'plain man', that we not only perceive ordinary objects but perceive them as they are, by a direct relation without sense data,

Perfection

interpretations, etc., and with 'as they are' raising no problems. There is a paradox in attributing any philosophical view to the 'plain' non-philosophical man, and in practice 'naïve realism' often starts by meaning whatever the plain man would say without reflection (i.e. discounting illusions, etc.) and ends, as the argument develops, by meaning simply realism..

Perceptual usually applies to things as they appear to the perceiver. Thus *perceptual consciousness* is the total conscious experience of the perceiver qua perceiver. *Perceptual objects* are whatever it is one perceives be it sense data, physical objects, or whatever, considered as having just those characteristics they are perceived as having. These are *perceptual characteristics* (what these are may be unclear, as in the penny case above). *Perceptible characteristics*, however, are those accessible to perception (e.g. colour but not magnetism). The *perceptual field* is the total of a person's perceptual objects at a given moment, not necessarily distinguished as separate objects. *Perceived object* refers usually to the physical or public object (or shadow, etc.) perceived, considered as having the characteristics it really has. *Percept* is similar to 'perceptual object'. It sometimes refers to sense data, but sometimes to the contents of perceptual consciousness for those *not* holding a sense datum theory (Firth). See also SENSES, SENSATION, SENSE DATA, SEEING, FEELING, PHENOMENALISM.

R. J. Swartz (ed.), *Perceiving, Sensing, and Knowing*, 1965.

G. J. Warnock (ed.), *The Philosophy of Perception*, 1967. (Two volumes of essays, both with bibliographies).

R. J. Hirst, *The Problems of Perception*, 1959. (Introduction, advocating one view.)

E. H. Gombrich, *Art and Illusion*, 1960.

E. H. Wolgast, 'The experience in perception', *Philosophical Review*, 1960. (These two argue against isolatability of experience in perception, Gombrich from point of view of art and with plentiful illustrations.)

R. Firth, 'Sense-data and the percept theory', *Mind*, 1949–50, reprinted with important addendum (p. 270) in Swartz. (Develops and discusses 'percept theory' as against sense datum theory, and discusses perceptual reduction.)

J. P. Day, G. N. A. Vesey, 'Unconscious perception', *Proceedings of the Aristotelian Society*, supplementary vol., 1960. (Cf. also A. R. White, *Attention*, 1964, pp. 52–6.)

J. Teichmann, 'Perception and causation', *Proceedings of the Aristotelian Society*, 1970–1. (See also Warnock and Swartz volumes.)

D. W. Hamlyn, *The Psychology of Perception*, 1957. (Discusses Gestalt and other theories from philosophical standpoint.) *Sensation and Perception*, 1961. (General history with own views in last chapter.) *The Theory of Knowledge*, 1970. (Has chapter on perception.)

Perfection (principle of). See SUFFICIENT REASON.

Performatives. See SPEECH ACTS.

Phenomenalism

Peripheric. See JAMES-LANGE THEORY.

Perlocutions. See SPEECH ACTS.

Person. Certain modern writers use 'person' in a technical way to stand for a type of entity different from material objects and disembodied spirits. P. F. Strawson (1919–) insists that persons are not reducible to these other things. He distinguishes *M-predicates*, applying to both material bodies and persons (e.g. weighing ten stone), from *P-predicates*, applying only to persons (e.g. thinking, going for a walk). Others have made a similar distinction. Some P-predicates, however, may apply to persons only because they have bodies (e.g. going for a walk).

P. F. Strawson, *Individuals*, 1959, chapter 3.
T. Forrest, 'P-predicates', in A. Stroll (ed.), *Epistemology*, 1967. (Discusses Strawson.)

Personalism. Any of a wide variety of views emphasizing the primacy, in the universe, of persons (non-technical sense), whether human or divine.

R. T. Flewelling, 'Personalism', in D. D. Runes (ed.), *Twentieth-Century Philosophy*, 1943. (General survey.)
P. A. Bertocci, 'The perspective of a teleological personalistic idealist', in John E. Smith (ed.), *Contemporary American Philosophy*, 2nd series, 1970.

Phase terms, universals. See IDENTITY.

Phenomena. See NOUMENON, PHENOMENOLOGY.

Phenomenalism. Literally, a theory based on appearances. Earlier phenomenalists analysed physical objects in terms of actual and possible sensations (Mill: 'Matter is the permanent possibility of sensations'). More recently phenomenalism has taken a linguistic form. Its main claim has been that sentences about physical objects can be analysed without residue into sentences about SENSE DATA, which Moore and Russell distinguish from SENSATIONS. Its point, in both earlier and later forms, is that we can only know appearances, but need not postulate unknowable objects lurking behind them, because belief or talk about such objects is really only a disguised form of belief or talk about the appearances themselves. The phenomenalist goal of providing detailed translations of statements about physical objects was vigorously pursued before and just after the Second World War, but is now widely regarded as unattainable, even in principle.

Like subjective IDEALISM, from which perhaps it developed, phenomenalism makes appearances central. Subjective idealism says physical objects are unreal. Phenomenalism says they are real, but are not what

157

Phenomenology

they seem—they are appearances, actual or possible. See also PERCEPTION, PHILOSOPHY.

Primarily phenomenalism is a doctrine about physical objects. More broadly, any view can be called phenomenalist which uses LOGICAL CONSTRUCTIONS.

J. S. Mill, *An Examination of Sir William Hamilton's Philosophy*, 1865, chapter 11, appendix to chapter 12. (Early version of phenomenalism.)

A. J. Ayer, *Foundations of Empirical Knowledge*, 1940. (Defence of modern phenomenalism. Cf. his later view in 'Phenomenalism', *Proceedings of the Aristotelian Society*, 1946–7, reprinted in his *Philosophical Essays*, 1954.)

J. Hospers, *Introduction to Philosophical Analysis*, 1956, chapter 8. (Discusses phenomenalism in relation to other theories.)

Phenomenology. Literally, the description or study of appearances. Any description of how things appear, especially if sustained and penetrating, can be called a phenomenology. The close attention given by linguistic PHILOSOPHY to the actual workings of language is sometimes called *linguistic phenomenology*. But more specifically 'phenomenology' refers to a movement starting with Brentano and associated especially with Husserl. This at first emphasized the description of human experience as directed onto objects, in the sense in which thoughts or wishes have objects, even if unreal ones ('intentional objects'; see INTENSIONALITY). In Husserl the emphasis shifted away from the mere description of experience towards a description of the objects of experience, which he called phenomena. Phenomena were things which appear. He saw them in fact as essences which the mind intuited, and the task of phenomenology was to describe them. This, however, was not an empirical task, but an a priori one. It resembled in fact what was later called conceptual analysis (see PHILOSOPHY), though it insisted that the essences were real things, not, for example, ways in which words were used. (We can still think of unreal things like unicorns; the essence of unicorn is real.) Phenomenology also led on to the study of being, associated with EXISTENTIALISM. Husserl thought that studying essences as they were intuited involved laying aside various preconceptions derived from science; this laying aside was called *reduction, epoche*, or *bracketing* the world.

E. Husserl, *Cartesian Meditations*, 1931 (French), 1950 (German), 1960 (English). Cf. also his *The Idea of Phenomenology*, 1907, transl. 1964, and *The Paris Lectures*, 1929, transl. 1964.

G. Ryle, *Collected Papers*, vol. 1, 1971. (Includes several relevant items. Chapter 10 brings out some connexions with conceptual analysis, and chapter 12 some with existentialism.)

M. Warnock, *Existentialism*, 1970. (Includes chapter on Husserl.)

H. Spiegelberg, *The Phenomenological Movement*, 1960. (Extended history, ending with philosophical summary.)

Philosophy and analysis. An embarrassment for the professional philosopher is that he cannot produce any succinct, or even agreed, definition of his profession. 'What is philosophy?' is itself a philosophical question.

Literally meaning 'love of wisdom', 'philosophy' came to stand for knowledge in general about man and the universe. The Stoics and Epicureans (c.BC 300) divided knowledge into logic (including also what is now called epistemology), physics (including all that we now call science), and ethics (including also what we now call philosophy of mind and psychology). *Natural philosophy*, dealing with the world of nature, and *moral philosophy*, dealing with man, were the descendents of physics and ethics, respectively, in these senses. 'Natural philosophy' is now, when used at all, limited to physics while 'moral philosophy' is normally limited to ETHICS. Metaphysics, which the Stoics and Epicureans had largely assimilated into physics, became assimilated to natural theology, and became the centre of philosophy, after Aquinas had separated natural from revealed or dogmatic theology.

Only in the last century or two have the sciences become so specialized that philosophy appears as simply one discipline among others. There are two main ways of distinguishing it, by its subject-matter or its methods. Many have held that its subject is in some way 'ultimate things', either about the universe as a whole or about matters affecting human fate and conduct in the most basic way. Now, however, philosophy is more commonly distinguished by certain methods, its subject being whatever is most suitably studied by them. In particular, philosophy avoids using the senses and relies on reflection. It is an a priori study. In developing from its older to its modern form it has shed the sciences one by one as they became amenable to systematic empirical study rather than armchair speculation—first physics and chemistry, and then the human sciences (economics, psychology, sociology). But philosophy also lacks any definite and systematic procedures for proving results. Mathematics has therefore always lain rather outside philosophy, and mathematical LOGIC, though needed more than ever as a tool by philosophy, is itself now becoming a separate subject, allied to mathematics.

All this circumscribes the subject-matter of philosophy. What particular things the world contains is for science to say, but philosophy can ask about the different ways in which we can classify *whatever* the world, or any world, contains (cf. CATEGORIES, METAPHYSICS). Again science gives us knowledge, but philosophy asks what we *can* know, and how (EPISTEMOLOGY).

One role, then, of philosophy is to look behind or after (*meta-*) the sciences and analyse the concepts (notions, ideas) and methods they use. A given science X, often has an associated 'philosophy of X' (or 'meta-X') which fulfils this role. METAPHYSICS, where 'physics' means the study of nature in general, is the most general of these studies, though questions of scientific *method* now form a separate study, philosophy of SCIENCE.

Analysis, in some sense, is always therefore an important part of philosophy. Under the influence of POSITIVISM and allied trends, much twentieth-century English-speaking philosophy has assumed that substantive results

Philosophy and analysis

in subjects like ethics, politics and aesthetics could not be reached by rational argument. These subjects were matters of attitude and persuasion. Philosophy, it was often thought, should simply analyse concepts (*conceptual analysis*). It should become *analytical philosophy*, using *philosophical analysis*.

Analysis, however, is ambiguous. It can mean simply the explication of concepts like *substance, cause, good, material object*, asking, for example, what things count as material objects and what they all have in common. In this ordinary sense all philosophy involves analysis. But two technical senses of 'analysis' are often contrasted. *Philosophical, reductive* or *new-level analysis*, analyses entities *away* into others at a deeper level which replace them. A stock example is the PHENOMENALIST analysis of material objects, which, while not denying their reality, reduces statements about them to statements about possibilities of sensation (cf. LOGICAL CONSTRUCTIONS). *Logical* or *same-level analysis*, claims simply to show the correct logical form of ordinary sentences (cf. theory of DESCRIPTIONS), and makes no metaphysical claims about material objects, etc. Even this, however, is in fact reductive, since it condemns some ways of speaking and replaces them. Both 'philosophical analysis' and 'logical analysis', however, can also mean simply conceptual analysis, of any of these kinds, as against physical analysis.

After the Second World War a reaction against the restrictions of logical positivism, and the failure of phenomenalism, suggested that any consistent outlook or set of concepts (e.g. in ethics or religion) was prima facie as good as any other, and that philosophy should analyse what is involved in everyday ways of speaking and thinking, without trying to judge between them. Like logical analysis this emphasizes ways of speaking, but it is no longer reductive. It is called *linguistic* or *ordinary language philosophy*, using *linguistic analysis*, and was often condemned as evading the real problems. Ordinary language philosophy need not, as its enemy Russell thought, be done *in* ordinary language, i.e. without technical terms. Philosophy of LANGUAGE is different, being a subject, not an outlook.

The *paradox of analysis* arose on analysing, for example, the concept *brother* into the concept *male sibling*. If they are the same concept, differently named, no analysis has occurred. If they are different concepts, how can one analyse the other? Hence the analysis must apparently be either trivial or wrong. This raised the question, among others, what CONCEPTS are.

Recent English-speaking philosophy (on which this entry has concentrated; for other kinds cf. PHENOMENOLOGY, EXISTENTIALISM, IDEALISM) is now bolder in making substantive claims. But it still, like linguistic philosophy, relies on the English language, and feels discomfort, if no more, at outraging common sense. It relies heavily on the techniques of formal logic, but is more sensitive to its debt to the empirical sciences, e.g. relativity physics and Freudian psychology—though the philosopher must still have an eye for the difference between questions for reflection and questions for observation. Observation may stimulate, but can never solve, philosophical problems.

See also AESTHETICS, EPISTEMOLOGY, ETHICS, LOGIC, METAPHYSICS, POLITICAL PHILOSOPHY, SOCIAL PHILOSOPHY, Philosophies of EDUCATION, HISTORY, LANGUAGE, LAW, MATHEMATICS, MIND, RELIGION, SCIENCE.

B. Russell, *The Problems of Philosophy*, 1912. (Dated in detail but still standard as introduction.)

A. Flew, *An Introduction to Western Philosophy*, 1971. (Rather traditionalist in approach, written in light of, but with little emphasis on, contemporary developments.)

J. A. Passmore, *100 Years of Philosophy*, 1957, 2nd (revised) edn 1966. (Full, documented and readable. Tends to conflate important and unimportant.)

J. O. Urmson, *Philosophical Analysis*, 1956. (Two main inter-war movements, LOGICAL ATOMISM and logical POSITIVISM. Ambiguity of 'analysis'.)

G. Ryle (ed.), *The Revolution in Philosophy*, 1956. (Philosophy as it saw itself about 1950.)

B. Russell, *My Philosophical Development*, 1959. (Final chapter attacks linguistic philosophy.)

C. H. Langford, 'Moore's notion of analysis', in P. A. Schilpp (ed.), *The Philosophy of G. E. Moore*, 1942. (Analysis in Moore. See p. 323 for paradox, and pp. 660 ff. for Moore's reply.)

Phrastic and neustic. Sentences like 'The door is shut', 'Shut the door!', 'Is the door shut?' seem to have something in common as well as differences. R. M. Hare (1919–   ) called what they had in common the *phrastic* (roughly, what is said, or the content) and what was peculiar to each of them the *neustic* (from the Greek for assenting or subscribing). The phrastic might be represented as 'The door being shut' and the respective neustics as 'Yes', 'Please', 'Query'. Thus the first sentence would be analysed as, 'The door being shut: yes.' Later Hare distinguished also the *tropic*, or sign of mood (from the Greek for 'mood'), from the neustic, which he kept for assent or subscription. See also SENTENCES, SPEECH ACTS.

R. M. Hare, *The Language of Morals*, 1952. (See index. Original distinction. For tropics see his 'Meaning and speech acts', *Philosophical Review*, 1970, pp. 19 ff., reprinted with appendix in R. M. Hare, *Practical Inferences*, 1971, pp. 89 ff.)

Physicalism. See POSITIVISM.

Physico-theological argument. See DESIGN.

Plato. 428–348 BC. Earliest European philosopher of whom substantial works survive. Pupil of SOCRATES. founder of Academy (probably c.385 BC), teacher of ARISTOTLE. Lived mostly in Athens, with occasional visits to Sicily where he tried unsuccessfully to put into practice the ideal state of his dialogue *Republic*. Contributed to all the main branches of philosophy, notably with his theory of 'FORMS' or 'IDEAS'. Wrote some thirty-four dialogues, which all survive. See also ALBERT, BEAUTIFUL, BEING,

Platonism

CONCEPT, DIALECTIC, EDUCATION, EMPIRICISM, IDEALISM, INCONTINENCE, LANGUAGE (PHILOSOPHY OF), MEANING, METAPHYSICS, NEOPLATONISTS, POLITICAL, PYTHAGORAS, SCEPTICISM, SOPHISTS, SUBSTANCE, UNIVERSALS.

Platonism. See UNIVERSALS, MATHEMATICS.

Pleasure. An agreeable quality of experiences or the experiences themselves. An ambiguity exists between 'pleasure' in general and 'pleasure' in the sense of a pleasant activity or experience, a source of pleasure in the first sense. 'Pleasure' can also mean something like 'will' as in 'at the king's pleasure'.

Philosophers discuss primarily the first sense, and start by asking what pleasure is. It has often, especially in connexion with HEDONISM, been regarded simply as 'agreeable feeling'. But competing accounts have been offered, especially recently. Pleasure has been thought to be a process, or a kind of activity, or to be essentially connected with attention or desire. *Adverbial theories* make pleasure a modification of activity, so that 'experiencing pleasure' means something like 'living pleasurably'. The relations between pleasure and enjoyment, liking, pain, etc., and the relations between terms like 'pleasing', 'pleasant', 'pleasurable', 'unpleasant', 'painful', are also much discussed. Special problems concern asceticism and masochism: Does anything count as disliking or failing to like pleasure, or as liking or failing to dislike pain?

Discussions of hedonism have raised the question whether pleasure can be measured. Can pleasures, or amounts of pleasure, whether of the same or different people, be compared and added together, or arranged in order of magnitude? Are there any bad pleasures? Can pleasure itself be bad, or only its source? *Qualitative hedonism*, a form of ethical HEDONISM, says pleasures differ in quality as well as quantity, and some are better than others. How pleasure relates to happiness is also important for hedonism and utilitarianism.

A particular set of problems concern pleasure and belief, and the notion of being pleased that. . . . How is pleasure related to what one is pleased at, by, etc., especially when the object is illusory? How are the object and the cause of a pleasure related? Can pleasures themselves ever be false, as against merely resting on false beliefs? Can one be mistaken about whether one is pleased, etc.? See also UTILITARIANISM.

D. L. Perry, *The Concept of Pleasure*, 1967. (General discussion of what pleasure is, and how it relates to neighbouring concepts and expressions.)

J. C. B. Gosling, *Pleasure and Desire*, 1969. (Discusses hedonism in light of modern treatments of pleasure.)

M. A. McCloskey, 'Pleasure', *Mind*, 1971. (Asymmetries between pleasure and pain.)

J. C. Hall, 'Quantity of pleasure', *Proceedings of the Aristotelian Society*, 1966–7. (Can pleasure be measured?)

J. S. Mill, *Utilitarianism*, 1861, chapter 2. (Qualitative hedonism. See J. Plamenatz, *The English Utilitarians*, 1949, p. 137; this volume includes Mill.)

D. A. Lloyd Thomas, 'Happiness', *Philosophical Quarterly*, 1968
J. Dybikowski, 'False pleasure and the *Philebus*', *Phronesis*, 1970.
(False pleasure and Plato. Fairly difficult, with occasional Greek, but
refers to other literature.)

Plenitude (principle of). Principle that the universe, to be as perfect as
possible, must be as full as possible: must contain the greatest possible
diversity of kinds in the greatest possible profusion compatible with the
laws of nature. Cf. the idea that existence is a perfection. An alternative
version is that nothing can remain a real but unactualized possibility
throughout eternity.

A. O. Lovejoy, *The Great Chain of Being*, 1936.
J. Hintikka, *Time and Necessity*, 1973, chapter 5. (Discusses principle in
Aristotle, criticizing Lovejoy.)

Poisson's theorem. See NUMBERS.

Polar concepts. Concepts which allegedly only have application if their
opposites have application, e.g. *good* and *evil*, if it is true that there could
be nothing good in the universe unless there were something evil for it to
contrast with, and vice versa.

C. K. Grant, 'Polar concepts and metaphysical arguments', *Proceedings of
the Aristotelian Society*, 1955–6. (Cf. also Heraclitus, fragments B23,
111 (Diels).)

Political philosophy. Often loosely called *politics*. Political philosophy
studies both substantive questions and concepts used in them. Substantive questions have returned to favour recently, as in ETHICS. The basic
concern is with authority and sovereignty in groups of people not subject
to further authority (sovereign states), and with associated organizational
questions.

The notions of authority and obedience lead to two groups of questions.
The first concerns the nature and purpose of the state, its ultimate justification or dispensability, and the relations between it and its citizens. Is the
state a real entity with a life of its own? Is it founded on divine right, natural
law, utility, or social contract—a contract whereby its citizens or their
ancestors have somehow, perhaps by not emigrating, pledged themselves
to behave in certain ways? Does the state exist for its own sake? Or to
promote the real or supposed interests of its citizens, or of some of them?
Or to guarantee its citizens maximum freedom from mutual interference?
Are there limits to the power it should have over its citizens, and can its
citizens ever properly disobey, secede, or engage in revolution?

The second group of questions, which is not independent of the first,
concerns different types of constitution, and where sovereignty lies within
them. Should only some citizens or inhabitants of the relevant area have
the right to participate politically, and if so, which? By what methods may
the sovereign body justifiably reach its decisions, and in particular,

Polyadic

especially in modern times, what are the forms of direct and representative democracy, and how acceptable are they? What rights should belong to minorities and those excluded from participation? What are the basis and limits of property and privilege?

The two groups come together in questions about ideal states or utopias and ideals in general, like the various forms of liberty and equality.

Further questions concern the use of force by the state and its citizens, both internally and externally, the relations of sovereign states with each other, and transfers of sovereignty both within and between sovereign states.

Political science studies actual past and present political institutions, and explains rather than justifies them. Political philosophy and political science are each often called *political theory*.

Plato, *Crito* (obedience), *Republic* (ideal state), *Statesman* (or *Politicus*: different constitutions; cf. *Republic*, book 8), *Laws* (second-best state).

Aristotle, *Politics*. (Books 4–6 discuss different constitutions, book 7–8 ideal state, while book 2 criticizes Plato.)

S. I. Benn and R. S. Peters, *Social Principles and the Democratic State*, 1959; American edn. 1964, entitled *Principles of Political Thought*. (Full-scale general introduction.)

A. Quinton (ed.), *Political Philosophy*, 1967. (Essays, with annotated bibliography.)

P. Laslett *et al.* (eds), *Philosophy, Politics and Society*, 4 vols, 1956, 1962, 1967, 1972. (Miscellaneous essays, reflecting development of subject since the war.)

Polyadic. See MONADIC.

Polymorphous. Literally, having many forms. Concept introduced by Ryle and applied, in particular, to THINKING. The general idea is that there is no particular action we must be engaged in to be thinking, and perhaps also that there is no overt action we could not engage in without thinking; but the detailed interpretation of polymorphousness is controversial.

J. O. Urmson, 'Polymorphous concepts', in O. P. Wood and G. Pitcher (eds), *Ryle*, 1970. (Cf. also ibid., pp. 77–8.)

D. L. Mouton, 'The concept of thinking', *Nous*, 1969. (Criticizes Ryle.)

Popper, Sir Karl R. 1902– . Austrian philosopher of science, and also political philosopher, born in Vienna. He was connected with the Vienna Circle (see POSITIVISM) in his youth but later migrated to New Zealand and then to England where he worked in London. He asserts that if a statement is to be scientific rather than metaphysical it must be falsifiable, but he does not, like the logical positivists, dismiss metaphysical statements as meaningless. He then bases his philosophy of science on the hypothetico-deductive method, claiming that enumerative INDUCTION is invalid, and indeed does not in fact occur, while verification and CONFIRMATION (as opposed to his own 'corroboration') are impossible. As his philosophy of

Positivism

science says we should aim to eliminate the false rather than establish the true, so, rather analogously, his political philosophy says we should aim to eliminate the bad rather than establish the good. *Logik der Forschung*, 1934–5, transl. with additions as *The Logic of Scientific Discovery*, 1959. *The Open Society and Its Enemies*, 1945. *The Poverty of Historicism*, 1957. See also BASIC STATEMENTS, CONCEPT, CONVENTIONALISM, EVIDENCE, FREE-WILL, HISTORICISM, INSTRUMENTALISM, PROBABILITY.

Positivism. Doctrine associated with Comte who adopted the term 'positive' to convey six features of things: being real, useful, certain, precise, organic, relative. He used it of his philosophy, which insisted on applying the scientific attitude not only to the sciences but also to human affairs. He saw the sciences as forming a natural sequence resting on mathematics and developing, both in order of logic and historically, through the physical and biological sciences to sociology (whose name he invented) and morals. Thought, he said, evolved from the theological attitude, explaining things by introducing gods, etc., through the metaphysical attitude involving a search for things-in-themselves and causes, to the scientific attitude stressing the observable. He emphasized synthesis, both of reason, feeling and action, which the two earlier attitudes had failed to balance, and of the various sciences, and even of the three attitudes, since the superseded ones still had their merits. This is why his list of features includes 'relative' and 'organic'. Positivism continued ever after to emphasize the unity of the sciences, and to confine science to the observable and manipulable. The evolutionary approach fitted well with nineteenth-century biological developments and with systems extending these to human affairs, like that of Herbert Spencer (1820–1903).

Comte, however, was more concerned to expound and apply scientific method than to examine it and ask what it presupposes. More critical, in the sense of stressing the limitations of what science can do, was Mach. For him, science aims at the most economical description of appearances, i.e. ultimately of our sense-experience, or sensations. Appearances are explained in the sense of being described in familiar terms, but no hidden entities or causes are postulated. Atoms, being unobservable are treated as a mere façon de parler (cf. PHENOMENALISM). This goes beyond the earlier positivism by criticizing notions (e.g. those of physical object and atom) that seem proper to science itself, not merely to metaphysics. Mach's outlook, and the similar one of R. Avenarius (1843–96), are sometimes called *empiriocriticism*.

Logical positivism is primarily associated with the *Vienna Circle* of the 1920s, whose most famous members were M. Schlick, Carnap, O. Neurath and Waismann. Wittgenstein and Popper were on its fringes. C. Hempel and H. Reichenbach in Berlin, and later Ayer in England, were its allies. It also influenced philosophy in America, Holland and Scandinavia. Schlick preferred the name *consistent empiricism*, and *logical empiricism* has a similar sense. The prefix 'logical' indicates partly that the topic for enquiry is meaning and partly that the doctrine is regarded as true as a matter of logic. Under the influence of Mach, and also of Hume, the Circle

165

Positivism

concentrated on the general problem of MEANING, and developed the *verification* or *verifiability* principle. This said that something is meaningful if and only if it is either verifiable empirically, i.e. ultimately (not necessarily directly) by observation through the senses, or is a TAUTOLOGY of logic or mathematics. The *verification theory* either *identifies* meaning with method of verification, or simply says that the verification principle is to be accepted.

Positivists have always tried to limit enquiry and belief to what can be firmly established. Following the empiricist tradition they have usually taken this to be primarily what we learn immediately from the senses. Metaphysics and theology they dismissed. Ethics and aesthetics they usually tried to assimilate as far as possible to sciences like psychology, later distinguishing different kinds of meaning (emotive, evaluative, prescriptive, etc.: see NATURALISM) to deal with what was left of them. But they found it difficult to deal with science, and most of everyday discourse (e.g. about material objects, other people, or the past), without letting metaphysics and sheer nonsense through. They sometimes required only verifiability in principle, not in practice. But then meaning can hardly be identified with the 'method' of verification, especially if in the end a statement is verifiable simply if we 'know what it would be like' for it to be true. And must verification be conclusive ('strong') or will mere provision of evidence ('weak' verification) suffice? Since few, if any, statements are strongly verifiable, much energy was devoted to elaborating 'weak' forms of the principle and a theory of CONFIRMATION, especially by Ayer and Carnap.

'Verify' may mean 'find to be true' or 'test for truth'. Carnap substituted 'test'. But Popper used the first sense, and argued that with universal affirmative statements like 'All swans are white', which he thought important for science, it is easier to falsify false ones than to verify true ones. He therefore emphasized falsifiability, not, however, as a criterion of meaningfulness but as demarcating scientific statements from metaphysical ones. He accepted both as meaningful.

Neurath and others thought that sentences could only properly be compared with sentences, not with the world. They therefore sympathized with the coherence theory of TRUTH. This sympathy was reinforced by the difficulty of verifying general laws.

Carnap emphasized the unity of science, and his *physicalism* claimed that all scientific statements could be translated into statements about physical objects, or space-time points (as against electrons, desires, social systems, etc.). He also insisted that meaningful statements must be verifiable publicly, not just by one person. 'Physicalism' is also used for the doctrine that all meaningful statements can be translated into the language of physics, and for the IDENTITY THEORY OF MIND.

Among questions facing the verification principle is whether it is itself a tautology, empirical or meaningless. One answer treats it as a recommendation. Other problems concern necessary statements (see MODALITIES): if, as logical positivists think, they assert nothing, of what use are they?

Operationalism or *operationism* stems from P. Bridgman and treats concepts rather as logical positivism treats statements: concepts must be defined in terms of the operations employed in applying them, e.g. length can be defined only in terms of techniques of measurement, so that length may be a different concept when applied to football pitches and stellar diameters.

Legal positivism names a complex variety of doctrines, only partly connected with positivism as above considered. The main connecting threads are emphasis on law as what is commanded or 'posited', and emphasis on law as it is (positive law) rather than as it should be (e.g. natural law). See also MEANING, REDUCTIONISM, CONFIRMATION, BASIC STATEMENTS, ANALYTIC, PRAGMATISM.

L. Kolakowski, *Positivist Philosophy*, 1966, transl. 1968. (Elementary introduction, mainly on earlier forms and related outlooks.)

A. Comte, *Discourse on the Positive Spirit*, 1844, transl. with analytical table of contents by E. S. Beesley 1903. (Popular exposition.)

E. Mach, *Popular Scientific Lectures*, 1898, pp. 186 ff. (Popular exposition.)

D. Hume, *Enquiry concerning Human Understanding*, 1748. (Last paragraph is famous forerunner of verification principle.)

M. Schlick, 'Meaning and verification', *Philosophical Review*, 1936, reprinted in H. Feigl and W. Sellars (eds), *Readings in Philosophical Analysis*, 1949. (Exposition and applications of verification theory.)

A. J. Ayer, *Language, Truth and Logic*, 1936, 2nd edn with important 'Introduction', 1946. (Classic statement in English of logical positivism.)

D. Makinson, 'Nidditch's definition of verifiability', *Mind*, 1965. (Difficulties in formulating verifiability principle. Moderately technical.)

J. L. Evans, 'Meaning and verification', *Mind*, 1953. (Critical discussion of development and presuppositions of logical positivism.)

A. J. Ayer (ed.), *Logical Positivism*, 1959. (General essays, including famous one by Hempel, and long bibliography.)

C. Hempel, 'On the Logical Positivists' theory of truth', *Analysis*, vol. 2, 1935.

R. Carnap, *The Unity of Science*, 1932, transl. with Introduction by M. Black, 1934. (Classic statement of physicalism.)

K. R. Popper, *The Logic of Scientific Discovery*, 1934, transl. with additions 1959. (Standard statement of Popper's falsificationist position.)

P. Bridgman, *The Logic of Modern Physics*, 1927. (Operationalism.)

A. C. Benjamin, *Operationism*, 1955. (General treatment.)

C. Hempel, 'A logical appraisal of operationism', *Scientific Monthly*, 1954, reprinted in his *Aspects of Scientific Explanation*, 1965. (Sympathetic discussion. Popper (above), p. 440, briefly criticizes operationalism. Cf. also C. Taylor, *The Explanation of Behaviour*, 1964, chapter 4.)

H. L. A. Hart, *The Concept of Law*, 1961, esp. p. 253. (Legal positivism.)

Possible. See MODALITIES.

Pour soi. See BAD FAITH.

Pragmatics. See SEMIOTIC.

Pragmatism

Pragmatism. Originally developed as a theory of meaning by Peirce who was concerned with the meaning of concepts affecting the intellect, especially scientific concepts, rather than those confined to the senses (like *red*) or emotions. He thought the meaning of such concepts, and of statements in which they appeared, was exhausted by the effects they could have on our experiences and actions. When the name became widely used for various related theories he used *pragmaticism* for his own particular version. This theory can be thought of as a looser form of operationalism (see POSITIVISM), and Peirce expressed an affinity for positivism.

Pragmatism is also often thought of as a theory of truth. Peirce made truth 'the opinion which is fated to be ultimately agreed to by all who investigate'. He seems to mean that truth is what would be believed if investigation continued indefinitely, whether or not it does continue; it is the limit where belief is finally stabilized. This side of pragmatism was developed by W. James, who differed from Peirce by including, and emphasizing, the effect of concepts on our senses and emotions. Truth, for James, is agreement with reality, but this means that it is what works or satisfies us. He seems to mean that the truth is whatever we ultimately find believable or consistent. But he allowed that our emotions might well, and properly, influence what we do ultimately find believable or consistent.

Other philosophers who have been labelled pragmatists include Dewey, F. C. S. Schiller (1864–1937) and C. I. Lewis (1883–1964). 'Pragmatism' is also sometimes used as a general label for views like CONVENTIONALISM and INSTRUMENTALISM, though these (especially instrumentalism) perhaps replace truth, at least in certain contexts, rather than define it.

J. Buchler (ed.), *The Philosophy of Peirce*, 1940. (Selections from Peirce. See especially chapters 2, 3 and 17, and for the quotation p. 38.)

W. James, *Pragmatism*, 1907.

W. James, *The Meaning of Truth*, 1909. (Selected essays, issued to clarify *Pragmatism*.)

A. Rorty (ed.), *Pragmatic Philosophy*, 1966. (Anthology.)

W. B. Gallie, *Peirce and Pragmatism*, 1952.

A. J. Ayer, *The Origins of Pragmatism*, 1968. (Treats Peirce and James.)

B. Aune, *Rationalism, Empiricism, and Pragmatism*, 1970. (Chapters 4 and 5 discuss modern versions of pragmatism.)

Predicate. What is said of (predicated of) a subject. In 'Grass is green' *grass* is the subject and *is green* is the predicate. (But in traditional formal logic, and loosely elsewhere, the predicate would be *green*, not *is green*.) A *subject/predicate sentence* is a sentence in which something is predicated of a subject as in 'Grass is green', as against, for example, conditional or existential sentences such as 'There are lions in Africa'. There is a certain ambiguity between whether a predicate is linguistic (a set of words) or non-linguistic (what the words in some sense stand for). See also MONAD.

Predicative. See ATTRIBUTIVE.

Prediction paradox. Some boys are told they will be examined next week, but will not know on which day until it arrives. It cannot be Saturday, or they would know on Friday night. But if Friday is the last possible day, it cannot be Friday either, or they would know on Thursday night. By repeating the argument the other days too are eliminated. Apparently, therefore, the examination cannot occur, under the conditions stated. Many other examples are used.

D. J. Connor, 'Pragmatic paradoxes', *Mind*, 1948, followed by discussions (still continuing) in subsequent issues of *Mind*.

Preface paradox. It seems paradoxical for an author to assert things in his book, and modestly add in his preface that his book probably contains errors. Can one coherently say, 'Some of my beliefs are false'?

Prescriptivism. See NATURALISM.

Presupposition. See IMPLICATION.

Price, H. H. (1899–) is an epistemologist and metaphysician who has written on PERCEPTION, BELIEF, THINKING and UNIVERSALS, and also on psychical research. See also SIDGWICK.

Price, Richard. 1723–91. Welsh philosopher and economist, born in Glamorgan, who worked as a clergyman in London. He supported the American and French revolutions. He was a leading representative of the 'intutionist' school of moral philosophy, which opposed the 'MORAL SENSE' theory of HUTCHESON and others. He insisted that our knowledge of right and wrong was derived from reason, and that right and wrong themselves were 'real characters of actions', not 'only qualities of our minds'. *A Review of the Principal Questions in Morals*, 1758.

Principle. See LAWS.

Private language. Anyone can invent a private Esperanto for his diary, but can languages, or parts of languages, be private in a more radical sense? In particular, can a language contain elements which it is logically impossible for anyone but its speaker to learn or understand?, e.g. can a language contain words which have meaning by standing for objects only accessible to the speaker? The importance of the question is that sensations, pains, etc., have been thought to be such objects, so that words which had meaning by standing for them would be private in the relevant sense. Three questions therefore are whether such a private language is possible, and, if not, how words like 'pain' do have meaning, and in what sense, if any, pains are private.

Wittgenstein seems to have argued that to use a language is to do something one may do correctly or incorrectly. One must therefore be able to check, at least in principle, that one is doing it correctly. But with a private

Probability

language no such checking would be possible. It is disputed whether this argument is sound, and also whether the alternative account that Wittgenstein himself gave of how words like 'pain' have meaning commits him to some form of behaviourism.

The issue is important in connexion with various kinds of scepticism. See also ACCESS.

O. R. Jones (ed.), *The Private Language Argument*, 1971. (Includes much of the important literature.)

J. T. Saunders and D. F. Henze, *The Private-Language Problem*, 1967. (Presents opposing attitudes in dialogue form, finally offering solution.)

Probability. *Probability theory* or the *calculus of chances* or *probabilities*, is the mathematical theory underlying probability arguments and most theories of induction with a mathematical basis. (See CONFIRMATION, where the relation between confirmation and probability is also discussed.) This calculus contains elementary rules governing results to be expected from tossing dice or drawing marbles from a bag. It also covers BAYES'S THEOREM, and topics like the law of large NUMBERS. Results within this theory are purely mathematical, and are not predictions about what actual dice, etc. will do. Use of the theory simply draws out the logical implications of assumptions already made.

Various theories have been offered about the nature of probability. The *classical theory* defines an event's probability as the proportion of alternatives, among all those possible in a given situation, that include the event in question. There are 36 possible results of tossing two dice, of which 11 include at least one six, so the probability of getting at least one six in a throw of two dice is 11/36. But the alternatives must be equiprobable (equally probable)—or equispecific, if 'equiprobable' seems question-begging in an analysis of 'probable'. This is hard to ensure. Attempts to ensure it have often used the principle of INDIFFERENCE. Other difficulties concern the probability of theories such as Darwinism, and cases where the alternatives are not obviously finite and definite in number, e.g. the probability that all swans including future ones are white. BERTRAND'S PARADOX and BERTRAND'S BOX PARADOX become relevant here. Kneale's 'range' theory attempts to answer some of these difficulties. *Range* is used elsewhere too. For Carnap a proposition's range is the set of state-descriptions compatible with it. See CONFIRMATION.)

The *frequency theory* defines probability in terms of the ratio of times something happens to times it might happen. If the proportion of smokers who die of cancer remains steady at 10 per cent then the probability of smokers dying of cancer is 10 per cent. If probability is defined in terms of frequency in a finite class one may be tempted into the GAMBLER'S FALLACY. For this and other reasons the probability is defined as the limit, in the mathematical sense, to which the frequency tends in the long run. We often talk of the probability of single events, e.g. that Smith will die of cancer, and it is disputed how, if at all, the frequency theory can account for this. Also the notion of a limiting frequency raises a problem because in an infinite or open-ended series, such as tosses of a coin, any limiting frequency is compatible with any result in a finite run. If a penny falls heads a million times running the limiting frequency of heads could still be a half if it fell tails the next million. Therefore in applying the theory we seem to have to say things like '*Probably* the limiting frequency is this' or '*Probably* present trends of cancer among smokers will continue', where 'probably' is unexplained.

The *logical relation theory* makes probability a logical relation between evidence and a conclusion, rather like entailment (see IMPLICATION) only weaker (cf. CONFIRMATION). Probability is therefore always relative to evidence. Apart from the difficulty of finding such a relation, one defect of this theory as an analysis of 'probably' is that if we know a true proposition, p, which entails another, q, we can assert q, but if p only makes q probable, we can at best say 'Probably q', which leaves 'probably' unanalysed—and even that we cannot say if we know there is another true proposition which makes q improbable.

The *subjectivist theory* analyses probability in terms of degrees of belief. A crude version would simply identify the statement that something is probable with the statement that the speaker is more inclined to believe it than to disbelieve it. Degrees of belief may be measured in terms of the bets the believer would be willing to place, and more refined versions of the theory say one is only entitled to use 'probably' if one's bets are 'coherent', in the sense that one does not bet on contradictory propositions in such a way that one is bound to lose whatever happens. This, however, still bases probability on the attitudes of the believer. Because 'coherence' is required, subjectivism is sometimes described as the view that probability is the degree of the rational man's belief. However, when this means that calling something probable is saying that it is rational to believe it, it is not subjectivist, since it no longer analyses probability in terms of beliefs actually held. It then has no special name.

Another version of the subjectivist theory is the *speech act theory*. To call something probable is not to describe one's belief but to express it. To say war is probable is to say, but only tentatively, that war will occur. Like other SPEECH ACT analyses (e.g. of 'good', 'true') this faces the objection that it ignores cases like 'If war were probable we would emigrate', where it is not being even tentatively asserted that war will occur.

Between them these theories try to account for the ideas that probability is objective and not of our choosing, and yet is somehow relative to our knowledge, since things in the world are either so or not so, and not probably so. Problems also arise over when to say something *was* probable, especially if eventually it never happened.

Many recent writers think that there is more than one kind of probability. They often distinguish between probability as a logical relation, where probability statements are true or false as a matter of logic (Carnap's *probability₁*), and probability as relative frequency, where probability statements are empirical statistical statements which form the material for the mathematical calculus of chances (Carnap's *probability₂*). Some, like the frequency theorist Reichenbach, hold the *identity conception of*

Probability

probability, saying that these two kinds are really one. Surely, however, one should distinguish at least three kinds of statement: empirical statistical statements, like 'The probability of an Englishman being a catholic is 10 per cent', where this just means that 10 per cent are so, purely mathematical statements, like 'The probability of a double six with two throws of a true die is 1/36, where this makes no prediction about any actual dice, and 'ordinary' probability statements, like 'The probability of Smith being a catholic is high', 'The probability of a six with this die is low', 'The probability of rain tomorrow is high', 'The probability of Darwinism being true is high'. These 'ordinary' statements may of course themselves be of various kinds, and may rest on statistical or mathematical statements.

Probabilities are called *absolute, a priori* or *prior* if they are considered as relative either to nothing or to the general background of knowledge rather than to some real or assumed set of evidence statements; otherwise they are *relative* or *conditional*. When a certain probability is assumed, e.g. the probability of an *a* which is *b* being *c*, the probability of an *a* which is *c* being *b* is called the *inverse* probability (cf. BAYES'S THEOREM). This notion raises no problems itself, but has been put to controversial uses, as a result of which LIKELIHOOD has been introduced.

Probabilism is the view that scientists can and should seek to attach positive probabilities to their hypotheses, i.e. to confirm them. Popper's opposing view that this is impossible and that the scientist should seek the most improbable, i.e. the most easily falsifiable, hypothesis is sometimes called *improbabilism*. See also CONFIRMATION.

H. E. Kyburg, *Probability and Inductive Logic*, 1970. (Part 1 gives basis of calculus of chances and discusses various theories of probability. Includes exercises and bibliographies.)

W. C. Kneale, *Probability and Induction*, 1949. (Includes brief treatment of calculus of chances and discussion (sometimes difficult) of various theories, as well as giving his own range theory. C. D. Broad's review in *Mind*, 1950 is helpful.)

R. Von Mises, *Probability, Statistics and Truth*, 1928, transl. 1939. (Nontechnical account of one version of frequency theory (first chapter), followed by discussion and applications.)

J. M. Keynes, *A Treatise on Probability*, 1921. (Chapter 1 defends logical relation theory. See also chapter 4 for principle of indifference.)

S. E. Toulmin, 'Probability', *Proceedings of the Aristotelian Society*, supplementary vol., 1950, reprinted in A. Flew (ed.), *Essays in Conceptual Analysis*, 1956, and in revised form as chapter 2 of Toulmin's *The Uses of Argument*, 1958. (Speech act theory.)

R. Swinburne, *An Introduction to Confirmation Theory*, 1973. (First two chapters discuss kinds of probability.)

R. Carnap, 'The two concepts of probability', *Philosophy and Phenomenological Research*, 1945, reprinted in H. Feigl and W. Sellars (eds), *Readings in Philosophical Analysis*, 1949, and in H. Feigl and M. Brodbeck (eds), *Readings in the Philosophy of Science*, 1953. (Cf. also his book *Logical Foundations of Probability*, 1950, and, for another version, J. O. Urmson, 'Two of the senses of "probable" ', *Analysis*, vol. 8, 1947, reprinted in M. Macdonald (ed.), *Philosophy and Analysis*, 1954.)

H. Reichenbach, *Experience and Prediction*, 1938. (§ 33 advocates identity conception, and discusses single events.)

A. J. Ayer, *The Concept of A Person*, 1963. (Chapter 7 discusses logical relation theory, and single events. Criticized by C. G. Hempel, *Aspects of Scientific Explanation*, 1965, pp. 65–6.)

I. Hacking, *The Emergence of Probability*, 1975. (Historical.)

Problematic. See MODALITIES.

Proof theory. See METAMATHEMATICS, LOGIC.

Proper. It is convenient to allow a whole to count as one of its parts, a class as one of its subclasses, etc. 'Proper' is used to exclude these special cases, e.g. a proper part is a part smaller than the whole.

Property. (i) Any characteristic. (ii) A characteristic relevant for the indiscernibility of identicals (see LEIBNIZ'S LAW). Tully is the same as Cicero, but 'Tully is hereby named by a five-letter name' is true, while 'Cicero is hereby named by a five-letter name' is false. *Being hereby named by a five-letter name* is therefore not a property in this sense. It may, however, be doubted whether it is a characteristic at all. (iii) A positive, as against negative, characteristic. (iv) A non-relational characteristic, e.g. *being red*, but not *being a brother*. (v) The Aristotelian and medieval *proprium*: a characteristic following from, and unique to, the essence of a species, but not part of its definition. *Able to laugh* is a proprium of man, if only man can have it but man is not defined as a laughing animal.

Propositional acts, attitudes, verbs. See SENTENCES.

Propositions. See SENTENCES.

Proprium. See PROPERTY.

Protocol statements. See BASIC STATEMENTS.

Psychologism. The practice of taking problems or concepts to be psychological when they are not, and failing to distinguish the psychological from the non-psychological. Adducing psychological evidence for philosophical, etc., theories, whether explicitly or through confusion.

Psychology (philosophical). See MIND.

Psychophysical parallelism. Doctrine that mental events and physical (in particular, bodily) events form separate chains, with causal relations holding or not holding within each chain, but not between the chains.

Pythagoras

The apparent connexions between the chains can be attributed to God. Associated in one form with Leibniz. See also OCCASIONALISM.

Pythagoras. Late sixth century BC. Born in Samos, he migrated to south Italy and founded Pythagorean 'brotherhood' whose doctrines, even centuries later, were often attributed to him. He was probably the first to see the connexion between musical harmonies and ratios of string lengths, and the idea that simple ratios underlay basic harmonies may be what led him and his followers to develop arithmetic and geometry (including 'Pythagoras' theorem'), and in various ways to try and explain reality itself in terms of numbers. They may have originated the ideas (though without providing compelling evidence) that the earth is spherical and not the centre of the universe. They also developed religious ideas about the soul and reincarnation, together with rules for a 'way of life'. Both their mathematical and their religious ideas considerably influenced Plato. See also METAPHYSICS, NIETZSCHE.

E. Schrödinger, *Nature and the Greeks*, 1954. (Contains sympathetic appreciation by famous modern physicist.)

Q

_____

Quality-word. See METAPHYSICS.

Quantification. Literally, specification as to quantity. Two kinds of proposition are very important for formal logic, those saying something about everything, or everything of a given kind, and those saying something about at least one thing, or at least one thing of a given kind. There are therefore two main *quantifiers*. (In what follows, x is an individual VARIABLE.) The *universal quantifier* 'binding' (see VARIABLE) x is read 'For all (any, every) x', and is symbolized '(x)' or '($\forall$x)', occasionally '(Πx)' The *particular* (or *existential*) *quantifier* is read 'For some (i.e. at least one) x' or 'There exists at least one x such that', and is symbolized '($\exists$x)' or '(Ex)', occasionally '(Σx)'). (Except with '(x)' the brackets are sometimes dropped.) Thus, using 'Rx' for 'x is red', typical sentences might be '(x)(Rx)' meaning 'For all x, x is red', i.e. 'Everything is red', and '($\exists$x)(Rx)' meaning 'For some x, x is red', i.e. 'There is at least one red thing'. The 'x' in the first bracket in each case is sometimes counted as part of the quantifier and sometimes not. The bracket immediately following a quantifier ('(Rx)' in the above examples) defines its *scope*, i.e. how much of the ensuing discourse it governs, or how much of what follows is being said of the variable in it. (Precise conventions about brackets, etc., again vary.) Either of these quantifiers can be defined in terms of the other plus negation.

Other quantifiers exist, such as 'For most x', 'For exactly one x' (the *singular quantifier*), 'For exactly 2 x', etc.

The values of a VARIABLE bound by a quantifier are said to be *quantified over*. In the above examples objects in general are quantified over, but sometimes the range of objects quantified over (the *universe of discourse*) is limited: see MANY-SORTED LOGIC. When predicates are quantified over, 'f' usually replaces 'x', i.e. '($\exists$f)' means 'There is at least one predicate such that.'

Quantification is *objectual* (or *referential*) if it is taken to imply the existence, as 'real objects', of the values of the variables (cf. the views of Quine). Otherwise it is *substitutional*. Consider 'John is tall'. Can we infer '($\exists$f)(John is f)'? To those who interpret quantification substitutionally

175

Quantifier shift fallacy

this is harmless, and merely says that John has some property. But those who interpret it objectually may reject the inference because it seems to imply a realist view of universals like tallness.

J. A. Faris, *Quantification Theory*, 1964. (Semi-elementary. See also any modern introduction to logic.)

R. B. Marcus, 'Interpreting quantification', *Inquiry*, 1962. (Objectual and substitutional quantification).

Quantifier shift fallacy. The fallacy of arguing from 'Every nice girl loves a sailor' to 'Some (one) sailor is loved by every nice girl', i.e. of confusing 'For all x there is a y such that . . .' with 'There is a y such that for all x . . . ' (see QUANTIFICATION). The latter implies, but is not implied by, the former.

Quantifier words. A group of words including 'all', 'any', 'each', 'every', 'some', 'no', 'a', all concerned in various ways with the notion of quantity (cf. QUANTIFICATION).

Traditional formal logic dealt mainly with four kinds of proposition, *universal affirmative* (called *A propositions*: 'All cats are black'), *universal negative* (*E propositions*: 'No cats are black'), *particular affirmative* (*I propositions*: 'Some cats are black'), and *particular negative* (*O propositions*: 'Some cats are not black'). These were pictured as the corners of the *square of opposition*, whose sides and diagonals represented logical relations between the propositions (provided all four had the same subject and the same predicate, 'cats' and 'black' in the above examples). *Singular propositions* ('This cat (or Tiddles) is black') were traditionally treated as universal, though complications arise. The affirmative/negative distinction is called one of *quality*, the universal/particular distinction one of *quantity* (cf. QUANTIFICATION).

Both in the square of opposition and in the SYLLOGISM it was assumed that 'All cats are black' entails (see IMPLICATION) 'Some cats are black'. 'Some' can mean 'Some and perhaps all' on inclusive interpretation, or 'Some but not all' on exclusive interpretation. Nearly all logicians have found the inclusive interpretation more convenient. It is also assumed that 'some' means 'at least one', i.e. 'Some cats are black' is still true if only one is. In 'Some tea is undrinkable' it means 'not none'. In the last century, however, a problem arose, known as that of *existential import*, about which, if any, of the above four propositions entail that there exist any cats (or any black things, though this was less emphasized). It appeared that no otherwise acceptable answer could preserve intact the square of opposition and the traditional list of valid syllogisms, though for purposes of formal logic it was, and still is, found convenient to interpret 'All cats are black' as *existentially negative*, i.e. as saying that nothing is a cat and not black. This is true if there are no cats, and so does not imply that there are any. But 'Some cats are black' was interpreted as *existentially affirmative*, i.e. as saying that there exists at least one thing which is both a cat and black. Clearly 'All cats are black' no longer then entails 'Some cats are black'.

To call 'All unicorns are black' true simply because there are no unicorns has caused dissatisfaction. One solution, suggested by Strawson, is to say that 'All unicorns are black' does not entail, but does presuppose, that there are unicorns (for this distinction see IMPLICATION). If there are none it will then fail to be true, but in a way that need not upset the square of opposition.

However, let us compare the following sentences: 'All coins in my pocket are silver.' 'All (of) the coins. . . .' 'Some coins. . . .' 'Some of the coins. . . .' 'No coins. . . .' 'None of the coins. . . .' The cases containing 'the' imply (i.e. entail or presuppose) that coins exist in my pocket. ('The' may be implicit, as in 'All John's children', i.e. 'All the children of John'.) But these cases say nothing about coins that might be, but are not, in my pocket. The other cases, however, are rather ambiguous. 'All coins . . .' is perhaps most naturally taken to mean 'Were you to find any coins in my pocket (which you might or might not) they would be silver (I throw coppers away on principle)'. 'Some coins . . .' most naturally means 'Some of the . . .' though I *could* use it to express my principle of never keeping copper coins by themselves in my pocket. But 'some' does not mean 'some of the' in 'There are some unicorns' or 'Some water is needed',—nor in 'Some foxes entered my garden last night', where it is what is said about them that implies their existence.

All this raises the question whether some or all of the quantifier words, in at least some of their uses, form part of referring expressions. Does 'No cats are black' refer to all cats and say of them that they are not black? Does 'Some cats are black' refer to all cats and say that they are not all not black, or does it perhaps refer only to those that are black? All these views have difficulties, and some writers say quantifier words never have a referring role (cf. DISTRIBUTION, REFERRING).

It seems that one role of 'any' is to make clear that what is being said is more like a law than a factual statement. 'Any body unacted on by forces moves in a straight line' carries less suggestion that there are such bodies than 'All bodies. . . .' 'Any', however, can imply existence when combined with 'the', as in 'Any of the ones in that box would have done', and has ambiguities of its own: Compare 'Is any (at least one) member ready to vote?' and 'Is any (old) member entitled to vote?' Only the latter can be answered with 'Yes, any member'.

Another main role of 'any' is to emphasize randomness or choice: 'Any you choose, no matter which.' This may explain why 'any' is allied to 'some' as well as to 'all', for choice may be relevant in either case. But it only partly explains the substitution of 'any' for 'some' in many negative, interrogative and conditional contexts: 'Have you any matches (I don't mind which, or of what kind)?' 'If I had any matches', 'I haven't any matches (no matter what kind you choose)', 'I have some matches (but I have no choice about which, or what kind they are)',—but why 'I want some matches' and not (by itself) 'I want any matches'? ('I want *any* matches' (stressed) means 'I want as many as you've got, no matter what they're like'.) The negation, etc., may be only implicit: 'It was too smooth to have any effect', 'I was ashamed to take any' (but: 'glad to take some'), 'The question whether (condition that) there is any'.

Quantifier words

'Any' tends, more than 'all', to focus attention on the individuals rather than the mass. Suppose we know that nearly all swans are white but a few are black. Then 'All swans are probably white', on its most natural interpretation, will be false, while 'Any swan (you choose) will probably be white' may be true. Note too that, though 'Any swan is white' implies 'All swans are white', 'Any of the candidates may win' does not imply 'All the candidates may win'.

'Each' too, emphasizes that the things in question are taken one by one, or distributively, while 'all' can be interpreted distributively ('All the soldiers were conscripts') or collectively ('I doubt if *all* the soldiers could defeat that enemy (much less each of them)'). 'They each gave a pound and presented him with a clock' is normally elliptical. The role of 'any', as against 'each', in selecting is seen by comparing 'I will take any of you on' with 'I will take each of you on'.

'Every' (from 'ever each', and apparently peculiar to English) is like 'each' in many respects. They both imply existence, and do not, like 'any', cover hypothetical cases, But whereas 'each' emphasizes taking the items separately, 'every' sometimes does not, but rather resembles 'all'. 'I told everybody to come', but not 'I told each person to come', is true if I told a crowd in which everybody was present. Similarly 'I will take every one of you on', like 'I will take all of you on', is ambiguous about whether I mean together or separately.

'A' is rather like 'any', though it only goes with the singular, and only with words that *can* be in the plural. Like 'any', though with these limitations, it can approximate to 'all' ('A whale breathes air') or to 'some' ('I met a man'). When approximating to 'all' it often signifies typicality rather than universality ('A cat usually likes fish'; in 'Any cat usually likes fish' the 'usually' limits the number of occasions, not the number of cats (unless there are commas round 'usually'), while in the former case it may limit either). 'A' also may or may not imply existence. 'I am looking for a dog' may or may not mean I have a definite dog in mind.

Other quantifier words include 'many', 'most', 'few', 'a few', 'several', 'one' (and numbers generally), and even 'the' in some uses ('The whale is a mammal'). 'The' perhaps gets its generalizing use from referring to species ('The species whale is a species of mammal').

J. N. Keynes, *Formal Logic*, 1884, 4th (revised) edn 1906. (Standard account of traditional formal logic.)

T. Czezowski, 'On certain peculiarities of singular propositions', *Mind*, 1955. (Cf. J. L. Mackie, ' "This" as a singular quantifier', *Mind*, 1958, L. Gumanski, 'Singular propositions and "this" as a quantifier', *Mind*, 1960.)

P. F. Strawson, *Introduction to Logical Theory*, 1952. (Chapter 6 discusses existential import.)

P. T. Geach, *Reference and Generality*, 1962. (Contains discussions of quantifier words in connexion with reference, and also with conjunction and disjunction, and with scope. Draws on medieval discussions.)

W. V. Quine, *Word and Object*, 1960, § 29. (Quantifier words and scope.)

Z. Vendler, 'Each and every, any and all', *Mind*, 1962. (Cf. also his article 'Any and all' in P. Edwards (ed.), *The Encyclopedia of Philosophy*, 1967, where he connects the topic with the philosophy of science.)
E. S. Klima, 'Negation in English' in J. A. Fodor and J. J. Katz (eds), *The Structure of Language*, 1964. (Elaborate and technical, but see p. 294 for 'too' and p. 314 for 'ashamed' and 'glad'.)

Quine, Willard V. O. 1908- . American mathematical logician, born in Akron, Ohio, and working in Cambridge, Mass. He has elaborated a system of logic, following RUSSELL, where singular terms can be eliminated, and has cast doubt upon the ANALYTIC/synthetic distinction and similar distinctions, and on the extent to which assured TRANSLATION is possible between, or even within, languages. He denies the possibility of a formalized INTENSIONAL logic. His slogan 'To be is to be the value of a variable' offers a criterion for distinguishing between realists and nominalists (cf. BEING, METAPHYSICS). *Methods of Logic*, 1950 (part 4 eliminates singular terms). *From a Logical Point of View*, 1953 (contains 'On What There Is', 1948 (the slogan), 'Two Dogmas of Empiricism', 1951 (analytic/synthetic), and articles relevant to meaning and intensional logic). *Word and Object*, 1960. See also AMBIGUITY, CONDITIONALS, INSCRIPTION, INTUITIONISM, LEIBNIZ'S LAW, MEANING, MODALITIES, QUANTIFICATION, QUANTIFIER, REFERRING, SATISFY, SENTENCES, TOKEN-REFLEXIVES.

R

Range. See PROBABILITY, VARIABLE.

Rationalism. Any view appealing to reason as a source of knowledge or justification. Reason can be contrasted with revelation, in religion, or with emotion and feeling as in ethics, but in philosophy it is usually contrasted with the senses (including introspection, but not intuitions). 'Rationalist' is to A PRIORI what EMPIRICIST is to empirical. Rationalism is an outlook which somehow emphasizes the a priori. 'Rationalist' has a variety of interpretations corresponding to those of 'empiricist'. A philosopher can be both rationalist and empiricist, in different though important respects (e.g. Kant); but such philosophers are often though to be best classified as neither.

'Continental rationalists' is a traditional label for Descartes, Spinoza and Leibniz, with various lesser figures of that period who are regarded as sharing their general outlook.

W. von Leyden, *Seventeenth-Century Metaphysics*, 1968. (Chapter 3 has general introduction to rationalism and empiricism.)

A. O. Lovejoy, *The Great Chain of Being*, 1936. (Chapter 5 brings out some features and conflicts of some developed rationalist philosophies (Leibniz and Spinoza). See also A PRIORI, EMPIRICIST.)

D. W. Hamlyn, *The Theory of Knowledge*, 1970. (Chapter 2 briefly discusses basis of rationalism as it appears in Descartes, Leibniz and Bradley (and then discusses empiricism).)

G. Ryle (see bibliography to EPISTEMOLOGY (last item).)

Realism. Like 'real', 'realism' gets its sense largely from what it is contrasted with. Any view can be called realist which emphasizes the existence, or role, of some kind of thing or object (e.g. material objects, propositions, UNIVERSALS), in contrast to a view which dispenses with the things in question in favour of words (nominalism), ideas (idealism, conceptualism), or LOGICAL CONSTRUCTIONS (phenomenalism). Cf. PERCEPTION, UNIVERSALS, IDENTITY.

In aesthetics realism emphasizes the nature of things as they are in themselves, not as we see them. A realist art-form aims to portray things as they are, not as mediated by some attitude, etc. of the artist.

Reason. As a noun, a general faculty, common to all or nearly all men, and sometimes regarded, either seriously or by poetic licence, as a sort of impersonal external power ('the dictates (truths) of reason', etc.) This faculty has seemed to be of two sorts, a faculty of intuition by which one 'sees' truths or abstract things ('essences' or universals, etc.), and a faculty of reasoning, i.e. passing from premises to a conclusion (*discursive reason*). The verb 'reason' is confined to this latter sense, which is now anyway the commonest for the noun too, though the senses are connected (to pass from premises to conclusion is to intuit a connexion between them).

Kant contrasts reason, which is concerned with mediate INFERENCES with understanding and power of judgment, which are concerned with acquiring concepts and passing judgments, respectively.

Practical reason has been distinguished from *theoretical* or *speculative reason* since Aristotle, and raises problems: Is reason in the practical sphere 'the slave of the passions' (Hume), i.e. is it limited to showing us means to ends which the passions dictate?

How far can reason be distinguished from feeling, emotion, etc.? (This problem parallels that of relating theoretical reason to the senses: cf. PERCEPTION.) Can reason mediate between morals and self-interest ('A sacrifice beyond all reason')? Also how many kinds of reasoning are there apart from deductive reasoning? (Cf. LOGIC.)

A second group of uses of 'reason' allows the plural and involves expressions like 'a (the, his) reason'. A reason may be a cause as in 'the reason for the explosion', or a factor in an explanation as in 'the reason why there are infinitely many prime numbers', and again problems arise over the practical sphere: how are reasons for believing related to reasons for acting? Only the former are evidence, but Smith's honesty may be a reason for believing him, and also for rewarding him.

Can the reason why someone acts be a cause of his acting? This depends on whether actions can be caused, but it is a further question whether *his* reason can be the cause. 'The' reason might be something he is unconscious of, which 'his' reason cannot be (cf. FREEWILL).

'He has a reason to act' may mean that acting would promote some purpose he has, or some interest he has, or some purpose he should morally have. An interest is perhaps a purpose he would or should rationally have if he knew certain facts. One can have a reason, even consciously, and act as it prescribes, without acting *from* it. Also *the* reason why Smith acted, whether or not it coincides with *his* reason, need not be *a* reason for acting; it may be not even a poor reason, but no reason at all, for acting.

I. Kant, *Critique of Pure Reason*, 1781, 1787. (See 'reason', 'understanding', 'judgment' in index to N. Kemp Smith's translation, 1929.)

Aristotle, *De Anima* (*On the Soul*), III, 4–8 (theoretical reason), III, 9–10; *Nicomachean Ethics*, VII, 1–10; *De Motu* (*Movement of Animals*), 701a, 7–25 (practical reason). (Classic though difficult discussions.)

Recursive

R. Edgley, *Reason in Theory and Practice*, 1969. (Defends practical reason, discussing its relations with theoretical.)

J. Kemp, *Reason, Action and Morality*, 1964. (The place of reason in morals and conduct. Includes historical material.)

Recursive. Applied to a procedure if it consists of rules for taking the first step and then rules for taking further steps on the basis of those already taken. *Recursion theory* is a branch of mathematical logic studying FUNCTIONS definable by such procedures. See also DEFINITION, INDUCTION.

Reduction. See PERCEPTION, PHENOMENOLOGY.

Reductionism. Also called *reductivism*. Tendency to reduce certain notions, whether everyday ones, like *physical object*, or theoretical ones in science, like *electron*, to allegedly simpler or more basic notions, or more empirically accessible ones, e.g. one might claim to dispense with the word 'electron' and talk only of vapour trails in cloud chambers. Reductionism is a feature especially of PHENOMENALISTS, and other empiricists, and of POSITIVISTS in philosophy of science. See also PHILOSOPHY.

Reduction sentences. A technical device introduced by Carnap, to avoid a difficulty that arises over definitions like ' "is soluble" means "dissolves if immersed" '. With 'if' interpreted in terms of material IMPLICATION, as is usual in logic, this definition would make anything soluble that was never actually immersed. The general idea is to avoid giving a definition, but to give instead conditions under which something is soluble, and conditions under which it is not, which do not imply that everything which is never immersed is soluble.

R. Carnap, 'Testability and meaning', *Philosophy of Science*, 1936 and 1937, § 8.

Reference. See REFERRING, MEANING.

Referent. See REFERRING.

Referring. There is a group of terms, including 'refer', 'denote', 'name', 'designate', 'stand for', 'mention', 'be about', 'talk about', 'say of', 'apply to', 'be true of', which somehow seem to connect language with objects in the widest sense. Some of these terms are used varyingly, and sometimes interchangeably, but all have peculiarities.

Referring is done primarily by people. Words and sentences refer only in so far as people use them to do so, and therefore often differently on different occasions. (Cf. MEANING for referring and denoting, and for sense and reference. A sentence can 'refer' in this derivative way without having a 'reference' in the technical sense, i.e. without referring as a whole and in its own right.)

When does referring occur? 'Smith is tall' is true of many people. But if I say the words 'Smith is tall' I normally refer only to some Smith I have in mind. The context shows which. Suppose, however, that I intend to refer to Smith, and in fact say things true only of him, but mistakenly use the name 'Jones'. Have I referred to Smith? If my audience realize the mistake, perhaps I have, although I referred to him as 'Jones'. But suppose they are deceived? Certainly I have not mentioned Smith, whereas I perhaps have mentioned one of the Joneses, at any rate if there is exactly one reasonably relevant in the context. (*Mentioning* something involves at least using some name or description which actually applies to it—or would apply to it if it existed; see 'Alaska' example below.) A further case is when I deliberately use 'Jones' because I know (or believe) my audience wrongly thinks of Smith as 'Jones'. These and other problems occur also when I use not names but descriptions, or words like 'someone' (cf. also QUANTIFIER WORDS).

So much for subjects, but do we refer in using predicates, and in identity statements? Suppose I say, perhaps mistakenly, 'That is my doctor': have I referred to, and have I mentioned, my doctor? Again we can mention and refer to universals ('Tallness is becoming commoner') but do I mention or refer to tallness in saying 'Smith is tall'? Confusions in this area may contribute to referential theories of MEANING. That we *can* refer to tallness, and that 'tall' as a predicate has *some* relation to tallness, may suggest that 'tall' always refers to tallness and has meaning by doing so. An ambiguity of *stand for* may also cause confusion here: ' "Tall" stands for tallness' may mean ' "Tall" refers to tallness', or ' "Tall" is the term to use when applying the concept tallness'. Another question bearing on referential theories of meaning is how we can understand propositions which involve reference to objects we are not acquainted with.

Many of these problems recur with *about*. 'Talk about' resembles 'refer to'. Talking *about* something may seem to involve more than 'merely referring' to it, but perhaps one can refer to something without talking about it only if one is interrupted in mid sentence, etc. 'Be about' applies mainly to statements, problems, etc., rather than people, and has a more technical air. It is not obvious where to draw the line between what a statement is and is not about, and there is a danger of any statement being about everything (Goodman).

So far we have distinguished referring from related notions, and have considered the effects of things like the role of the speaker's intentions and mistakes, and of the speaker's and hearer's beliefs. A special group of problems concern referring and existence. How can we refer to or talk about what does not exist, be it fictional (Pickwick), future (one's own death), a LOGICAL CONSTRUCTION (the average man), or simply a muddle (the round square)? Do such things have some sort of BEING so (Meinong), or do we not 'really' refer to them (Russell. Cf. theory of DESCRIPTIONS)? Or is referring not, or not always, a relation (which requires real terms to relate)? Is the use of the 'objects' mentioned in the first sentence of this entry simply a linguistic device? Perhaps 'The king of Alaska is tall' mentions that non-existent king, but perhaps this simply means that a certain

Reflexive

phrase is used—a phrase suitable for mentioning a real king if there were one.

The 'king of Alaska' example introduces a further group of problems: how far are notions like referring essential to language? Does the fact that the phrase is suitable for mentioning a real king if there were one mean that 'mentioning the king of Alaska' is a phrase we can only understand because we understand 'mentioning the Queen of England', where there is one? Are non-designative names possible only because we have designative names? We have asked whether it is only because their objects are sometimes real objects that referring etc. are possible. One can also ask whether at least some of these objects must be particulars and not UNIVERSALS. But one can further ask whether referring, etc., could be dispensed with, either in a language spoken by people who already knew a language containing them, or (more radically) in a people's first language. Could other devices in language, like predicating, be understood without these notions? Or could there be a language with quite different devices altogether?

A *referent* is what is referred to. A *reference class* (probability theory) is the population serving as a basis for statistical statements. In '10 per cent of Englishmen are Catholics' Englishmen form the reference class; in 'The probability of a double six is 1/36' the reference class may be throws of a die, or of a double die, according to context. For *divided reference* see MEANING.

J. W. Meiland, *Talking about Particulars*, 1970. (General discussion of nature of referring.)

P. T. Geach, *Reference and Generality*, 1962. (Referring and allied notions, including discussion of QUANTIFIER WORDS. See especially 'denoting' in index. Cf. also his *Mental Acts*, 1957.)

N. Goodman, 'About', *Mind*, 1961. (Mainly rather technical, but § 2 is good introduction to paradox concerning 'about'.)

D. Holdcroft, 'A principle about "about" ', *Mind*, 1968.

M. Hodges, 'On "being about" ', *Mind*, 1971. (Both concerned with 'about' and existence. See Holdcroft, pp. 515–17 for whether sentences have references.)

L. Linsky, *Referring*, 1967. (Discusses referring in connexion with existing and describing. More historical than Meiland, discussing Meinong, Frege, Russell, Strawson.)

W. V. Quine, *Methods of Logic*, 1952. (Part 4 tries, following Russell, to eliminate singular terms, i.e. to eliminate referring except by bound variables (see QUANTIFICATION).)

P. F. Strawson, *Individuals*, 1959. (Part 2 distinguishes referring and predicating. Stresses role of particulars and discusses eliminability of referring. Fairly difficult.)

Reflexive. Applied to a relation which, if a term has it to something it must have it to itself (*as old as*). A relation is *irreflexive* or *aliorelative* if a term cannot have it to itself (*older than*), and *non-reflexive* if it may or may not have it (*fond of*).

184

Refute. Successfully show to be false. But it is not necessary for hearer to be convinced.

A. Flew, *An Introduction to Western Philosophy*, 1971, pp. 21–3.

Reid, Thomas. 1710–96. Born at Strachan, he worked mainly in Aberdeen and Glasgow. He is generally known as the founder of the 'Scottish school of common sense', which reacted against the sceptical conclusions of the 'British EMPIRICISTS'. Reid, like KANT, was particularly influenced by HUME (whom some scholars think he misinterpreted). Being unable to accept Hume's sceptical conclusions, he attacked the basis from which Hume began, and substituted one based on our common-sense assumptions. *Essays on the Intellectual Powers of Man*, 1785 (epistemology). *Essays on the Active Powers of Man*, 1788 (psychology and ethics).

Relations (external and internal). A relation is internal to its terms when they would not be the things they are unless related by it. Otherwise it is external. 'Orange is between red and yellow' expresses an internal relation, presumably, because these colours would not be what they are unless related in this way. Alternatively a relation is internal if without it its terms would not have the qualities they have. If crimson is a dark colour and pink is a light colour, *being darker than pink* is internal to crimson, for if crimson were not darker than pink it would not be a dark colour. In a looser sense whether a relation is internal may depend on how its terms are described. *Being married* is internal to a husband, described as such, but not, presumably, to Smith. For the husband would not be a husband unless married, but Smith could be Smith whether married or not. Some philosophers, notably Bradley, held the *doctrine of internal relations*, that all relations are internal in one or both of the stricter senses. Bradley added that ultimately relations are unreal.

F. H. Bradley, *Appearance and Reality*, 2nd edn 1897, Appendix B. (Cf. also chapter 3.)
G. E. Moore, *Philosophical Studies*, 1922, chapter 9. (Criticizes doctrine.)

Religion (philosophy of). The study of general philosophical problems about religion and God. Particular religious doctrines belong rather to *revealed* or *dogmatic theology* or to *comparative religion*, though their logical, metaphysical, etc., implications belong to philosophy of religion.

An initial question is, what counts as a religion? Must there be one or more gods involved? What counts as a god, and in particular as the God of monotheism?

Natural theology is a part of philosophy of religion. Without using revelation it examines the existence, nature, properties and abilities of God, and His relations to the world. Are there limits to His power? Can He perform logical impossibilites, or set Himself problems that He cannot solve (*paradox of omnipotence*)? Can He be omniscient compatibly with human, or indeed His own, freewill (*paradoxes of omniscience*)? Can He be both omnipotent and benevolent, the world being as it is (*problem of evil*)?

185

Resemblance

Concerning His nature one can ask whether He exists necessarily, how His essence relates to His existence, and whether He has His predicates in the ordinary sense or analogically.

Arguments for God's existence include the ONTOLOGICAL ARGUMENT, the COSMOLOGICAL ARGUMENT, the argument from DESIGN, and the argument from religious experience. The last has it that there is a special religious experience which guarantees or lets us infer the existence of God as its object.

On God and the world one can ask: Did He create the world, and if so, in what sense? Does He determine laws of nature, or of logic, or of morality? Does He intervene in the world with miracles, and what counts as a miracle?

Religious questions have been affected by the recent dominance of logic and semantics. How do religious words and discourse have meaning? Are religious statements to be interpreted literally or in some other way (the modern version of the medieval problem about analogical predication; see above)?

The field of religious experience suggests questions about mysticism, awe, the numinous, and also faith: what is faith, how is it related to rational evidence and superstition, and can it be justified? Can there be a duty to believe? Religions promising immortality engender questions shared with philosophy of MIND. Problems peculiar to Christianity arise over concepts like the Incarnation, transubstantiation, salvation, grace and prayer, and their bearings on substance, causality, and freewill again.

J. Hick, *Philosophy of Religion*, 1963. (General introduction.)

A. Kenny, *The Five Ways*, 1969. (Aquinas' proofs for God's existence.)

J. L. Mackie, 'Evil and omnipotence', *Mind*, 1955. (Problem of evil and paradox of omnipotence. Cf. discussions in succeeding volumes.)

N. Smart, *Philosophers and Religious Truth*, 1964. (Early chapters have good points on miracles, freedom, God's existence. Fifth chapter contrasts mystical and numinous.)

A. Flew and A. MacIntyre (eds), *New Essays in Philosophical Theology*, 1955. (Representative of philosophical outlook at that date.)

Resemblance. See UNIVERSALS.

Results. See CAUSATION.

Richard's paradox. One of what are sometimes called the semantic PARA-DOXES (cf. RUSSELL'S PARADOX, TYPES). Take all decimal numbers between 0 and 1 specifiable in finitely many words. Each will have infinitely many digits. Those which apparently terminate are followed by endless 0's. Arrange these numbers in some order in a table, so that each number occupies a row and its digits appear in successive columns. Take the number formed by the diagonal of the table, starting from the top left. For any n, the n-th digit of this number will be the n-th digit of the n-th row in the table. Replace each digit in this number by its successor. (Assume the successor of 9 is 0.) The resulting number cannot appear in the table, yet is specifiable in finitely many words (we have just specified it).

This *diagonal procedure* was originally used by G. Cantor (1845–1918) to prove that there must be more decimal numbers than can be put in a table as above, even though such a table has infinitely many rows. Since the infinite number of decimals thus exceeds the infinite number of rows in such a table, in the sense that these numbers cannot be paired off with each other, there must be more than one 'transfinite' (i.e. infinite) number. This last result is not affected by solutions to Richard's paradox, which only concerns numbers specifiable in finitely many words.

Rousseau, Jean-Jacques. 1712–78. Political philosopher and philosopher of education, he was born in Geneva and lived largely in France, often under patronage (including that of HUME in England). He emphasized the corrupting effects of society on man in his natural condition. He thought that society must be considered to be founded on a social contract between men, and he elaborated a notion of the 'general will', which would be represented in the decisions made in a properly ordered society. The sovereign's decisions were legitimate only when they represented this general will, not (as with HOBBES) whenever the sovereign had effective power. He also set forth principles of education in line with his other views. *Discours sur les sciences et les arts*, 1750. *Discours sur l'origine et les fondements de l'inégalité parmi les hommes*, 1755. *Le Contrat social*, 1762. *Émile*, 1762 (on education).

Russell, Bertrand A. W. 1872–1970. Worked mainly in England (especially Cambridge), sometimes in America. His early fame rested on two main contributions to logic, the theory of DESCRIPTIONS and the theory of TYPES. He taught Wittgenstein at Cambridge before the First World War. His later work concentrated mainly on EPISTEMOLOGY, metaphysics and philosophy of mind, where he based himself mainly on the empiricist tradition of HUME, MILL, etc., though he was notorious for changing his views. He also stressed the importance to philosophy of modern scientific developments. A prolific writer, Russell was also famous for his great political and social commitment. 'On Denoting', *Mind*, 1905 (theory of descriptions). *Principia Mathematica*, 1910–13 (with WHITEHEAD. Theory of types. Different from his *The Principles of Mathematics*, 1903). *Our Knowledge of the External World*, 1914. 'The Philosophy of Logical Atomism', *Monist*, 1918. *The Analysis of Mind*, 1921. *An Inquiry into Meaning and Truth*, 1940. See also BROAD, CALCULUS, CATEGORIES, CAUSATION, CLASS, FREGE, IMPLICATION, INDUCTION, INTENSIONALITY, LANGUAGE (PHILOSOPHY OF), LOGICAL ATOMISM, LOGICAL CONSTRUCTIONS, MATHE-MATICS, MEANING, MONISM, PARADIGM CASE, PARADOX, PHENOMENALISM, PHILOSOPHY, QUINE, REFERRING, RUSSELL'S PARADOX, SENSE DATA, SENTENCES, STRAWSON, SUFFICIENT REASON, TOKEN-REFLEXIVES, TRUTH, UNIVERSALS, VARIABLE.

Russell's paradox. Most classes are not members of themselves (the class of cats is not a cat), but some classes are members of themselves (the class

187

Ryle, Gilbert

of classes is a class). Is the class of all classes that are not members of themselves a member of itself? If yes, no. If no, yes. This is the most famous of the logical PARADOXES. Russell invented his theory of TYPES in order to answer it.

Ryle, Gilbert. 1900– . British philosopher working in Oxford, who was one of the early protagonists of 'linguistic PHILOSOPHY'. His main work has been in philosophy of MIND and in philosophical LOGIC. He is particularly famous for criticizing the 'ghost in the machine' view of mind and body, which he attributed primarily to DESCARTES, and he analyses various mental concepts in terms of dispositions to behave in certain ways. In his youth he felt some affinity for PHENOMENOLOGY. *The Concept of Mind*, 1949. *Dilemmas*, 1954. See also CATEGORIES, CONDITIONALS, DIALECTIC, EPISTE-MOLOGY, FEELING, FREEWILL, HETEROLOGICAL, INFERENCE, LIAR, MATHE-MATICS, NEGATION, POLYMORPHOUS, RATIONALISM, SCEPTICISM, SEEING, SENSATION, SENTENCES, THINKING, TOPIC-NEUTRAL.

S

Salva Veritate. See INTENSIONALITY.

Sartre, Jean-Paul. 1905– . Born in Paris, he has worked mostly in France, with some study in Germany. Famous both as a writer of novels and plays and as a philosopher, he represents one form of EXISTENTIALISM, though his later work tends towards Marxism. He is the most explicitly atheistic of existentialists, and has taken an active part in politics. *Esquisse d'une théorie des émotions*, 1939. *L'Être et le néant*, 1943. *L'Existentialisme est un humanisme*, 1946 (popular, but often regarded as not representing his main thought). *Critique de la raison dialectique*, 1960 (Marxist in tendency). See also BAD FAITH, MARCEL, MERLEAU-PONTY.

Satisfy. In logic a formula containing one or more VARIABLES is usally said to be *satisfied* by those sets of one or more values (see VARIABLES) which produce a true proposition when assigned to those variables, e.g. if John and James are brothers they satisfy the formula 'x is brother to y'. A formula is *satisfiable* if there are such sets of values. But defining satisfaction involves some of the problems of defining TRUTH and satisfaction is sometimes made prior to truth.

A rule or command is satisfied when the situation it prescribes exists, even if by accident. It can therefore be satisfied without being obeyed.

W. V. Quine, *Philosophy of Logic*, 1970, chapter 3. (Satisfaction as prior to truth.)

Saturated. See CONCEPT.

Scepticism. Any view involving doubt about whether something exists, or about whether we can know something, or about whether we are justified in arguing in certain ways. Throughout the ages many philosophers have held that unless we know some things for certain we cannot know anything at all, or even legitimately think anything probable. Many of them, especially the Greek sceptics and Descartes, have therefore sought a sure mark or 'criterion' of when a proposition is true.

One can doubt whether knowledge can be had in certain spheres, or

Scepticism

whether it can be had by certain methods. An extreme rationalist like Plato, sometimes, may doubt whether we can ever get knowledge through the senses. An extreme empiricist like Hume may doubt whether we can ever get it through reason, or through any reasoning except deductive (Hume again; see INDUCTION). Particular arguments may attack the reliability of particular kinds of alleged knowledge, e.g. memory, precognition, intuition.

The sceptic may doubt whether we can know something, or even have any reason to believe it (cf. agnostics). Or, more rarely, he may deny that certain things exist, or that they could exist, even though he must then claim to know negative propositions (cf. atheists). Sceptics have doubted or denied that subjects like ethics contain any truths to be known (logical POSITIVISTS; cf. NATURALISM), and that certain things exist. These things include God, the past (Russell asked how we know we did not spring into existence, complete with 'memories', five minutes ago), other minds than one's own, objects when not being experienced (Berkeley), any objects at all beyond our experiences themselves, i.e. beyond our SENSATIONS or SENSE DATA (Hume; cf. PERCEPTION). Descartes even tried, unsuccessfully, to doubt his own existence. Milder forms of scepticism allow that we can know something, but only by certain methods. Perhaps we can know that ordinary objects, or others' feelings, exist, but only by inference, not by direct observation.

The views that nothing exists outside one's own mind, or that nothing such can be known to exist, are called *solipsism* (literally, 'only-oneself-ism'). A weaker version of solipsism concerns merely the existence of other minds (one form of the *other minds problem*, though this problem also concerns what we can know, and how, *about* other minds, e.g. what others are thinking and feeling).

One particular form scepticism takes is the question how I can know that I am not now dreaming.

Methodological scepticism or *methodological solipsism* is the adoption of these views not to defend them but as a starting point, departures from which are to be justified. Thus Descartes' *method of doubt* involves doubting everything until something necessarily undoubtable is found, on which knowledge can be built.

Radical forms of scepticism are currently unpopular on the grounds that they cannot coherently be stated without presupposing their own falsity. See also PRIVATE LANGUAGE ARGUMENT, ACCESS, INCORRIGIBLE, PERCEPTION.

A. A. Long, *Hellenistic Philosophy*, 1974. (Includes treatment of Greek sceptics.)

D. Hume, *Treatise*, 1739, and *Enquiry concerning Human Understanding*, 1748. (Nearest among great philosophers to scepticism.)

G. E. Moore, *Philosophical Papers*, 1959. (Several items attack scepticism.)

J. L. Austin (see bibliography to SENSE DATA).

G. Ryle, *Dilemmas*, 1954, chapter 7. (Scepticism and perception.)

J. Wisdom, J. L. Austin and A. J. Ayer, 'Other minds', *Proceedings of the*

Aristotelian Society, supplementary vol., 1946, Wisdom reprinted in his *Other Minds*, 1952, and Austin in A. *Flew* (ed.), *Logic and Language*, 2nd series, 1966.
M. Macdonald, 'Sleeping and waking', *Mind*, 1953. (Dreaming.)
A. P. Griffiths, 'Justifying moral principles', *Proceedings of the Aristotelian Society*, 1957-8. (Tries to rescue morals from sceptic.)

Schopenhauer, Arthur. 1788–1860. Born in Danzig and educated partly in France and England, he worked mostly in Germany. He admired KANT, but, like KIERKEGAARD, reacted against the prevalent philosophy of HEGEL. His chief contribution to philosophy lay in emphasizing the role of will in the world, both animate and inanimate. His treatment of unconscious willing partly anticipates Freud. He combined this with an ethic of pessimistic resignation strongly influenced by Indian thought, and with somewhat complementary aesthetic views. *Die Welt als Wille und Vorstellung* (*The World as Will and Idea* (or *Representation*)), 1819. *Parerga und Paralipomena* 1851 (miscellaneous essays).

Science (philosophy of). Primarily the study of how science works, or should work. The study of how it does is normally taken as a fair guide to how it should. This study is often called *methodology*, a term which can also be relative, e.g. methodology of history. *Inductive logic*, or *the logic of induction*, is normally limited to the study of INDUCTION as a mode of reasoning. Whether strictly there is any inductive *reasoning* is a question philosophy of science shares with logic. But philosophy of science itself studies the process, taken as a whole, whereby we start from premises about the world and reach, by rational means, conclusions about the world which cannot be reached from those premises by deduction alone. Everyday thinking also uses this process, but science is more systematic and method-conscious, and so more often studied.

The 'mathematical' sciences, especially physics, need special mathematical techniques, but scientific argument in general has been widely taken to presuppose a mathematical apparatus for applying the notions of PROBABILITY and CONFIRMATION, both of which themselves raise many problems. The calculus of chances (see PROBABILITY), which underlies probability, is often, but not universally, taken as the basis for scientific procedure.

When studying the nature of scientific reasoning we naturally ask how it can be justified, and what are its purposes. In what circumstances can a scientific statement properly be accepted? In particular what role does simplicity play, and when is one hypothesis simpler than another? Apart from prediction and control the main purpose of science is perhaps EXPLANATION, and an important part of philosophy of science concerns what this is and how it is achieved. LAWS of nature, CAUSATION and scientific necessity (see MODALITIES) are important concepts here.

The difficulties about acceptability, and about what laws of nature are, lead to questions about the nature of scientific systems. Are they perhaps abstract systems which we fit to the world as we might choose between alternative geometries (see SPACE)? Just as there are problems about a system as a whole, so there are about the terms in it. What sort of meaning and definition can they have? (cf. POSITIVISM for operationalism). Are so-called theoretical entities such as electrons, which cannot be directly observed, postulated as really existing things, or are they LOGICAL CONSTRUCTIONS? These problems about the terms and structures of scientific hypotheses lead one to ask about the properties a good hypothesis should have, and about the respective roles of observation and experiment, and the nature and types of measurement (see MAGNITUDES).

Moreover, how does science develop? Is it through the orderly replacement of hypotheses found to be false by better ones, or in some other way? And how far does science extend? Do geology, astronomy, psychology, sociology, even history, have equal claims with physics, chemistry and biology to be called sciences (cf. SOCIAL PHILOSOPHY, philosophy of HISTORY), and can they be reduced to a common basis, as physicalism (see POSITIVISM) asserts?

S. E. Toulmin, *The Philosophy of Science*, 1953. (What science is, with particular reference to scientific laws. INSTRUMENTALIST approach.)

L. J. Cohen, *The Implications of Induction*, 1970. (Develops alternative to calculus of chances as basis of confirmation.)

L. W. Beck (see bibliography to LOGICAL CONSTRUCTIONS).

T. S. Kuhn, *The Structure of Scientific Revolutions*, 1962. (One, controversial, view of how science develops. For criticism see I. Lakatos and A. Musgrave (eds), *Criticism and the Growth of Knowledge*, 1970.)

Scope. See QUANTIFICATION.

Scotus, John Duns. c.1266–1308. Scottish theologian and philosopher who probably worked in Cambridge, Oxford and Paris. His interests were in the same general area as those of AQUINAS, though somewhat less closely tied to ARISTOTLE. He held distinctive views on such questions as the nature of being, of matter, of relations, of transcendentals (see BEING), and on how individual members of a species are distinguished (where he introduces his notion of *haecceitas* ('thisness')). He also introduced a fresh proof for God's existence. Among his authentic works are the *Opus Oxoniense* (a commentary on the *Sentences* of Peter Lombard), *Quaestiones Quodlibetales* (miscellaneous questions), *De Primo Principio*, and commentaries on Aristotle's metaphysics and logic. His philosophy, with that of his followers, is called *Scotism*. See also OCKHAM.

John Scotus Erigena (ninth century) was an Irish theologian and philosopher whose *De Divisione Naturae* shows NEOPLATONIC influence, and develops (following earlier Greek thinking) an idea similar to that of the analogical predication discussed by later thinkers.

Seeing. Cf. PERCEPTION throughout. With both one must distinguish philosophical from psychological questions (see philosophy of MIND).

In general, seeing is having sight. We normally use eyes, but sight cannot be defined as perception through eyes if we allow that we might see with artificial eyes, or none. Would a man without eyes count as seeing if he consistently knew the colours of surrounding objects? We see objects, shadows, flashes, properties like 'the blue of her dress', relations, events, states of affairs, facts. We may see literally or metaphorically ('the point of the joke', 'that his wits were failing'), and these can be hard to distinguish.

Normally what we see must exist, though we see pink rats and 'see in the mind's eye' (see below). We 'see stars', but are not normally said to 'see' visual SENSE DATA. However, it is disputed whether we see whole objects in the same sense in which we see the parts of their surfaces in our line of vision.

Sometimes 'see' means 'catch sight of' or 'come to see', and so means something momentary ('suddenly he saw it'). But, as 'come to see' suggests, in another sense we can go on seeing something. This raises the question how far 'see' is a 'success' or 'achievement' word, i.e. a word which does not, or not simply, refer to an activity, like 'run', but refers to a success or achievement, like 'win'.

Does seeing something involve noticing and identifying it? *Seeing as* is important here. We can switch from seeing a certain ambiguous drawing as a picture of a duck to seeing it as a picture of a rabbit. Does this involve a change in belief, or in judgment, or what? How are seeing X, seeing X as Y (which may or may not be the same as X), judging X to be Y, and taking X to be Y, related together? The role of judgment or inference arises in other cases too. Our retinal image is two-dimensional. Must we therefore use inference in seeing the world as three-dimensional? We judge that a pillar-box looking grey in sodium light is red. But when the sun looks larger at sunset than at noon, though we know that even the visual image it subtends is not, is any judgement involved?

Is visualizing a sort of inner seeing? If so, what is seen? Does it involve seeing or having mental images, and how, if so, are these related to what is visualized (which may be real or imaginary)?

Seeing differs from some of the other SENSES in certain ways. Colours seem to be 'in' objects in a way sounds, smells, or feels (see FEELING) are not. We 'catch sight of', or 'like the look of', something, but 'sights' and 'looks' are not things we see, in the way sounds are things we hear. How analogous is seeing the colour of something to hearing the sound of it? (cf. SENSATION).

G. J. Warnock, 'Seeing', *Proceedings of the Aristotelian Society*, 1954–5, reprinted (with postscript) in R. J. Swartz (ed.), *Perceiving, Sensing and Knowing*, 1965. (Senses of 'see'.)

T. Clarke, 'Seeing surfaces and physical objects', in M. Black (ed.), *Philosophy in America*, 1965.

F. N. Sibley, 'Seeking, scrutinizing and seeing', *Mind*, 1955, reprinted in G. J. Warnock (ed.), *Philosophy of Perception*, 1967. (How far is 'see' an 'achievement' verb?)

L. Wittgenstein, *Philosophical Investigations*, 1953, II, xi, pp. 193–214. ('Duck/rabbit', etc. Cf. review by P. F. Strawson in *Mind*, 1954,

Self-deception

pp. 95–7, reprinted in G. Pitcher (ed.), *Wittgenstein*, 1966, pp. 59–61.

G. N. A. Vesey, 'Seeing and seeing as', *Proceedings of the Aristotelian Society*, 1955–6, reprinted in Swartz (above).

J. M. Shorter, 'Imagination', *Mind*, 1952, reprinted in O. P. Wood and G. Pitcher (eds), *Ryle*, 1970. (Seeing and visualizing.)

Self-deception. See BAD FAITH.

Self-regarding. Attributed to desires or actions if aimed at affecting oneself. If aimed at affecting others, these are other-regarding. Self-regarding aims need not be selfish (e.g. improving one's own moral character is not), nor need other-regarding aims be altruistic (e.g. sadism is not). Actions may also be divided, irrespective of their aims, into *self-affecting*, affecting only the agent, and *other-affecting*, affecting others too; both individual actions and types of action may be so divided.

C. D. Broad, 'Egoism as a theory of human motives', *Hibbert Journal*, vol. 48, 1949–50, reprinted in his *Ethics and the History of Philosophy*, 1952, and in D. Cheney (ed.), *Broad's Critical Essays in Moral Philosophy*, 1971; cf. also chapter 12 in this last.

J. S. Mill, *On Liberty*, 1859. (Advocates self-affecting/other-affecting distinction as basis for state interference with individual, but calls it self-regarding/not self-regarding.)

Semantics. See SEMIOTIC.

Semiotic. Literally, 'theory of signs'. A relatively unimportant term denoting the genus of three important species. *Syntax* or *syntactics* studies signs independently of their interpretation. It studies the properties of formal systems (see AXIOM), and the formal aspects of natural languages (e.g. words like 'and', 'the'; see FORM). (This usage is rather different from that where syntax, as the study of sentences, contrasts with grammar, as the study of individual words.) *Semantics* studies signs in relation to what, or how, they signify. It is the general study of meaning, though philosophers study the nature of meaning, while for linguists semantics is the study of empirical and historical questions about particular natural languages, changes of meaning, etc. *Pragmatics* studies signs in relation to what we do with them, given that they have the meaning they have (cf. pragmatic IMPLICATION). It also studies meaning itself in so far as this depends on what we do with the signs (e.g. SPEECH ACT theories of meaning); here it fuses with semantics. (In this entry SIGN is used in its wide sense.)

C. W. Morris, *Signs, Language and Behaviour*, 1946, chapter 8, § 1.

Sensa. See SENSE DATA.

Sensation. Either a kind of experience or a faculty, the latter including, in philosophy, the faculty of having 'pure experiences' (see PERCEPTION).

Usually SENSE DATUM means an alleged object of experience distinct from the experiencing, while 'sensation' means the experience itself. We hear sounds, but 'have' auditory sensations. When we 'have' or 'feel' a sensation, 'sensation' is an 'internal accusative', like 'blow' in 'strike a blow'; whatever the case with sense data, sensations must presumably be had by some person or animal. Experiences seem to be called sensations primarily when either they have no external cause, or they are of something rather general or obscure. Hearing a ringing in the ears is an auditory sensation. 'Seeing stars' and being dazzled, and perhaps being hallucinated, having after-images, and seeing a pure blue sky, are visual sensations. We seldom talk of visual sensations of colour; cf. SEEING on the nature of colour. 'Sensation of' usually means 'consisting of' as in 'sensation of pain, giddiness, nausea', but it can mean 'apparently, or as if, caused by' as in 'sensation of hardness, falling'; 'sensation of warmth' may be of the 'consisting of' kind as in fever or of the 'caused by' kind as when extending a hand to fire. 'Sensation' can apparently refer to a *kind* of experience like 'the sensation of falling' or to something datable such as 'the sensation I had just now', but phrases like 'I keep feeling that sensation' suggest that the 'datable' cases should really be analysed as 'kind' cases where 'had' means 'had an instance of'. This affects the question whether several people can have the same sensation. (For a related important problem concerning sensations see PRIVATE LANGUAGE.)

Most sensations seem to be bodily, but some, like the sensation of being followed, are hard to classify. See also PERCEPTION, FEELING, SEEING.

G. Ryle, 'Sensation', in H. D. Lewis (ed.), *Contemporary British Philosophy*, 3rd series, 1956, reprinted in R. J. Swartz (ed.), *Perceiving, Sensing, and Knowing*, 1965. (One view of ambiguity of 'sensation' and role of sensations.)

D. L. Perry, *The Concept of Pleasure*, 1967, pp. 91–3. (Do sensations 'occur'?)

D. W. Hamlyn, *The Theory of Knowledge*, 1970. (Chapter 6 has general discussion of sensations, sense data and perception.)

G. N. A. Vesey, 'Berkeley and sensations of heat', *Philosophical Review*, 1960. (Why we can call both objects and sensations hot.)

Sensationalism. Also called *sensationism*. An extreme form of EMPIRICISM whereby all our knowledge rests ultimately on SENSATIONS or on SENSE DATA, which initially are given to us free from any element of interpretation or judgment.

P. Alexander, *Sensationalism and Scientific Explanation*, 1963.

Sense. See MEANING.

Sense data. Generally, entities which exist only when, and because, they are sensed. Many philosophers throughout history have felt that perception shares with memory, imagination, dreams, hallucinations, etc., a basis in 'pure experience' that is free from interpretation and error. This was

Sense data

usually treated as a special and infallible direct or immediate awareness, recently often called *sensing*, of things variously described as impressions, ideas, perceptions or sensations until Moore and Russell introduced the term 'sense data' (plural of 'sense datum', literally 'given to sense'). *Sensa*, plural of 'sensum', is also used (but see Price, p. 19). For them, to exist *is* to be sensed. They have all the properties they appear to have, and no others, and can only be sensed by one person or animal. Colour patches, sounds, smells, tastes, feelings of hardness or heat would be typical examples. After-images, dream images, mental images, pains, kinaesthetic sensations, feelings of nausea, etc., are sometimes included, sometimes not.

In practice, however, it is hard to pick out and describe sense data, and to base our knowledge of physical objects on them (see PERCEPTION), and so conceptions of them vary. Sometimes they are said to be public, and parts either of objects or of the surfaces of objects. They may lack some properties they seem to have, or have others as well, discoverable on further inspection. Or they may be intrinsically vague in some respects. When one catches a quick glimpse of a speckled hen, does one's sense datum have a definite number of speckles? Those who try to connect sense data with physical objects sometimes suppose there could be merely possible sense data (*sensibilia*, plural of 'sensibile'), and that objects, even when not being perceived, consist of these. It is also hard to individuate sense data, i.e. say where one ends and the next begins, and hard to say whether they can change. And are they substances, qualities, events, or what?

The *act/object view* of sensing so far discussed, where sensing is an act directed upon sense data as objects, is sometimes replaced by the allegedly less objectionable *adverbial view*, where 'I am sensing a red sense datum' is replaced by 'I am sensing redly'. Another view is that talk of sense data is a mere linguistic convenience, providing a noun for talking about appearances, so that on seeing a red dress in sodium light one says 'I sense a grey sense datum' instead of 'I seem to see something grey'. See also SENSATION, PHENOMENALISM.

B. Russell, *Problems of Philosophy*, 1911.

H. H. Price, *Perception*, 1932. (Chapter 1 introduces and defends sense data, which form basis for rest of book.)

A. J. Ayer, *The Central Questions of Philosophy*, 1973. (See pp. 70–2 for some terminological points.)

G. J. Warnock (ed.), *Philosophy of Perception*, 1967. (Various articles, including R. J. Hirst, R. Wollheim, 'The difference between sensing and observing', *Proceedings of the Aristotelian Society*, supplementary vol., 1954, and A. M. Quinton, 'The problem of perception', *Mind*, 1955, who criticizes the role sense data can play.)

R. J. Hirst, *Problems of Perception*, 1959. (First four chapters criticize arguments for sense data.)

R. J. Swartz (ed.), *Perceiving, Sensing and Knowing*, 1965. (Part 2 contains relevant articles, including G. A. Paul, 'Is there a problem about sense data?', *Proceedings of the Aristotelian Society*, supplementary vol., 1936 (defending linguistic view), and Quinton (above).)

J. L. Austin, *Sense and Sensibilia*, 1962. (Attacks sense datum theory held by A. J. Ayer, who replies in 'Has Austin refuted the sense-datum theory?', *Synthese*, 1967, reprinted in Ayer's *Metaphysics and Common Sense*, 1969, and (with discussions) in K. T. Fann (ed.), *Symposium on J. L. Austin*, 1969.)

Senses. Normally the faculties of sight, hearing, touch, taste, smell. Occasionally the sense organs are called 'senses'. The kinaesthetic sense, sense of muscular movement, can be included, though not normally the sense of balance, nor the MORAL SENSE, nor things like a sense of rhythm, beauty, responsibility, etc.

Should the senses be distinguished and defined in terms of their objects, or of their organs, or of how they operate? How far do they parallel each other?, e.g. do we hear and smell objects as directly as we apparently see them? How can they apparently trespass on each other's territory. How can ice which *feels* cold, *look* cold? (cf. SEEING, SENSATION).

Because of problems like 'trespassing', various philosophers since Aristotle have distinguished the senses' *special* or *proper objects* (or *special* or *proper sensibles*; but for 'sensibilia' see SENSE DATA) from others. Various views of these proper objects are possible. They may be (i) those primarily accessible only to one sense, such as tastes, sounds, etc.; or (ii) those a sense cannot be mistaken about; or (iii) those a sense must perceive if it perceives anything (perhaps we cannot see without seeing shapes, though shapes can also be felt); or (iv) those a sense perceives directly, without interpretation or inference. (i) is the commonest view. Those objects accessible to more than one sense, as shape is accessible to sight and touch, are called *common sensibles*. Aristotle postulated a *common sense* (*sensus communis*) for them to be the proper objects of. The nature and roles of this 'common sense', which has no connexion with shrewdness, etc., are disputed. It seems to have been a sort of unifying general sense which acted through all the sense organs.

R. Sorabji, 'Aristotle on demarcating the five senses', *Philosophical Review*, 1971.

D. W. Hamlyn, *Sensation and Perception*, 1961. (Proper objects, etc. See index under 'sense-objects'.)

Sensibilia. See SENSE DATA.

Sensing. See SENSE DATA.

Sentences, propositions, statements. A *sentence* is a set of one or more words in a natural or artificial language, provided the set is constructed according to the grammatical rules and can be used by itself for asserting, asking, commanding, etc. It need not be meaningful and one sentence may have different meanings. 'I saw wood' may mean I cut it, or I sighted it; but

Sentences, propositions, statements

some see different sentences here. One sentence may play different roles: 'The company will parade at noon' may be a prediction or an order. In artificial languages of the kind used in formal logic, sentences are often called *well-formed formulae* (see AXIOM), and the grammatical rules are called *formation* or *syntactical rules*. Such languages are normally designed to exclude as ungrammatical the meaningless, and also the paradoxical (e.g. 'This sentence is false'). An *open sentence* is a sentential FUNCTION. An *eternal sentence* (Quine) is one without tenses and other TOKEN-REFLEXIVES, and having its verbs in the 'timeless present' ('Chaucer comes before Shakespeare'), so that if anyone using it on a certain occasion says something true, anyone else using it on any other occasion will also say something true. (Contrast 'The weather is hot', which may be true today and false tomorrow.) Philosophers have in fact been mainly concerned with indicative or *declarative sentences*, i.e. those fitted for making assertions.

In natural languages, sentences have usually been defined and distinguished in ways allowing them to suffer from various kinds of ambiguity and meaninglessness. *Propositions* have therefore been introduced. They have provided something common to sentences, in the same or different languages, which mean the same ('I am hot' and 'J'ai chaud'), or to utterances which do not mean the same, but say the same thing ('I am hot' said by me and 'You are hot' said to me by you), or to an assertion and the corresponding question or command, etc. ('The door is shut'/'Is the door shut?'/'Shut the door!') In this last use propositions resemble PHRASTICS, but are expressed in the indicative, and so, unlike phrastics, can represent what is assertible but unasserted ('Snow is white' can be asserted, but is unasserted in 'If snow is white . . .'). Whether propositions can similarly represent unasked questions, uncommanded commands, etc., is another problem. Propositions have also served as what can be true or false, and what logical relations like entailment relate. Finally they have served as what is believed, wished, judged, etc. (Believing and wishing, etc. are *propositional attitudes*. Things like judging, which occur at a definite time, are *propositional acts*. All these verbs are *propositional verbs*.)

A big difficulty with propositions is how they are to be individuated, i.e. when do we have one and when another? This difficulty can be avoided, or at least mitigated, if we take a proposition to be a sentence in one of its meanings, assuming it is clear when a sentence has one meaning and when another. This is how propositions were usually treated before the problems they were later supposed to solve became urgent. It makes them less useful for explaining things like translation and wordless thoughts where either more than one sentence, or no sentence, seems to be involved. Another difficulty concerns how many roles propositions can play at once. To take the above examples, can they provide both something common for 'I am hot' and 'J'ai chaud', and something common for 'I am hot' and 'You are hot', when the latter is said to me by you? Earlier this century Moore and Russell had much to say about propositions. Ayer has treated them as LOGICAL CONSTRUCTIONS out of synonymous sentences. Propositions are standardly represented by 'that'-clauses ('That all cats are black').

Sentences, propositions, statements

Some of these difficulties have led to the introduction of *statements*, either instead of or in addition to propositions. Statements, which are usually thought to be what is true or false, are either datable statings which are fairly easy to individuate ('His statement was made before lunch'), or, more usually, they are the content of such statings, or what is stated ('That statement has been often made'). The flavour of the 'datable statings' view lingers on in the feeling that something assertible but unasserted (cf. 'Snow is white' above) is better called a proposition than a statement, and in the fact that statements, rather than propositions, are contrasted with questions, commands, etc. A way of accepting both statements and propositions is to treat statements as what is common to 'I am hot' and 'You are hot', said of the same person, and propositions as what is common to 'I am hot' and 'J'ai chaud', or 'I am hot' said by different people (Lemmon).

Individual uses of 'proposition' and 'statement' are legion (for a further use of 'statement' see Ayer), but it is largely in connexion with natural languages that they need to be distinguished from each other and from 'sentence'. This is because of TOKEN-REFLEXIVES, whereby a sentence may not only be ambiguous, but may be true or false, or neither, according to who utters it when. Therefore the distinctions are not needed in formal systems (see AXIOM), nor in discussing ordinary language so far as we can assimilate this to formal systems by translation, or ignore the differences. For many purposes the three terms, and especially 'proposition' and 'statement are used interchangeably.

Singular statements or propositions predicate something of a single subject as in 'Socrates is wise', 'Socrates is not wiser than Plato', and are contrasted with *general* ones, which may be *universal:* 'All cats are black' ('All John's cats ...' is universal for most but not all purposes), or *particular:* 'Some cats are black', 'There exist black cats' (cf. QUANTIFIER WORDS). A *multiply general* statement contains each of the two main quantifiers (see QUANTIFICATION) or their defined equivalents ('Every man has some faults'). 'General' is sometimes used for 'universal'. For *atomic* and *molecular* see LOGICAL ATOMISM. See also JUDGMENT, FACTS, SPEECH ACTS.

G. Ryle, 'Are there propositions?', *Proceedings of the Aristotelian Society*, 1929–30. (Pros and cons of substantial propositions.)

G. E. Moore, *Some Main Problems of Philosophy*, 1953, written much earlier. (Contains important discussions of propositions. See pp. 262–6 for a difficulty over false propositions.)

B. Russell, *Logic and Knowledge*, 1956. ('The Philosophy of logical atomism' and 'On propositions' in this volume discuss propositions, the latter giving his later view. See pp. 222–4 for difficulty over false propositions.)

R. Carnap, *Introduction to Semantics*, 1942, § 37. (Ambiguity in 'proposition'.)

A. Church, 'On Carnap's analysis of statements of assertion and belief', *Analysis*, vol. 10, 1950, reprinted with Carnap's reply, 'On belief sentences', in M. Macdonald (ed.), *Philosophy and Analysis*, 1954. (Pro substantial propositions.)

Serial relation

A. J. Ayer, *Language, Truth and Logic*, 1936. (See index to second edition, 1946.)

E. J. Lemmon, 'Sentences, statements and propositions', in B. A. O. Williams and A. Montefiore (eds), *British Analytical Philosophy*, 1966. (Criticized by R. T. Garner, 'Lemmon on sentences, statements and propositions', *Analysis*, vol. 30, 1970.)

A. Stroll, 'Statements' in A. Stroll (ed.), *Epistemology*, 1967.

W. V. Quine, *Word and Object*, 1960. (See pp. 35–6 for accounts of *occasion* and *standing sentences.*)

Serial relation. Relation which is CONNECTED, TRANSITIVE and asymmetric (see SYMMETRIC), thus uniting a series. *Less than* is a serial relation which unites the natural numbers into a single series.

Set. See CLASS.

Set theory. See CALCULUS.

Sextus Empiricus. Floruit c.200 AD in unknown location. Generally considered the main representative of ancient SCEPTICISM, of an agnostic rather than dogmatic kind (i.e. he rejected the view that knowledge was demonstrably impossible, and insisted on keeping an open mind on this as on other questions). He was influenced by the earlier sceptic Pyrrho of Elis (flor. c.300 BC) and used logical modes of argument ('tropes') deriving from Aenesidemus of Knossos (1st century BC). He is also a major source for our knowledge of STOIC logic (which he opposed). His main works are the *Pyrrhonian Hypotyposeis* (*Outlines of Pyrrhonism*) and *Adversus Mathematicos* (*Against the Learned*), this latter having subdivisions with various titles.

Shaftesbury, Third Earl of. 1671–1713. Also called Anthony Ashley Cooper, he was born in London, lived mostly in England, and died at Naples. His early education was entrusted to LOCKE. He was an early representative of the MORAL SENSE school, believing in a 'natural sense of right and wrong'. He emphasized the existence of altruistic sentiments, and gave a utilitarian basis for morality, which could be reinforced by religion but was not dependent upon it. *An Inquiry concerning Virtue or Merit*, 1699. *Characteristics of Men, Manners, Opinions, Times*, 1711 (collected treatises, including the *Inquiry*). See also HUTCHESON.

Sidgwick, Henry. 1838–1900. Born in Yorkshire, he worked in Cambridge, and is best known as a leading UTILITARIAN. He made an elaborate attempt to show that a kind of HEDONISTIC utilitarianism underlies common sense morality. He also wrote on economics, and took an interest in psychical research (cf. BROAD, H. H. PRICE). *The Methods of Ethics*, 1874 (revised 1901). See also INTUITION.

Sign and symbol. The main distinction is that signs operate through a natural or causal connexion as in 'Clouds are a sign of rain', while symbols are conventional as in 'A broken line is a symbol for a footpath'. The convention need not be explicit. Symbols may be chosen, or arise, because of their causal associations: a scarifying bang may be used as a danger-warning. Symbols relying on resemblance are sometimes called *icons*. But 'sign' is often used in a wide sense to include symbols.

H. H. Price, *Thinking and Experience*, 1953, esp. chapter 6.

Sinn. See MEANING.

Smith, Adam. 1723–90. Moral philosopher and economist, who was born at Kirkcaldy and worked mainly in Scotland, including Glasgow University. Though primarily known for his economic theory based on an individualistic system of free enterprise, he also developed a system of moral philosophy in his first book. This system was primarily founded on that sympathy which, he said, we feel for the motives of moral agents and for the gratitude or resentment of those affected by the actions of such agents. He also criticized the 'moral sense' theory of his teacher HUTCHESON. There is some dispute about how far a single view of human nature underlies Smith's two main books. *The Theory of Moral Sentiments*, 1759. *An Inquiry into the Nature and Causes of the Wealth of Nations*, 1776.

Social philosophy. The study of philosophical problems arising from economics, anthropology, sociology and social psychology. It borders on philosophy of mind since it studies concepts involved in action like motive, intention, freewill, responsibility. However, it emphasizes the agent's role as a member of a group, and the group as itself an agent. Hence it considers ethical problems like that of collective responsibility, and metaphysical and methodological problems concerning the nature of groups and features of their behaviour. How far can group behaviour be caused or predicted, or described in terms of general laws? How far can it be reduced to the play of economic forces, and what kinds of EXPLANATION can be given of it? How does a social scientist form the concepts he uses? What counts as a society or social behaviour, and how are these related to individuals and individual behaviour? How far can one be objective in collecting and assessing evidence in the social sciences, and in general how far can or should these sciences resemble the natural sciences?

The 'rational man' is often used as a model in economics. This leads to problems about his behaviour, especially in competitive situations (game theory, DECISION THEORY). The notions of preference and voting behaviour can be studied by means of logical systems which formalize these notions. Such systems show how various electoral procedures work and study problems like the VOTING PARADOX.

Social philosophy shares further problems with ethics and political philosophy. These cover things like the rights of a group acting in self-defence against members or outsiders, what constitutes the interests of a group as such, how these interests relate to members' and outsiders' interests, how it is legitimate to achieve them, and how decisions are to be taken.

Socrates

The methodological, as against ethical, political and psychological, parts of the subject are often called the *philosophy of the social sciences*. See also HISTORY.

J. Feinberg, *Social Philosophy*, 1973. (Mainly on freedom, rights, justice.)

A. Ryan, *The Philosophy of the Social Sciences*, 1970. (Emphasizes connexions with general methodology.)

R. S. Rudner, *Philosophy of Social Science*, 1966. (Emphasizes classificatory questions, objectivity, functionalism.)

M. Brodbeck (ed.), *Readings in the Philosophy of the Social Sciences*, 1968.

Socrates. c.469–399 BC. Mentor of PLATO and of several so-called 'Socratic schools' (Megarians, Cynics, Cyrenaics). Probably scarcely left Athens except on military service. Executed for 'corrupting the youth and introducing strange gods'. He apparently wrote nothing, and is known to us mainly through Plato and Xenophon (and a caricature in Aristophanes' contemporary comedy *The Clouds*). ARISTOTLE, who never met him, regards him as mainly interested in ethics, but as laying the basis for Plato's theory of 'Forms'. See bibliography to SOPHISTS, DIALECTIC, INCONTINENCE.

Socratic paradox. See INCONTINENCE.

Solipsism. See SCEPTICISM.

Sophists. A movement of itinerant professional lectures on many topics, including philosophical ones, who flourished in Greece, mainly in the last half of the fifth century BC. They differed widely in outlook, though many shared a tendency to scepticism. They emphasized the study of human affairs rather than natural science or abstract metaphysics, and they were responsible for many initiatives in ethics and political philosophy, and also philosophy of language, philosophy of mind and epistemology. They were accused, especially by PLATO, of logic-chopping and subversiveness, but also of pandering to popular tastes. Leading sophists, all active in this period, include Protagoras of Abdera, Gorgias of Leontini, Prodicus of Ceos, Hippias of Elis, Antiphon of Athens. After the fifth century the movement continued but declined in quality.

W. K. C. Guthrie, *A History of Greek Philosophy*, vol. 3, 1969. (Covers Sophists and Socrates in two sections, which are also published separately.)

Sortal. A UNIVERSAL which provides a principle for distinguishing, counting and reidentifying particulars (see UNIVERSALS), i.e. for saying of what sort they are. If a sortal applies to an object at any time, then it applies to that object throughout its existence. *Cat* is a sortal. *Thing, red thing, snow* are not sortals (but *patch of snow* perhaps is: Strawson, p. 202). Cf. COUNT NOUN.

P. F. Strawson, *Individuals*, 1959. (See 'universals' in index. Cf. also M. Dummett, *Frege: Philosophy of Language*, 1973, p. 76. For potentially wider usage cf. J. Locke, *An Essay concerning Human Understanding*, 1690, 3.3.15.)

Sosein. See BEING.

Sound. See VALID.

Space and time. Some problems concern space or time individually, while others concern both. These latter have become more prominent in recent times.

How are space and matter related? Parmenides (see ELEATICS) thought that to say empty space exists would be to say that what is not exists. Aristotle and Descartes too, among others, rejected the void. Modern physics blurs the issue by allowing matter and energy to be intertransformed in certain circumstances, and emphasizing fields of force. General relativity theory treats gravity as a property of space rather than of matter, and quantum mechanics complicates the distinction between space and matter.

Until about two centuries ago, Euclidean geometry was thought to be unique, and so *the* geometry of space. It relied on the *axiom of parallels*, that through a given point not on a given straight line exactly one straight line could be drawn parallel to the given one. But then it was realized that not only was this independent of the other axioms, but consistent systems could be developed if it were replaced by an axiom saying either that more than one such line, or that none, could be drawn. These replacements yield geometries often called hyperbolic or Lobachevskian (N. I. Lobachevsky, 1793–1856) and elliptic or Riemannian (G. F. B. Riemann, 1826–66) respectively. In these systems space is regarded as curved, negatively in Lobachevskian and positively in Riemannian geometry, because it has in three dimensions properties analogous to those of a saddleback and sphere, respectively, in two dimensions. It now becomes an open question what kind of geometry applies to real space, and geometries can be developed for imaginary spaces, which need not be limited to three dimensions. Real space evidently has three, but is this logically necessary (cf. MODALITIES, ANALYTIC)? Spaces studied by mathematics are *metrical* if they allow of measurement and *topological* if they do not. Some transformations of spatial things affect shape and size, and so disturb measurements, but leave relations of betweenness undisturbed. If *b* was between *a* and *c* before the transformation, it remains so afterwards. Topology studies these transformations. The topological transformations of a rubber ball, for example, are those possible with stretching and squeezing but without tearing.

Logical space is a term used by Wittgenstein in his difficult discussion of logical possibility. A place in logical space is given by the sense of an atomic sentence (see LOGICAL ATOMISM), which then describes that place. A rough example: the question whether my cat is black constitutes a place in logical space. When I say that it *is* black I describe that place as being of a certain sort. The logical relations between propositions and between the terms in them can then be treated as having some analogy with spatial relations. Later this 'mapping' of relations between concepts was often called *logical geography*.

The notion of empty space suggests the corresponding notion of time

Space and time

without change. This, however, has been more generally rejected, presumably because there seems to be no analogue here of the effects of perspective. Would the progressive fading of memory serve as an analogue? But this is unreliable and seems to depend in fact, though not in principle, on changes.

Time, more than space, seemed not to be real or measurable because most, if not all of it, so far as it consists of periods rather than moments, seems not to exist at any given moment, and what fails to exist *now* has seemed less real than what merely fails to exist here (Augustine).

A famous attack on the reality of time was made by McTaggart, who distinguished two series of temporal positions. The *A series* contains notions like *past, present, future*, which apply to different events at different times. The *B series* contains notions like *earlier than, simultaneous, after*, which permanently link whatever events they do link. He then argues that the B series by itself, without the A series, cannot account for change, and so for time, while the A series involves either a contradiction or a vicious regress. Some try to make the B series basic by defining 'present' as 'simultaneous with this utterance'.

It is hard to describe the 'passing of time', for whether time itself flows or we move in time, how fast do these things happen? They seem to need a second-order time to occur in (Dunne), but this makes doubtful sense, and only leads to a regress. A further problem arises over our consciousness of change, if we can only experience the present and this is strictly momentary (cf. Augustine's problem about measuring time). To deal with this, the *specious present* was used by various psychologists who claimed empirical evidence for it, and philosophers. 'Specious' suggests it only appeared to be present. It was usually claimed that the specious present was some short period ending at the present and forming the object of an act of awareness occurring at the present instant. The awareness itself was momentary, but it was awareness of a period of time. The stream of experience was then founded, in complex and controversial ways, on such acts. It has been argued, however, that the whole idea of analysing experience into successive units is mistaken; perhaps the momentary present is only a myth. There still remains the general question of how we acquire our ideas of time and space—e.g. are memory and perception involved?

Time, unlike space, has only one dimension, and an apparently irreversible direction. This irreversibilty is connected with the second law of thermodynamics, which says that entropy, or lack of organization, tends towards a maximum in isolated systems. For time to be reversed would be for this law to be broken. However, this law can be analysed as an effect of the statistical probabilities governing matter in motion: of all the possible configurations of a set of particles that can follow after a given initial state the vast majority correspond to a higher degree of disorder than exists in that state. The subject is, however, controversial.

Einstein's special theory of relativity treats space and time together as space-time. The main point of this is that in certain cases one event's preceding another depends on the observer's motion relative to the two events, and motion involves both space and time.

A different and historically earlier, though not completely separate, issue is whether space and time are absolute or relational ('relative' is also used, but often kept for the Einstein view). Are space and time independent of the objects in them, as the absolute view says, or are they merely sets of relations between objects, so that it does not make sense to talk of absolute directions or absolute motion? The questions mentioned above about empty space, and time without change, are relevant again here. The question about motion has largely centred round rotation and centrifugal force, i.e. the relations between force and acceleration.

Another question concerning space and time is whether they are parallel, in the sense that all, or nearly all, that can be said of the one can be said of the other, e.g. can a thing move around in time as it can in space?

A question discussed recently is whether space and time are necessarily unique. Could there be a set of objects spatially and temporally related to each other but not to us? And could there be duplicate universes in space or time? If we went off in a rocket, travelling in what by all available tests was a straight line, and eventually reached what appeared to be a second earth, could we decide whether it really was another one or whether we had somehow come back to this earth? Similarly, could there be a 'mirror universe', i.e. could the universe contain a point or axis of symmetry? (Cf. INCONGRUENT.) The 'duplicate universe' question was asked earlier about time than about space (cf. METAPHYSICS for the doctrine of eternal recurrence, and in general cf. LEIBNIZ'S LAW).

On the infinite divisibility of space and time see ZENO'S PARADOXES.

J. J. C. Smart (ed.), *Problems of Space and Time*, 1964.
R. Gale (ed.), *The Philosophy of Time*, 1968. (These two volumes contain, with some overlap, many relevant discussions, with editorial introductions. Several of the authors mentioned above are included.)
Aristotle, *Physics*, IV. (Place, void and time.)
J. E. Wiredu, 'Kant's synthetic a priori in geometry and the rise of non-Euclidean geometries', *Kant-Studien*, 1970. (Presupposes some knowledge of Kant.)
L. Wittgenstein, *Tractatus*, 1921, transl. D. F. Pears and B. F. McGuinness, 1961. (Logical space. Very difficult.)
J. W. Dunne, *An Experiment with Time*, 1927, 3rd (revised) edn 1934.
C. D. Broad, *Examination of McTaggart's Philosophy*, vol. 2, 1938, pp. 281-8. (Specious present.)
H. G. Alexander (ed.), *The Leibniz-Clarke Correspondence*, 1956. (Clarke defended Newton's absolute view in a series of letters to Leibniz, who defended the relational view. Alexander's introduction discusses later writers too.)
H. M. Lacey, 'The scientific intelligibility of absolute space', *British Journal for the Philosophy of Science*, 1970. (Distinguishes relative and relational views and discusses Newton's position from modern standpoint.)
R. Taylor, 'Spatial and temporal analogies and the concept of identity'

Specious present

Journal of Philosophy, 1955, reprinted in Smart. (Defends parallelism of space and time.)

A. Quinton, 'Spaces and times', *Philosophy*, 1962. (Are space and time unique? See also R. G. Swinburne, 'Times', *Analysis*, vol. 25, 1965, discussed by A. Skillen and Swinburne, vol. 26, 1965. Cf. also K. Ward, 'The unity of space and time', M. Hollis, 'Box and Cox', *Philosophy*, 1967.)

F. Reif, *Statistical Physics*, 1965 (vol. 5 of Berkeley Physics course), chapter 1. (Elementary account of how irreversibility of time is related to statistical physics.)

L. Sklar, *Space, Time and Spacetime*, 1974. (Extended introduction to effects of modern science on philosophy of space and time. Requires some fairly elementary mathematics.)

Specious present. See SPACE.

Speech acts. When we speak there are many things we may be doing. We are normally saying something meaningful. We may be stating, ordering, promising, etc. And we may hope to achieve certain ends such as frightening someone. The systematic study of these things we do in or by speaking dates mainly from J. L. Austin, who distinguished three main levels of what he called 'speech acts': *Locutionary acts*, or *locutions*, are acts of uttering meaningful sentences. *Illocutionary acts*, or *illocutions*, are what we do in saying things, e.g. stating, promising, urging. *Perlocutionary acts*, or *perlocutions*, are what we do *by* saying things, e.g. persuading, frightening, embarrassing. (The words 'in' and 'by' are only rough guides: Austin, chapter 10.) Austin thinks illocutions rely on conventions and can usually be made explicit with 'hereby': 'I hereby warn (urge, command) you ...' Perlocutions depend on natural or causal processes, etc.; we cannot say, 'I hereby persuade you'.

These distinctions grew out of the breakdown, or apparent breakdown, of an earlier distinction between *constatives*, or utterances which state something, and so can be true or false, and *performatives*, or utterances which do something other than stating. To say 'I promise' is to promise, not to say *that* one is promising.

The related notions of performatives and illocutions have been used to try and explain the meaning of certain terms like GOOD, TRUE, PROBABLE, by reference to the 'force' of utterances containing them, i.e. what these utterances normally achieve (cf. NATURALISM.) To explain a term's meaning in this way is to offer a *speech act analysis* of its meaning.

Of Austin's three main terms 'illocution' is the most important, but whether meaning can ever be explained in terms of illocutionary force is disputed. Whether illocutionary force is something distinct from meaning, and whether there are locutions, as distinct from illocutions, have also been disputed. Other problems concern how successful a speech act must be to count as a speech act, and what the speaker must intend. Must the hearer hear and understand the speaker? Must the speaker intend the hearer to believe or understand something, and if so, what? (cf. REFERRING). The use of 'act' in this way has been objected to as a term of art which here rests on confusion (Cerf, § IV, in Fann).

J. L. Austin, *How to Do Things with Words*, 1962.

J. R. Searle (see bibliography to GOOD).

J. R. Searle, 'Austin on locutionary and illocutionary acts', *Philosophical Review*, 1968. (Criticizes notion of locution.)

K. T. Fann (ed.), *Symposium on J. L. Austin*, 1969, part 4. (Six relevant discussions.)

H. Fingarette, 'Performatives', *American Philosophical Quarterly*, 1967.

J. D. B. Walker, 'Statements and performatives', *American Philosophical Quarterly*, 1969. (Both these defend Austin's earlier constative/performative distinction.)

J. R. Searle (ed.), *The Philosophy of Language*, 1971. (First four items are relevant.)

Spinoza, Baruch (Benedict). 1632–77. Jewish philosopher who was born and lived in Holland, working as a lens-grinder. He is usually counted among the 'Continental RATIONALISTS', and his main work is his *Ethics*. In this he sets out to give a systematic exposition of philosophy in general, culminating in ethics, on the model of Euclid. The result concerns metaphysics at least as much, and shows considerable Cartesian influence, though he replaces DESCARTES' body/mind dualism by a monism in which there is but a single SUBSTANCE, which he pantheistically calls 'Deus sive natura' ('God or nature'). He was also a rigid determinist. *Tractatus Theologico-Politicus*, 1670. *Ethica Ordine Geometrico Demonstrata*, 1677. *Tractatus de Intellectus Emendatione* (*Treatise on the Improvement of the Understanding*), 1677. See also DOUBLE ASPECT, IDENTITY THEORY.

Square of opposition. See QUANTIFIER WORDS.

Stadium. See ZENO'S PARADOXES.

Stand for. See REFERRING.

State-description. See CONFIRMATION.

Statements. See SENTENCES.

Stochastic. Concerning or involving conjecture or randomness.

Stoics. Movement founded by Zeno of Citium (c.336–c.264 BC; different from Zeno the ELEATIC), and named from the porch ('stoa') in Athens where he taught. Stoics treated knowledge under three heads: logic, physics, ethics. They developed propositional LOGIC and the theory of IMPLICATION, and tried to discover a sure mark ('CRITERION') of truth. They developed a thoroughgoing materialism, treating matter as a continuum (as opposed to Epicurean atomism), but added a rather non-material flavour with their

Strawson, Peter F.

pantheism and notions such as the 'tension' ('tonos') that matter was subject to. In ethics (to which the later Stoics largely confined themselves) they held determinist views and advocated acceptance of fate, based on self-sufficiency and a realization that 'virtue' was the only ultimate value. Leading Stoics include also Chrysippus (c.280–c.206 BC), Posidonius (c.135–c.51 BC), Cicero (106–43 BC), Seneca (c.4 BC–AD 65), Epictetus (c.AD 50–c.138), Marcus Aurelius (AD 121–80). See also CATEGORIES, DIALECTIC, EPICUREANS, IDEA, METAPHYSICS, NIETZSCHE, PHILOSOPHY, SEXTUS.

A. A. Long, *Hellenistic Philosophy*, 1974.

Strawson, Peter F. 1919– . British philosopher working in Oxford, who has been a leading member of the later phase of 'linguistic philosophy'. He has both earned the strictures of RUSSELL for his attention to 'ordinary language' in criticizing Russell's theory of DESCRIPTIONS, and has cautiously led linguistic philosophy back to METAPHYSICS along lines laid down by KANT. He has also made notable contributions to the theory of truth and to the mind/body problem (cf. MIND, NO-OWNERSHIP, PERSON). 'On Referring', *Mind*, 1950 (criticizes Russell). *Individuals*, 1959 (return to metaphysics). *The Bounds of Sense*, 1966 (commentary on Kant). See also CATEGORIES, CONDITIONALS, CONJUNCTION, FACTS, FEATURE-PLACING, FORM, IMPLICATION, INDIVIDUALS, LANGUAGE (PHILOSOPHY OF), LEIBNIZ'S LAW, LOGIC, QUANTIFIER, REFERRING, SEEING, SORTAL.

Structure (deep and surface). The *surface structure* of a phrase or sentence, studied by *surface grammar*, is its grammatical analysis as it stands. Its *deep structures*, studied by *depth grammar*, are the abstract structures underlying given interpretations of it and determining them, e.g. 'Little girls' camp' has one surface structure (adjective + noun + noun) but two possible deep structures: it has two interpretations, according as 'little' qualifies 'girls' or 'camp'. See also GRAMMARS.

N. Chomsky, *Cartesian Linguistics*, 1966, pp. 31 ff. (See n. 80 for deep structure and logical form.)
L. Wittgenstein, *Philosophical Investigations*, 1953, § 664.

Structure-description. See CONFIRMATION.

Sub-contraries. See CONTRADICTION.

Subjectivism. View or views which claim that what appear to be objective truths or rules in certain spheres, notably ethics, are really disguised commands or expressions of attitude, etc., e.g. 'Lying is wrong' would be regarded not as stating an objective fact, but as really being the command 'Never lie!', or an expression of the speaker's hostility to lying, like 'Lying! Grr!' (cf. NATURALISM). An alternative version of subjectivism says that the utterances in question do express objective truths, but only about human minds, wishes, beliefs, experiences, etc., whether these be of the speaker or of people in general. 'Lying is wrong' would then mean 'I, or perhaps people generally, disapprove of lying'. Berkeley's IDEALISM is called 'subjective' because it holds that physical objects are really ideas in the mind, even though the mind in question is that of God.

Objectivist views, by contrast, claim of certain things that they exist independently of the mind, or that there are, in the relevant sphere, truths independent of human wishes and beliefs, or that there are similarly independent ways of establishing certain truths or answering certain questions (e.g. on how to act, or how to argue rationally).

Subsist. See BEING.

Substance. Parmenides (cf. ELEATICS) gave an apparent logical demonstration that reality must be one. He seems to have thought that anything real must exist at all times and in all places, and there were many attempts in the next century or so to distinguish between the real, which obeyed one or both of these demands, and the merely apparent or derivative. In the EPICUREAN system the atoms of which things were made were real, while their shifting colours and temperatures were merely attributed to them by us. Against this background, the notion of substance as one of the CATEGORIES is first explicitly discussed by Aristotle. ('Substance' is the traditional translation, followed here, for the Greek *ousia*. Some scholars, however, think 'substance' a bad translation, partly because of its later treatment by Locke (see below). They prefer terms like 'being' or 'entity'.)

Aristotle seems to use 'substance' in two main senses (though some see instead two *kinds* of substance here). In the first sense a substance is a particular concrete object, like Socrates or this horse, while in the second sense it is the FORM or essence which makes a substance in the first sense the thing it is. Socrates is what he is because the flesh of which he is made has taken on the form of man and not, say, that of horse. In his *Categories* Aristotle uses *primary substance* for the former sense of 'substance' and *secondary substance* for the latter sense. Socrates is a primary substance and *man* is a secondary substance. There is, however, a problem about this second sense of 'substance', where a substance is a form, for it is not clear how forms are related to UNIVERSALS. Aristotle denies, in his *Metaphysics*, that anything universal can be a substance. The modern sense of 'substance' as 'stuff' (water, iron, etc.), though uncommon in philosophy, seems to be an amalgam of these two senses.

There is, however, a third possible sense of 'substance', which Aristotle mentions but dismisses, namely matter, or what remains when one removes the form or properties of something. This largely dominates Locke's view, whereon the substance of something is what remains when we remove *all* its properties. Locke called this rather mysterious entity 'something ... we know not what' which underlies the 'accidents' or properties of things.

Descartes, like Locke, took substance to be the *subtrate* of, or what underlies, accidents or properties, but did not emphasize its distinction from them so much that it became unknowable. We can only know something by describing it, i.e. giving its properties, which is impossible if it itself

Substance

has none. Leibniz, who thought of substances as living things, connected substance with the notions of actuality and activity. But all these thinkers emphasize that substances are what can exist in their own right, in contrast to attributes and modes. *Modes* are, roughly, ways in which an attribute can be possessed. Red might be called a mode of the attribute colour. They disputed about the number and kinds of substances, the main classification being into material and spiritual substances, though Spinoza claimed that there could be only one substance, which he called 'God or nature'.

This notion of a substance as what exists in its own right or independently raises certain difficulties. Firstly, what things are distinguishable and definite enough to count? Clouds? rainbows? shadows? Secondly, what sort of independence is in question? Is a hand a substance although it must be a hand of someone? Is a father a substance when described as 'father', or only when described as 'man', since a father must be the father of children? In other words, do fathers as such form one kind of substance as men or horses do? Or is the independence not logical, as here, but of some other kind—perhaps metaphysical, as Descartes thought in calling God the only substance in the full sense, other things being only derivatively so because they owe their existence to God? How is the priority of substance to be explained, since one can no more have a substance without attributes than attributes without a substance? How indeed is *substance* related to *attribute*? Is a substance a mere bundle of attributes? If so, what binds the bundle together? Or does a substance underlie all its attributes, which leads to Locke's unsatisfactory view of an unknowable substance? If substances are what attributes apply to, what can be said about attributes of attributes? Surely we can say of an attribute, as well as of a substance, that it is desirable, or rare, or say that scarlet is brighter than crimson.

These considerations suggest a further ambiguity in the term 'substance'. Is there perhaps an absolute or metaphysical sense where the contents of the world are divided into substances and other things (attributes, relations, etc.), and a relative or logical sense where whatever we are talking about is the substance and what we say about it are the attributes? (cf. CATEGORIES). Some philosophers have rejected the metaphysical sense and supposed that substance is at bottom a linguistic notion (cf. METAPHYSICS. This is one form of *nominalism*). But if we accept the metaphysical notion of substance, should we count among substances any abstract things like UNIVERSALS or propositions (see SENTENCES)?

Aristotle, *Categories* (transl. with commentary by J. L. Ackrill in Clarendon Aristotle series, 1963), esp. chapter 5 but cf. chapter 7, *Metaphysics*, books 7 (or Z), 8 (or H), 12 (or Λ).

D. M. MacKinnon, 'Aristotle's conception of substance', in R. Bambrough (ed.), *New Essays on Plato and Aristotle*, 1965.

W. Sellars, 'Substance and form in Aristotle', R. Albritton, 'Forms of particular substances in Aristotle's *Metaphysics*', *Journal of Philosophy*, 1957. (Two rather more technical discussions of Aristotle, concentrating on notion of form.)

Descartes, *Principles of Philosophy*, part I, §§ 51–3, 56.Cf. also §5 of appendix to *Replies to Objections*, II.
Locke, *Essay*, book 2, chapter 23.
W. C. Kneale, 'The notion of a substance', *Proceedings of the Aristotelian Society*, 1939–40. (General historical discussion, followed by tentative defence of substance.)
G. Martin, *Leibniz: Logic and Metaphysics*, 1960, transl. 1964, § 28. (Leibniz on substance.)
A. Quinton, *The Nature of Things*, 1973. (Extended modern treatment of four relevant problems.)

Substrate. See SUBSTANCE.

Sufficient conditions. See NECESSARY AND SUFFICIENT CONDITIONS.

Sufficient reason (principle of). Principle that nothing can be so without a reason, causal or otherwise, why it is so. Nothing occurs by 'blind chance', and, in particular, two apparent alternatives such as our universe and a 'mirror universe' like ours but with right and left interchanged, are not really alternatives unless there is enough difference between them for God to have had a reason to create one rather than the other. The principle is associated mainly with Leibniz, for whom it forms one of the two main principles of reasoning, and governs 'truths of fact'. His other principle is the principle of CONTRADICTION, which governs 'truths of reason'. A third principle, the *principle of the best*, or of *perfection*, explains what is actual rather than merely possible by saying that the actual world is the best of all possible worlds.

G. W. Leibniz, *Monadology*, 1714, esp. §§ 32–6, 53–4. (Leibniz's 5th paper to S. Clarke, 1716, § 21 (in H. G. Alexander (ed.), *The Leibniz-Clarke Correspondence*, 1956) derives identity of indiscernibles (see LEIBNIZ'S LAW) from sufficient reason principle.)
B. Russell, *A Critical Exposition of the Philosophy of Leibniz*, 1900, §§ 14–15. (Claims Leibniz only partly distinguishes sufficient reason and perfection principles. Cf. G. H. R. Parkinson, *Logic and Reality in Leibniz's Metaphysics*, 1965, pp. 105–6.)
N. Rescher, *The Philosophy of Leibniz*, 1967, chapter 2. (Schematizes relations between the three principles.)

Supervenient. See CONSEQUENTIAL CHARACTERISTICS.

Support. See CONFIRMATION.

Sustain. See CONDITIONALS.

Syllogism. A valid or invalid argument in which a conclusion connecting two terms is deduced from two premises connecting those terms to a third term, called the *middle term*. The subject of the conclusion is called the

Syllogism

minor term, and is connected to the middle term in the *minor premise*. The predicate of the conclusion, the *major term*, is connected to the middle term in the *major premise*, conventionally written first. Only four types of proposition are allowed (see QUANTIFIER WORDS). In 'All men are mortal; all Greeks are men; so all Greeks are mortal', *men* is the middle term, *Greeks* the minor term, and *mortal* the major term.

The middle term may be either subject or predicate in each premise, giving accordingly four different *figures* of syllogism (Aristotle, who first formalized the syllogism, only recognized three as distinct). Since the three propositions in a syllogism can each be of four kinds, each figure will contain $4^3 = 64$ kinds of syllogism, called *moods*, giving 256 moods for the four figures together.

Only a few moods are valid (the number can be predicted mathematically, given certain assumptions. Cf. also DISTRIBUTION). If some of these are assumed to be valid the rest can be derived from them, or *reduced* to them, in an AXIOM SYSTEM. The gist of the assumed moods, especially the only valid mood with universal affirmative conclusion, exemplified above, can then be summed up as the *syllogistic principle*. The traditional *dictum de omni et nullo* is one form of this principle; taking two first-figure moods as basic it says that whatever applies to all, or none, of a given class applies, or fails to apply, respectively, to all of a given sub-class of it. In the above example *mortal* applies to all men, and so to all Greeks.

Modal syllogisms contain at least one modal term (see MODALITIES), e.g. '*Necessarily* all cats are black'.

All the above syllogisms are *categorical*. 'All' is closely related to the material IMPLICATION sense of 'if'. 'All cats are black' is similar in meaning to 'If anything is a cat, it is black'. *Hypothetical syllogisms* have at least one premise in this hypothetical form (but see Keynes).

Three main criticisms have been made of the syllogism: that as an argument it begs the question because the conclusion is already contained in the premises (cf. INFERENCE); that it is unclear whether the four allowed kinds of proposition entail the existence of things of the kinds they mention (the problem of *existential import*: does 'All unicorns are black' entail that there are unicorns? cf. QUANTIFIER WORDS); that it is very limited in scope, and in particular ignores the logic of relations by using 'be' as its only verb (cf. LOGIC).

Aristotle's *practical syllogism* is a subject of dispute. It is like an ordinary syllogism but has for conclusion an action, or perhaps an utterance closely related to one, such as a resolve: 'All sweet things are good to eat; this is sweet; therefore let me eat it.' Cf. practical REASON, INCONTINENCE, IMPERATIVE.

J. N. Keynes, *Formal Logic*, 1884, 4th (revised) edn 1906. (Full treatment from classical viewpoint.)

J. Lukasiewicz, *Aristotle's Syllogistic*, 1951. (Treats Aristotle historically and from viewpoint of modern logic. 2nd edn 1957 includes modal syllogisms.)

L. E. Rose, 'Aristotle's syllogistic and the fourth figure,' *Mind*, 1965.

J. S. Mill, *A System of Logic*, 1843, book 2, chapter 3. (Famous attack on syllogism's usefulness.)

G. H. von Wright, *Explanation and Understanding*, 1971. (Practical syllogism. See index under 'practical inference'.)

Symbol. See SIGN.

Symmetric. A relation holding from *a* to *b* is *symmetric* if it must hold from *b* to *a* (*sibling of*). It is *asymmetric* if it cannot (*parent of*), and *non-symmetric* if it may or may not (*brother of*). 'Non-symmetric' occasionally includes 'asymmetric'. It is *anti-symmetric* if its holding from *b* to *a* implies that *a* and *b* are the same object. *Not greater than* among numbers is anti-symmetric, but *not older than* among people is non-symmetric: different people can have the same age, but different numbers cannot have the same size, so if *a* is not greater than *b*, nor *b* than *a*, then *a* and *b* are the same number.

Symptom. See CRITERION.

Syncategorematic. See CATEGORIES.

Synonymy. See MEANING.

Syntax, syntactics. See SEMIOTIC.

Synthetic. See ANALYTIC.

T

Tarski, Alfred. 1902– . Mathematician and logician, born in Warsaw where he worked until 1939, and since then has been at Berkeley, California. His work relevant to philosophy has been mainly in his formalization of semantics. This has led to his 'semantic theory' of TRUTH, whose formulation was importantly affected by the LIAR paradox. He has also contributed to the formal treatment of logical and mathematical MODELS. 'Der Wahrheitsbegriff in den formalisierten Sprachen', *Studia Philosophica*, 1935 (translated from Polish book of 1933). 'The Semantic Conception of Truth and the Foundations of Semantics', *Journal of Philosophy and Phenomenological Research*, 1944 (shorter version of above). *Logic, Semantics, Metamathematics*, 1956 (collected logical papers from 1923 to 1938 in translation, including 'Wahrheitsbegriff'). *Introduction to Logic and to the Methodology of the Deductive Sciences*, 1941 (translated and revised from Polish original of 1936).

Tautology. Literally, saying the same thing. Loosely, any ANALYTIC truth. More strictly, and usually, either any logical truth, i.e. any statement true in virtue of its form (see ANALYTIC), or a truth-FUNCTIONAL logical truth, such as 'Snow is white or snow is not white'. (Not 'Everything is white or not white', which is logically true, but is not such that its truth can be inferred from the truth or falsity of its parts for it has no relevant parts.) The sense of mere repetition, whereby 'I took his life and killed him' becomes a tautology, does not occur in philosophy.

Teleological. Having to do with design or purpose. See also ETHICS, EXPLANATION.

Teleological argument. See DESIGN.

Term. Sometimes a word or phrase ('Always define your terms'), and sometimes objects or things, such as the terms of a relation. (If John loves Joan the relation *loving* has the people John and Joan as its terms.)

Tertiary qualities. See CONSEQUENTIAL CHARACTERISTICS.

Theorem. See AXIOM.

Theory. See LAWS.

Theory-laden. Applied to a term if its use can only be understood in terms of some theory. 'He has an anal-retentive personality', for example, only makes sense against a background of Freudianism. It is sometimes claimed that many more terms are theory-laden or theory-loaded than appear so at first sight.

N. R. Hanson, *Patterns of Discovery*, 1958. (See index.)

Thing-in-itself. See NOUMENON.

Thing-word. See METAPHYSICS.

Thinking. A few examples will best show the wide range of uses of 'think' and 'thought': 'I think it's raining'. 'What do you think of the Government?' 'Think of a number'. 'It's your welfare I'm thinking of'. 'I'm thinking of going abroad'. 'I'm thinking what to do'. 'I'm thinking about my childhood'. 'My first thought on waking was . . .'. 'Thoughts for the day'. 'Beautifully written, but the thought is obscure'. 'A little thought is needed here'. As well as thinking of, in several senses, one can think about things, think in English, or in images, think with one's hands like a sculptor, or gesticulator, and think things over, through, out, and up.

In the seventeenth century 'thinking' was often used to cover mental phenomena in general, including feeling, with the result that Descartes and others could distinguish between substances according as they had extension or thinking as their main attributes (giving material objects and minds respectively). This usage is no longer current.

From the examples we can see that thinking can take at least the forms of believing, imagining, pondering, calculating, deliberating, ruminating, assuming, evaluating; that it can be something occurring at a given time or a state we can be in; and that it can concern theoretical or practical matters (cf. practical REASON). Whether or not all these cases are equally central (Urmson), it seems hopeless to try and isolate any one activity as that of thinking. Moreover, it may be that thinking is never manifested except in other activities that could occur without it. Kicking a football involves thinking, but the same leg-movements could result from a reflex. Here one can in various degrees be 'thinking what one is doing', but the thinking is not, or need not be, a separate activity. For these reasons thinking is sometimes called POLYMORPHOUS. This in turn suggests an 'adverbial' view of thinking, whereby there is no activity, or even set of activities, to be called thinking, but activities in general can be carried out thoughtfully or thoughtlessly, intelligently or unintelligently, etc. However, this will hardly cover all cases. One cannot calculate thoughtlessly, except in the sense of 'He thoughtlessly went on calculating while the kettle boiled dry'. This example shows that intelligence or thoughtfulness,

Thinking

like care, deliberation, etc., can be manifested in the fact that something is done, as well as in the manner in which it is done. But it also shows that calculating, even if done hastily or carelessly, essentially involves thinking.

Such activities, and especially silent thought, and occasions when thoughts dawn on one or flash across the mind, have occupied much attention. A recently popular theory is that we have here simply physical events in the brain seen from a certain point of view (IDENTITY THEORY OF MIND). More longstanding are disputes about the role of mental images, language, and behaviour. Behaviour, if it involves overt movements, seems irrelevant in many of the cases we are considering. Hypothetical behaviour might seem to be involved, in the sense that the thinker would behave in certain ways if certain things happened, e.g. would give certain answers if asked certain questions. But this does not explain what does happen at the definite time when the thought occurs. Language seems involved in that any thought must presumably be expressible in language. But we often have the thought before finding words to express it. It may be true however that thoughts involving abstract things can only occur to a being possessing a language which could express them. Mental images here need not be full-blooded pictures, but may be confused patches of colour, or sounds, or incipient sensations of moving the vocal chords, or anything that might be called material for experience. It seems hard to conceive of thought occurring without any such elements at all. But it seems equally hard to see what relevance such imagery has if it does occur, since it seems that one could have any amount of such imagery without having the relevant thought.

All this suggests two further questions. First, how is thinking related to time? A train of thought takes time, and can be interrupted and left incomplete, but can any of this happen in the case of a single thought that flashes on one? In expressing a thought one may, for example, first say the subject and then the predicate, but does one think them in this or any order? How, in fact, is the structure of a thought, if it has one, related to that of a sentence expressing it? We must distinguish here a thought as a datable occurrence from a thought as the content common to many such occurrences. But how are they related? Have they a common structure? The second question is how far thoughts, in either sense, can be described. Thoughts as contents can be true, valid, fallacious, misleading, sombre, illuminating, commonplace, though some of these terms will only apply to them relative to a context. Thoughts as occurrences can be dated and put into words, but descriptions of them seem either to borrow from descriptions of the content, or to be peripheral and not reaching the heart of the thought itself. Descriptions like 'hasty', 'sudden', 'unexpected' seem to presuppose other descriptions, which yet are not forthcoming.

The question of the structure of a thought raises the question of how thinking a whole thought or proposition is related to thinking of an object, e.g. something which the thought was about. In particular, which is prior? Does one think thoughts by, for example, thinking of objects and attributes and somehow putting them together, as by thinking of the cat and of black, and putting them together to get the thought that the cat is

216

black? Or is thinking of an object something that can only be abstracted from a whole thought, so that one can only think of an object by thinking something about it?

Another important question about thinking concerns the things we think about. If I think about Caesar, does this constitute a relation between me and him? But perhaps Caesar never existed, so that I could not have been related to him, yet my thinking surely remains what it was. Also what happens if I think something false of him, e.g. that he had a beard when in fact he did not? This, with the fact that Caesar no longer exists to be thought of, may suggest that I must use a representative of him to do my thinking with, e.g. a mental image, which can exist now, and be bearded. But even if such an image were always present on these occasions, how would the image itself be related to Caesar? What would make it an image *of* him? For it is Caesar, not the image, that we are supposed to be thinking about, and we must surely know what we are thinking about, which would be difficult if there were just the image. This whole question remains wide open. With the idea that thought requires a representative cf. the representative theory of PERCEPTION. For further questions about thinking and the objects it has cf. INTENSIONALITY (see the 'Cicero' example there).

A further question we can ask is what it is that thinks? Must a thought belong to a continuing thinker? When Descartes said 'I think, therefore I am', what sort of an 'I' did he prove the existence of? See also JUDGMENT, REFERRING.

F. N. Sibley, 'Ryle and thinking', in O. P. Wood and G. Pitcher (eds)' *Ryle*, 1970. (Thinking and the many uses of 'think'. Cf. J. O. Urmson, 'Polymorphous concepts', in same volume, and also A. R. White, *The Philosophy of Mind*, 1967, chapter 4.)

H. H. Price, *Thinking and Experience*, 1953. (General study.)

W. J. Ginnane, 'Thoughts', *Mind*, 1960. (Clear exposition of the problem of analysing sudden thoughts.)

P. T. Geach, *Mental Acts*. (Exploration of the analogy between thinking and speaking. Cf. also his *God and the Soul*, 1969, chapter 3.)

D. L. Mouton, 'Thinking and time', *Mind*, 1969. (Refers to Ginnane and Geach.)

A. N. Prior, *Objects of Thought*, 1971. (Part I discusses the direct objects ('accusatives'), if any, of thinking (propositions, etc.) and requires a fair knowledge of logic. Part II uses less logic (but with some Polish notation) to discuss examples like the Caesar one above.)

J. W. Reeves, *Thinking about Thinking*, 1965. (Mainly on psychological questions, but with some reference to philosophical ones. Discusses imageless thought *inter alia*.)

T. L. S. Sprigge, *Facts, Words and Beliefs*, 1970. (Complex and sophisticated attempt to analyse thinking in terms of images.)

R. M. Chisholm, 'Sentences about believing', *Proceedings of the Aristotelian Society*, 1955–6. (Discusses cases like the 'Cicero' example in INTENSIONALITY.)

Time

Time. See SPACE.

Token. See UNIVERSALS, TOKEN-REFLEXIVES.

Token-reflexives. When a sentence contains phrases like 'here', 'now', 'this', 'I', 'last year', 'in January', or tenses of verbs, we cannot fully know what was said by someone uttering the sentence, unless we know something about that particular utterance like its date, place, utterer, etc. Particular utterances of a word or sentence are called *tokens* (see UNIVERSALS), and so these phrases, which as it were point back to the token sentence in which they appear, are called token-reflexives. Alternative names for them include *egocentric particulars* (Russell), *indicator terms, indexicals*.

An important issue, which affects what propositions (see SENTENCES) are, and what sort of things can be true or false, is whether token-reflexives can be eliminated, i.e. whether sentences containing them can be translated into what Quine calls eternal SENTENCES.

B. Russell, *An Inquiry into Meaning and Truth*, 1940. (Chapter 7 claims that 'egocentric particulars' can be eliminated.)

W. V. Quine, *Word and Object*, 1960. (Largely follows Russell. See index under 'indicator word'. See § 36 for tenses, and p. 107n. for terminology.)

J. N. Findlay, 'An examination of tenses', in H. D. Lewis (ed.), *Contemporary British Philosophy*, III, 1956. (Difficulties in eliminating tenses.)

C. Sayward, 'Propositions and eternal sentences', *Mind*, 1968. (Token-reflexives in general cannot be eliminated.)

Topic-neutral. 'We may call English expressions "topic-neutral" if a foreigner who understood them, but only them, could get no clue at all from an English paragraph containing them what that paragraph was about' (Ryle). Identifying such expressions raises problems. They might be called the subject-matter of logic. See also FORM.

G. Ryle, *Dilemmas*, 1954, chapter 8. (Quotation on p. 116.)

Topological. See SPACE.

Total evidence requirement. See CONFIRMATION.

Transcendental arguments. Roughly, an argument which shows of some proposition, not that it is true, but that it must be assumed to be true if some sphere of thought or discourse, especially an indispensable sphere, is to be possible. An early example is Aristotle's argument that the law of contradiction cannot be proved, since any proof involves it, but must be assumed by anyone who asserts anything at all, and therefore by anyone asserting that the law is false. Kant thought such arguments could also justify non-formal conditions of objective thought (his CATEGORIES). The law of contradiction is a formal condition: see FORM.

Since Kant, transcendental arguments have been popular as a weapon against various kinds of sceptic. The sceptic, it is claimed, cannot state his position without assuming what he is claiming to be sceptical of. His position is therefore parasitic on that of his opponent.

However, there is much dispute about exactly how transcendental arguments work, how they are to be distinguished from other kinds of argument, how many kinds of them there are, and what sort of things they can be used to establish. They may concern not only whether propositions are true, but whether terms are meaningful, whether concepts have application or usefulness, and whether arguments are valid.

Transcendental arguments are perhaps a strengthened form of PARADIGM CASE ARGUMENTS. A transcendental argument for something like the legitimacy of INDUCTION would say that a whole sphere of our thought or language presupposes its legitimacy, whether or not we have even heard of induction. A paradigm case argument for it points simply to the fact that we *regard* some arguments as legitimate inductive ones.

Aristotle, *Metaphysics*, book 4 (or *Γ*), chapter 4.
A. P. Griffiths, J. J. MacIntosh, 'Transcendental arguments', *Proceedings of the Aristotelian Society*, supplementary vol., 1969. (Griffiths defends them with examples. MacIntosh is critical.)
R. Rorty, 'Verificationism and transcendental arguments', *Nous*, 1971. (Moderate defence, but stressing limitations. M. S. Gram, 'Transcendental arguments', ibid., is relevant but difficult.)

Transcendentals. See BEING.

Transformation rules. See AXIOM.

Transitive. A relation holding from *a* to *b* and from *b* to *c* is *transitive* if it must hold from *a* to *c* (*ancestor of*). It is *intransitive* if it cannot (*father of*), and *non-transitive* if it may or may not (*fond of*). 'Non-transitive' occasionally includes 'intransitive'.

Translation (indeterminacy of). Quine claims that assured translation between any two languages, or even within one language, is impossible in principle. There are certain exceptions, namely certain occasion sentences, which are covered by stimulus synonymy, and also truth-FUNCTIONAL TAUTOLOGIES. To translate, in general, we must construct *analytical hypotheses*, which say that an element in one language is equivalent to, or analysable in terms of, an element in the other. But Quine thinks we may find it impossible in principle to justify choosing one such hypothesis against another, and our choice may affect not only the meaning, in any plausible sense, but the truth of the sentence being translated. Quine claims that this raises difficulties for accounts of meaning, synonymy and translation.

W. V. Quine, *Word and Object*, 1960, chapter 2 (see pp. 35–6 for occasion sentences, and pp. 32–3, 46, for stimulus synonymy.)
R. Kirk, 'Translation and indeterminacy' and 'Quine's indeterminacy thesis', *Mind*, 1969. (Critical. Answered by A. Hyslop, 'Kirk on Quine

Transparent

on bilingualism' and R. Harris, 'Translation into Martian', *Mind*, 1972.)
A. C. Lambert and P. D. Shaw, 'Quine on meaning and translation', *Mind*,
1971. (Critical.)

Transparent. See INTENSIONALITY.

Transposition. See CONTRAPOSITION.

Tropic. See PHRASTIC.

Truth and falsity. The *correspondence theory* is perhaps the commonest
theory of truth, partly because 'correspondence' can be interpreted strictly
or loosely. In its strictest form, primarily associated with Moore and
Russell, this theory involves a relation between two things, that which is
true (a proposition, belief, judgment, etc.) and that which makes it true
(a fact, or perhaps a state of affairs or event). The fact has a structure which
the proposition, etc., copies or pictures. But finding pairs of things which
correspond in this way is difficult, especially since the sort of structure that
a proposition might have, involving the relations between things like
nouns and verbs, or subjects and predicates, seems entirely different from
any features of the outer world. Similar difficulties confront correspondence, or picture, theories of how sentences or propositions have MEANING.
Also if all we know is propositions, and propositions picture the world,
how can we compare the propositions with the world itself to see if they
picture it accurately?

There is a less strict form of the theory, which no longer requires that
each part of the proposition should correspond to a part of reality. On this
view something is true if it can be correlated with a fact and false if not, or
if its negation can be correlated with a fact. A still looser form calls something true if it simply 'says things as they are'. This leads naturally to
F. P. Ramsey's *redundancy* or *no truth* theory, whereby to call something
true is simply to repeat what it says. On this view truth is not a property
of anything, but the use of 'true' provides a shorthand way of referring
to things said. A development of this is Strawson's *performative* or *ditto*
theory, which is a SPEECH ACT theory. Here when we call something 'true'
we perform an act of agreeing to, repeating, or conceding it—we say
'ditto' to it. These theories have, however, been criticized as unable to
cover all senses of 'true', and loose correspondence theories have been
returned to and defended by Austin and, in a modified form, Hamlyn.

A recent variant of the correspondence theory is Tarski's *semantic
theory*. This is primarily designed for, though not confined to, artificial
languages, whose elements or 'words' may be infinitely many but are of
definite kinds and have definite roles. Sentences in a given language, L, are
called 'true-in-L' (not to be be confused with 'L-true', Carnap's symbol for
'logically true': see ANALYTIC, VALID) when their elements are so combined
as to state what is the case, e.g. 'Snow is white' is true in English if and only
if snow is white. This avoids treating propositions and facts as entities, and
is easy to develop in a rigorous and formal way. But there are limits to how

Truth and falsity

far it can be applied, even to formal languages, for reason connected with the LIAR PARADOX and GÖDEL'S THEOREMS.

The correspondence theory suits philosophers who make a sharp distinction between knower and known. Those who refuse to do this, notably IDEALISTS, often favour the *coherence theory*. The basic idea of this is that something is true if it coheres or is logically consistent with a wider system than any of its rivals cohere with. This theory presupposes that CONSISTENCY can be defined independently of truth, and also that one of the various possible consistent systems of propositions is wider than any of the others. Idealists who hold this theory, however, say that strictly only the system taken as a whole is true. Single propositions in it give only partial approximations to the truth. Can we really understand 'Caesar crossed the Rubicon', it might be asked, and so be in a position to call it true, until we appreciate all its causes and consequences, even to the end of time? The theory is therefore sometimes called a *degrees of truth* theory. Another reason for thinking truth has degrees is that we cannot know whether something belongs to the widest coherent system, if there is one, without examining every proposition, so in practice we must be satisfied with something less. Moreover, in advanced sciences like cosmology it is often difficult to decide between different but inconsistent ways of describing the universe. All the known celestial movements *can* be explained on a geocentric theory, if it is sufficiently complex. The coherence theory can be supplemented by devices like adopting the simplest out of several competing hypotheses. It is then attractive in those regions of science where immediate verification is impossible. Perhaps partly for this reason it was favoured by some positivists (Neurath, Hempel). Cf. also CONVENTIONALISM, INSTRUMENTALISM, POSITIVISM.

This sort of consideration also lies behind the *pragmatic theory*, for which see PRAGMATISM.

What sort of things can be true? Is 'true' properly or primarily applied to mental acts and states such as acts of utterance, judgments, beliefs, or to linguistic things, such as indicative sentences, or to certain abstract things such as propositions (see SENTENCES)? 'Statement' can be a convenient non-committal word. How we answer this will affect what we say about how truth is related to time and tense: can something, like the sentence 'I am hot', *become* true?

Is everything which is of the right kind to be true or false actually true or false, as one form of the law of EXCLUDED MIDDLE asserts? Is 'My wife is asleep', said by a bachelor, false (Russell) or neither true nor false (Strawson)? Strawson's view claims that there are 'truth-value gaps', i.e. an absence of TRUTH-VALUES where one might expect them. Similarly it has been said that certain statements about the future are neither true nor false, since the future is not yet determined. Cf. FREEWILL (for logical determinism).

Compare also cases in fiction and mythology, like 'Unicorns are vegetarian', where the legends give no evidence. There are other things which seem to be of the right kind to be true or false but are sometimes thought to be neither, or to be not really of that kind. Examples include value

Truth conditions

statements, laws of nature and counterfactual CONDITIONALS. It seems, then, that some things fail to be true or false because they are not of the right kind, while others may be not false but wrong for some other reason ('My wife is asleep', said by a bachelor, 'You are a nigger' said to a negro). Metaphors and comparisons, etc., raise again the question of degrees of truth, e.g. should exaggerations be described as nearly true, or fairly true, or containing some truth?

Special problems arise in certain cases. What is it for a logical or mathematical statement to be true? How is 'true' related to 'provable'? (cf. GÖDEL'S THEOREMS, mathematical INTUITIONISM).

A distinction is often drawn, though also often ignored, between the meaning of 'true' and the CRITERIA of truth. It is sometimes unclear to which of these a given theory is intended to apply.

Another use of 'true' and 'false' is that whereby predicates can be true or false *of* subjects. Linguistic PHILOSOPHERS sometimes ask what significance there is in such facts as that artificial teeth, but not artificial silk, are called false, while no teeth are true. See also SATISFY, TRUTH-VALUE, FACTS, VALID, LIAR PARADOX, Philosophy of MATHEMATICS.

G. E. Moore, *Some Main Problems of Philosophy*, 1953, written much earlier.

B. Russell, *Problems of Philosophy*, 1911, chapter 12. (Cf. also Russell in bibliography to LOGICAL ATOMISM.)

G. Pitcher, (ed.), *Truth*, 1964. (Contains papers by J. L. Austin, P. F. Strawson, G. J. Warnock, M. Dummett, with excerpt from F. P. Ramsey. On Dummett cf. bibliography to TRUTH-VALUE.)

D. W. Hamlyn, 'The correspondence theory of truth', *Philosophical Quarterly*, 1962. (Fairly difficult defence of loose correspondence theory.)

A. Tarski, 'The semantic conception of truth', *Philosophy and Phenomenological Research*, 1944, reprinted in H. Feigl and W. Sellars (eds), *Readings in Philosophical Analysis*, 1949.

M. Black, 'The semantic definition of truth', *Analysis*, vol. 8, 1948, reprinted in M. Macdonald, *Philosophy and Analysis*, 1954. (On Tarski.)

H. Joachim, *The Nature of Truth*, 1906. (Coherence.)

P. F. Strawson, *Logico-Linguistic Papers*, 1971. (Includes several relevant items. For truth-value gaps see chapters 1, 4.)

Truth conditions. Conditions for a given sentence, proposition, etc., to be true, e.g. where p and q represent propositions which we assume must be true or false, the truth conditions of 'Not (p without q)' are that p and q be both true, or both false, or p be false and q true. To call something 'one of the truth conditions' of something else is ambiguous. It may mean that the first thing is adequate by itself to guarantee the truth of the second, but other things would be so too. (In the above example three such alternative truth conditions are given.) Or it may mean that the first thing is one of a set of things which are adequate for this if taken together (e.g. the truth of p is one of the truth conditions for 'p and q').

Truth table. One among the decision procedures (see DECIDABLE) for the propositional CALCULUS. The TRUTH-VALUE, normally true or false, of a complex expression in the propositional calculus depends on the truth-values assigned to the VARIABLES in it. A truth table consists in a systematic exposition of all possible combinations of such assignments for the expression in question. Each combination occupies a row in the table, with the resulting truth-value for the whole expression placed, for example, at one end of the row. These truth-values for the whole expression thus form a column, from which various properties of the expression can be read off, e.g. the expression is logically true whenever this column contains no truth value but *true*.

Truth-value. *True* and *false* are known as the two main truth-values. For a *two-valued logic* they are in practice the only truth-values, though theoretically any two could be chosen. *Three-valued* and in general *many-valued logics* use three or more values accordingly, adding to *true* and *false* or replacing them. When they add to them, as in the first example below, they reject one form of the law of EXCLUDED MIDDLE. Examples are *true/false/indeterminate*, *known to be true/known to be false/unknown*, *necessarily true/necessarily false/contingent*, *certainly true/99 per cent probably/ . . . /certainly false* (this last group could contain infinitely many values). Sometimes a set of truth-values fall into two groups with important logical properties analogous to those of *true* and *false* respectively. Those analogous to *true* are then called *designated values*, and those analogous to *false* are called *undesignated values*.

M. Dummett, 'Truth', *Proceedings of the Aristotelian Society*, 1958–9, reprinted in G. Pitcher (ed.), *Truth*, 1964, and in P. F. Strawson (ed.), *Philosophical Logic*, 1967. (Includes explanation of designated and undesignated values.)

Truth-value gaps. See TRUTH AND FALSITY.

Types (theory of). Towards the end of the last century interest revived in the logical PARADOXES, from which the semantic ones were not yet distinguished. To cope with RUSSELL'S PARADOX and others, Russell enunciated the *vicious circle principle*: 'If, provided a certain collection had a total, it would have members only definable in terms of that total, then the said collection has no total', i.e. we cannot talk of the *totality* of its members. Classes form such a collection, for him. There are, he said, first-type, or first-level, classes whose members are ordinary objects, second-type classes whose members are first-type classes, and so on. The class of cats and the class of dogs are animal classes. They are first-type classes themselves, and are members of the second-type class of animal classes. There is a class of all classes of a given type which will itself be one type higher, but no class of *all* classes (see also CATEGORIES). Ordinary objects are of type zero. The hierarchy of types also applies to properties: A property of properties of objects belongs to the second type. *Black* is a property of

Type/token

cats. It has the property of applying to cats. *Applying to cats* is therefore a second-type property of the first-type property *black*.

In 'Napoleon had all the properties of a great general', *having all the properties of a great general* is a property of Napoleon, and so is of the first type. But since it refers to a totality of properties, it is said to be of the second *order*. It attributes to Napoleon only the relevant first-order properties (on this theory). The addition of the hierarchy of orders to that of types gives us the *ramified* as opposed to *simple theory of types*. (But words like 'second-order' are normally used more loosely.) Propositions too are distinguished into orders. A proposition referring to no other propositions is of the first order. One referring to propositions of the first order (e.g. 'Some first-order propositions are false') is of the second order, and so on. The ramified theory was used to solve the semantic PARADOXES, e.g. the LIAR.

Since the ramified theory invalidates certain mathematical procedures, Russell introduced the controversial *axiom of reducibility*, saying that any higher-order property or proposition could be replaced by some first-order one.

Classes, etc., defined in ways violating the vicious circle principle are said to have *impredicative definitions* (for an example see Carnap, pp. 37–8).

One disadvantage of the theory is that many words, e.g. 'class', 'proposition', 'true', become systematically, or 'typically' AMBIGUOUS, with different senses for each type or order.

R. Carnap, 'The logicist foundations of mathematics' in P. Benacerraf and H. Putnam (eds), *Philosophy of Mathematics*, 1964, pp. 31–41. (Elementary but illuminating.)

I. M. Copi, *The Theory of Logical Types*, 1971. (Fuller treatment.)

Type/token. See UNIVERSALS.

U

Uncertainty principle. See CAUSATION.

Unexpected examination paradox. See PREDICTION.

Universalizability. An important part of morality seems to lie in the idea that what is right for one person must be right for anyone else in the same position. This can be expressed by saying that a moral judgment must be universalizable. If I say that you ought not to lie, I commit myself to saying that anyone else in that position ought not to lie. Similarly, if I call someone's action a good deed I must allow that anyone else who did the same thing in the same circumstances did a good deed.

Universalizability is not the same as generality. 'Everyone ought to give 1 per cent of his income to blind cripples over sixty' is very specific but quite universal. It refers to *all* who have an income and *all* blind cripples over sixty, since all such cripples are put on a level. In spite of this, 'generalize' is sometimes used for 'universalize', as by Singer.

Judgments may be universal in a stricter or a looser sense. The looser kind may mention individual people, places, etc. Thus 'Everyone should fight for his country' is universal in the stricter sense, since no particular country is mentioned. On the other hand, 'Everyone should fight for England', 'Every Englishman should fight for England', 'Every Englishman should be kind to animals', are all universal only in the looser sense.

Those who make universalizability important for ethics may hold either of two views. The first view uses universalizability to distinguish the MORAL from the *non-moral*. Someone's principle is a moral principle, on this view, if he is willing to universalize it. In this way universalizability helps to define morality, providing either a necessary condition for it (Hare) or a sufficient condition, or both (see NECESSARY AND SUFFICIENT CONDITIONS). The second view (Kant, Singer) tries to distinguish the moral from the *immoral*, by saying that what makes a principle moral is basically that it is universalizable, in the sense that there is no inconsistency in supposing everyone to act on it. 'Inconsistency' here may mean a kind of logical inconsistency (it is inconsistent to suppose that all promises are broken, if they would then no longer be regarded as promises). Or it may mean

225

Universalizability

simply the frustration of something which is, or should be, a general end of human action, e.g. maximizing happiness.

There are difficulties in the notion of universalizing. What counts as universalizing a judgment? Suppose that whatever applies to me must apply to everyone like me: how like me must they be? Can I not describe my case in such a way that no one *is* like me? Remembering that very specific judgments can still be universalized, I might say: 'Although people in general ought not to lie, I myself may lie, because I will allow that anyone may lie if he is just six feet tall, has a scar on his left knee, etc., etc.', listing so many of my characteristics that no one else has them all. Also do desires, etc., count as relevant characteristics? If so, I might say: 'You ought to help the poor, and so ought anyone like you, but I need not because I am not like you. I do not desire to help them, as you do.'

One way of expressing the need for universalizability is by saying that whatever is a reason for one person to act must be a reason for anyone else in the same position to act in the same way. This may give a necessary condition for morality, but it is not peculiar to morality, since it is a mere principle of logical consistency. If danger to health is a reason for Smith not to smoke, it is presumably a reason for everyone like him not to smoke —though again it may be hard to describe how 'like' him they must be.

Philosophers are at present hotly disputing about how many kinds of universalizability there are. Universalizability in the sense of mere logical consistency is, as we have just seen, too wide to define morality completely. Universalizability in the sense of impartiality (in particular, not favouring oneself) seems to be a principle which marks the moral from the immoral, rather than the moral from the non-moral. But this principle too, as we have seen, is not easy to formulate. How far universalizability is relevant to morality, therefore, whether as helping to define it or as contributing to its content, is unclear. (Another notion important here is that of CONSE-QUENTIAL CHARACTERISTICS.)

H. J. Paton, *The Moral Law*, 1948. (Probably best translation of Kant's *Grundlegung*, 1785, earliest and most famous major attempt to base morality on universalizability. Difficult.)

R. M. Hare, *The Language of Morals*, 1952, *Freedom and Reason*, 1963. (Claims universalizability gives necessary condition (not sufficient, but important) for defining morality.)

M. G. Singer, *Generalization in Ethics*, 1963. (Elaborate modern development of Kant's view, claiming that generalization (i.e. universalization) is 'the fundamental principle of morality' (*Preface*). Studies in detail the implications of the question 'What would happen if everyone did that?' Shorter version in his 'Moral rules and principles', in A. I. Melden (ed.), *Essays in Moral Philosophy*, 1958, stressing difference between rules and principles.)

D. H. Monro, 'Impartiality and consistency', *Philosophy*, 1961 (cf. his *Empiricism in Ethics*, 1967, chapter 16.) (Distinguishes these. Criticized by S. B. Thomas, 'The status of the generalization principle', *American Philosophical Quarterly*, 1968.)

Universals and particulars

A. Gewirth, 'Categorial consistency in ethics', *Philosophical Quarterly*, 1967. (Discusses how far universalizability can be used for moral attack on racialism. Criticized by N. Fotion, 'Gewirth and categorial consistency', *Philosophical Quarterly*, 1968.)

D. Locke, 'The trivializability of universalizability', *Philosophical Review*, 1968. (Distinguishes several senses of 'universalizability', and claims that most of them are of little importance to ethics.)

W. D. Hudson, *Modern Moral Philosophy*, 1970. (General introduction, including discussion of universalizability in connexion with Hare.)

Universals and particulars. Objects around us share features with other objects. It is in the nature of most such features that they can characterize indefinitely many objects. Because of this the features are called universals and the main problem is to describe their status. Exceptions, such as 'being the tallest of men', can be included for convenience. The objects are called their instances. The problem is often called, especially in Greek philosophy, the *one-many* or *one-over-many problem*.

Traditionally three kinds of answer have been given: realism, conceptualism and nominalism. *Realism* in this sense is primarily associated with Plato, who treated universals as objects (cf. FORM, IDEA), separate from their instances, and faced great difficulties over what they were like and how they related to these instances. Plato's Forms, in so far as they are treated rather as particulars (see below), are often said not to be universals, though doing duty for them. *Platonism* is nowadays any view which treats things like universals, propositions, numbers, etc., as independent objects. Frege is a noted modern Platonist. Another form of realism, often attributed to Aristotle though the interpretation of Aristotle is very controversial, denies that universals are objects or separate from their instances, but nevertheless makes them real things which somehow exist just *by* being instantiated. It is unclear how this view treats things like unicornhood. The labels *universalia ante rem* or *res*: universals prior to the object(s) and *universalia in re* or *rebus*: universals in the object(s), are often applied to Plato's and Aristotle's views respectively. *Universalia post rem* or *res*: universals after, or derivative from, the object(s), normally applies to nominalism, though it could apply to conceptualism. The term *substantial* universals is applied, like 'realism', primarily to Plato's view, though sometimes also to Aristotle's. It could, but usually does not, denote universals corresponding to substances, e.g. tablehood as against hardness, which would be a qualitative universal.

For *conceptualism*, universals are thoughts or ideas in and constructed by the mind. This view, summarily rejected by Plato, is largely associated with the British EMPIRICISTS. It may explain human thinking and the MEANING of many words, but it can no longer explain why the world itself is as it is (which Plato claimed his Forms explained). The view thus avoids Plato's dilemma that the universal is either outside its instances and so irrelevant to them, or inside them and so split up. But what sort of thing is this thought or idea? Does it involve images, and if so, of what sort? Can the same idea be shared by different people, which splits the universal up

227

Universals and particulars

again, or have they similar but distinct ideas, which leads to the difficulty associated with PRIVATE LANGUAGES?

For *nominalism*, represented especially by Ockham in the middle ages and by many recent writers, there are only general words like 'dog', and no universals in the sense of entities like *doghood*. Cf. MEANING, and also below on 'types' and 'tokens'. (For N. Goodman (1906–), nominalism means recognizing only INDIVIDUALS (second sense), which may be abstract but cannot include classes.)

There are two ways of defining a class of objects. One can define it *extensionally*, or *in extension*, by listing its members, or one can define it as containing all those things which have a certain property or set of properties (called defining it *intensionally*, or *in intension*; see INTENSIONALITY). The former way makes it impossible for a class, once it is defined, to acquire new members, and is of little use. The latter way leaves it open how many members, if any, a class has; the class of dogs contains whatever things have the properties necessary for being a dog. Nominalism now faces a difficulty, for if there are no universals, i.e. no properties, what determines whether something belongs to the class of dogs or not? This is another version of Plato's demand for Forms to account for the world's being as it is. The main nominalist answer to this difficulty uses the notion of resemblance. An object is a dog if it resembles some given dog which is chosen as a standard or paradigm. Two disputed objections to this are that resemblance itself seems to be an indispensable universal, and that resemblance involves partial identity, for to resemble something is to have something, though not necessarily everything, in common with it; the common feature is then presumably a universal.

A variant on the use of resemblance is Wittgenstein's notion of *family resemblance*, whereby there need be nothing common to all the members of a class, nor need any member be taken as the paradigm, but the members form 'a complicated network of similarities overlapping and criss-crossing' like the fibres that make up a thread. A somewhat related notion is that of *clusters* (Gasking).

Particulars, which are not always the same as INDIVIDUALS, cannot be instantiated, and cannot appear as a whole at separated places simultaneously though their parts may be spatially separate. A particular can appear as a whole at different moments of time, but these must normally be linked into a stream—though an intermittent sound may constitute one and the same particular. A particular's parts may be constantly changing, as with a flame, and it need not be 'solid' (shadows, rainbows, clouds, can all be particulars, and perhaps the sky). It must, however, be identifiable and distinguishable from other particulars, so clouds, etc., are not always particulars. Particulars can be abstract, provided the conditions about space and time are preserved (e.g. an action or event, like the Renaissance). *Bare particulars* are particulars considered as independent of all their properties. It is therefore hard to identify or refer to them.

Particulars are like SUBSTANCES in the first Aristotelian sense of that term, though the emphasis is on being unique in space and time rather than, as with Aristotle, on existing in their own right as the bearers of attributes

Universals and particulars

and subjects of change. Therefore shadows and actions are more easily called particulars than substances, while Platonist universals are more naturally called substances than particulars, especially since particulars cannot be instantiated.

As an adjective 'particular' has its everyday sense, and also that given under SENTENCE.

We have seen that universals are sometimes treated rather as particulars. Idealism's *concrete universal* is also a kind of particular. It is a system of instances, treated as a developing individual, e.g. *man* in 'Man has evolved slowly'. Bradley treats ordinary particulars as concrete universals, since they are developing individuals, though really the universe is the sole individual. He uses 'particular' in a more restricted sense than the present entry.

So far we have treated the notions of universal and particular as if they were tolerably clear. However, both are of many kinds. Some universals (relations) can only be instantiated in pairs or triplets, etc., of objects. Others, like 'round square', cannot be instantiated at all, even in thought. Some can be instantiated together with their opposites: an object can be both beautiful and ugly, in different respects; or the object may instantiate the universal only if described in a certain way: something may be large if described as a mouse, but not if described as an animal; and the instances may themselves be universals, for a universal may have universals as its instances: red may have the property of being beautiful. Moreover, stuffs, like water, are not particulars but presumably instantiate universals, though *wateriness* rather characterizes other things resembling water. Logically, then, it is the notion of an instance that is correlative to that of a universal, though instances are no doubt usually particulars.

A distinction closely related to that between universals and particulars, and revealing some of the complications in this field, is that between *types* and *tokens*, introduced by Peirce. The word 'in' appears twice in the present sentence, yet it is only one word. Peirce would call these two appearances in any one copy of the present book, two tokens of a single type. A word as found in the dictionary is therefore a type with indefinitely many tokens (written, spoken, etc.). Only types can be derived from Latin. Only tokens can be illegible. A token may be ambiguous, and then so must its type. A type may be polysyllabic, and then so must all its tokens. The distinction is significant for nominalists, for when they say there are only words and no universals, do they mean types or tokens? Also the distinction is not sufficient by itself, for the words in a speech cannot be types, for types are not limited to a single speech, nor yet tokens, since the same speech, and therefore the same words, can be recorded many times (Cohen). It is disputed how closely this distinction resembles that between universals and particulars, and also to what spheres, apart from words, it is relevant. Is the Union Jack, or the lion in 'The lion is carnivorous', a type or a universal or what? Spheres where the distinction has been used include aesthetics, in the analysis of works of art. See also REALISM, CONCEPT, IDEA, SENTENCES.

H. Staniland, *Universals*, 1972. (Elementary introduction.)

Universe of discourse

Plato, *Phaedo, Republic,* § 596, *Parmenides,* esp. down to § 135c. (These are among the important passages. The *Parmenides* includes what seems to be strong self-criticism, including the 'third man argument'.)

Aristotle, *Metaphysics,* book 7 (or Z), chapters 13–16, *Posterior Analytics,* book 2, chapter 19. (Cf. also Aristotle references under SUBSTANCE.)

M. J. Loux (ed.), *Universals and Particulars,* 1970. (Selected readings.)

R. I. Aaron, *The Theory of Universals,* 1952, 2nd (revised) edn 1967. (Universals as 'natural recurrences' and 'principles of grouping'. Some history.)

N. Goodman, 'A world of individuals', in I. M. Bochenski *et al., The Problem of Universals,* 1956, reprinted in P. Benacerraf and H. Putnam (eds), *Philosophy of Mathematics,* 1964 (cf. also ibid., pp. 21–3), and in C. Landesman (ed.), *The Problem of Universals,* 1971. (Goodman's nominalism.)

H. H. Price, *Thinking and Experience,* 1953, chapter 1, reprinted in Landesman (above). (Moderate defence of resemblance theory, reconciling it with 'universalia in rebus' theory.)

L. Wittgenstein, *Philosophical Investigations,* 1953, §§ 65–77 (Family resemblance view.)

R. Bambrough, 'Universals and family resemblances', *Proceedings of the Aristotelian Society,* 1960–1, reprinted in Landesman and Loux (above). (Sympathetic discussion of family resemblance view, and its relation to nominalism.)

M. A. Simon, 'When is a resemblance a family resemblance?', *Mind,* 1969. (Critical discussion of family resemblance view.)

D. Gasking, 'Clusters', *Australasian Journal of Philosophy,* 1960.

E. B. Allaire, 'Bare particulars', *Philosophical Studies,* 1963, reprinted with discussions in Loux (above).

F. H. Bradley, *The Principles of Logic,* 1883, book 1, chapter 2, § 4, chapter 6, §§ 30–6. (Concrete universals. Cf. R. M. Eaton, *General Logic,* 1931, pp. 269–72.)

L. J. Cohen, *The Diversity of Meaning,* 1962, pp. 4–5. (Brief discussion of types and tokens.)

W. Charlton, *Aesthetics,* 1970, pp. 27–9. (Types and universals. Relevance to aesthetics.)

Universe of discourse. See QUANTIFICATION.

Utilitarianism. Moral theories about what we ought to do are commonly, if not uncontroversially, divided into deontological and teleological ones (see ETHICS). The main, if not the only, teleological theory is utilitarianism, which in its most general form is to the effect that we always ought to do what will produce the greatest good.

But 'utilitarianism' is sometimes restricted to *hedonistic utilitarianism,* which holds that the good is pleasure, or perhaps happiness. Early utilitarians seldom distinguished these. *Ideal utilitarianism,* notably represented by Moore, allows other things to be good, or even to be the main goods (for Moore personal relations and aesthetic experiences). Most early utilitarians were hedonistic, though contemporary ones are harder to classify. Utilitarianism has never held, as its name may suggest, that one should pursue only the useful and not the good in itself.

Though the idea of utilitarianism goes back to the Greeks, its most famous exponents have been Bentham and J. S. Mill. Bentham's *greatest happiness principle* says that one should pursue 'the greatest good, or greatest happiness, of the greatest number'. This formula is imprecise, because if we try to spread happiness to many people we may produce less happiness overall than if we confine it to fewer people. Faced with this difficulty, utilitarians have usually said that one should aim for the greatest happiness overall, however distributed. It is therefore often objected that they cannot account for our intuitions about justice. It is also doubted whether they can account for our normal views on promise-keeping, truth-telling, etc.

Utilitarianism may be attacked in a weak or a strong way. The weak way grants that we always ought to aim for the greatest happiness, but says we have other duties too, e.g. to distribute it in certain ways. The strong attack says that some of our duties not only go beyond utilitarianism, but are inconsistent with it, because they involve producing less happiness than other courses of action would produce.

Recently utilitarians have split into two camps. *Act utilitarians* (also called *extreme* or *direct utilitarians*; notably J. J. C. Smart) say that on each occasion we should do whatever act will produce the greatest good. *Rule utilitarians* (also called *restricted* or *indirect utilitarians*) say that we should obey those rules which would produce the greatest happiness if generally followed. There are other versions of rule utilitarianism. Suppose I ignore a red traffic light and, by some fluke, thereby prevent an accident which would otherwise have occurred. Then, whatever my motive, on act utilitarianism I did right, but on rule utilitarianism I did wrong, assuming that general obedience to the traffic laws produces better results than general disobedience to them.

One difficulty for utilitarianism is how we can ever know what we ought to do. Not only can we never know the total consequences of any act, but much may depend on what others do, and they in turn must take account of what we may do (cf. DECISION THEORY, FREEWILL (on self-prediction)). Rule utilitarianism is partly intended to overcome this difficulty, but has difficulties of its own.

The question whether we should aim at what we think best or at what is really best raises a difficulty shared by other theories.

An interesting recent question concerns population policy. Normally utilitarians have concerned themselves with problems about creating goods and distributing them among a given population, but further questions obviously arise when we can decide how large that population shall be.

Negative utilitarianism says we should aim only to remove evil, not to produce good. Ordinary utilitarianism says we should both remove evil and produce good, aiming at the greatest overall balance of good. See also HEDONISM, PLEASURE, UNIVERSALIZABILITY, CONSEQUENTIALISM.

Utilitarianism

J. S. Mill, *Utilitarianism*, 1861. (Classic and provocative defence.)

G. E. Moore, *Principia Ethica*, 1903. (Ideal utilitarianism.)

J. J. C. Smart, 'Extreme and restricted utilitarianism', in P. Foot (ed.), *Theories of Ethics*, 1967. (Act utilitarianism. See also J. Rawls, 'Two concepts of rules', ibid.)

J. J. C. Smart and B. Williams, *Utilitarianism For and Against*, 1973. (Debate, with annotated bibliography.)

D. Lyons, *Forms and Limits of Utilitarianism*, 1965. (Discusses relations between versions of act and rule utilitarianism. Discussed by B. A. Brody, 'The equivalence of act and rule utilitarianism', *Philosophical Studies*, 1967.)

M. D. Bayles (ed.), *Contemporary Utilitarianism*, 1968. (Essays on utilitarianism, especially on the act/rule distinction.)

G. E. M. Anscombe, 'Modern moral philosophy', *Philosophy*, 1958, reprinted in G. Wallace and A. D. M. Walker (eds), *The Definition of Morality*, 1970, with additional bibliography, and in W. D. Hudson (ed.), *The Is/Ought Question*, 1969. (Criticizes utilitarianism.)

J. Narveson, 'Utilitarianism and new generations', *Mind*, 1967. (Population control. Discussed by T. L. S. Sprigge, 'Professor Narveson's utilitarianism', *Inquiry*, 1968 (§ 2), and H. Vetter, 'Utilitarianism and new generations', *Mind*, 1971.)

H. B. Acton, J. W. N. Watkins, 'Negative utilitarianism', *Proceedings of the Aristotelian Society*, supplementary vol., 1963.

V

Vacuous. In logic certain statements, notably universal statements (see SENTENCES) and CONDITIONALS, are often interpreted more widely than in ordinary thought. 'All unicorns are black' means 'There are no non-black unicorns' and so is true if there are no unicorns. 'If p then q', where p and q are propositions, means 'Not (p without q)', and so is true if p is false. Statements true simply because their subject terms are empty or their antecedents false, or for certain other 'irrelevant' reasons, are called *vacuously true*. Their contradictories can be called *vacuously false*. A term *occurs vacuously* in a statement if the truth or falsity of the statement remains unaffected when the term is replaced by any other term grammatically admissible in that context. 'Red' for instance occurs vacuously in 'This table is either red or not red'. Normally (though not always: see Quine) a term not occurring vacuously *occurs essentially*.

W. V. Quine, 'Truth by convention', in H. Feigl and W. Sellars (eds), *Readings in Philosophical Analysis*, 1949. (Vacuous occurrence.)

Vagueness. See AMBIGUITY, OPEN TEXTURE.

Valid. An inference or an argument is *valid* if its conclusion follows deductively from its premises. The premises may be false, but if they are true the conclusion must be true. An inference is *invalid* if it is not valid. It is *contravalid* if an inference from the same premises to the opposite conclusion would be valid. With inductive, etc., inferences, 'valid' may be used as above, in which case they are all invalid, but it may mean simply 'meeting the standards proper to them'. A formula (propositional FUNCTION, open SENTENCE) is valid if it is true for every value of its VARIABLES. It is contravalid if it is false for every value. Otherwise it is invalid. Logically true propositions, i.e. propositions instantiating valid propositional functions, are sometimes called valid, and logically false ones contravalid. *Sound*, applied to an inference, means either 'valid, and having all its premises true' or just 'valid'. An interpretation of an AXIOM SYSTEM is sound if, under it, all the axioms and theorems are truths. Alternatively, it is sound if whatever is derivable in it from certain premises really follows from those premises. A proof calculus of any kind can similarly be called sound. Soundness is similar to but not identical with CONSISTENCY.

B. Mates, *Elementary Logic*, 1965. (See index. Soundness and consistency.)
A. Church, *Introduction to Mathematical Logic*, vol. 1, 1956, p. 55. (Soundness.)

Value. See VARIABLE.

Variable. Symbol used to stand indefinitely for any one of a set of things or notions. It *ranges over* the members of the set. The members are its *values* and the set is its *range*. *Individual variables, propositional variables,* etc., range respectively over INDIVIDUALS, propositions, etc. *Syntactical* variables range over syntactical (i.e. logical) OPERATORS. A symbol assumed to stand for one thing alone throughout a given context is a *constant*. The thing in question may be unspecified. But with *logical constants* it is specified. The logical constants are terms like 'and', 'or', 'not', 'implies'. They are a sub-class of logical operators (which go beyond them by including things like quantifiers (see QUANTIFICATION)). In school algebra x, y, etc., are numerical variables, ranging over numbers; a, b, etc., are numerical constants; and '+', '×', etc., correspond to logical constants.

A variable is *bound* or, occasionally, *apparent*, if it occurs within the scope of a quantifier containing the same variable (see QUANTIFICATION). Otherwise it is *free* or, occasionally, *real*. In mathematics a 'real variable' is one ranging over 'real', as against complex, numbers.

For *intervening variables*, see LOGICAL CONSTRUCTIONS.

A. N. Whitehead and B. Russell, *Principia Mathematica*, vol. 1, 1910, pp. 16–18. (Bound and free variables (called 'apparent' and 'real' respectively).)

Vicious circle principle. See TYPES (THEORY OF).

Vico, Giambattista. 1668–1744. Born in Naples, he worked mainly there. His main work lay in speculative philosophy of HISTORY, where he elaborated a theory of how civilizations independently undergo a certain kind of development, which occurs under divine providence. He influenced CROCE among others. *Principi di una scienza nuova d'intorno alla comune natura delle nazioni (The New Science),* 1725 (revised in later editions).

Vienna circle. See POSITIVISM.

Vindication. See INDUCTION.

Voting paradox. Let three issues A, B, C, be voted on by three voters whose respective orders of preference are ABC, BCA, CAB. If the first vote is on two issues, and the second vote on the winner and the third issue, the third issue will always win, so that the winner will depend on the order in which the issues are voted on. This example also shows that majority preference is not TRANSITIVE; for a majority prefers A to B, and a majority prefers B to C, but also a majority prefers C to A.

W

Waismann, Friedrich. 1896–1959. Austrian logical POSITIVIST who migrated to Oxford. He was originally a member of the Vienna Circle, but in Oxford he became a leader of 'linguistic PHILOSOPHY', emphasizing the fuzziness in various respects of ordinary language. In particular, he criticized the sharpness of the ANALYTIC/synthetic distinction, and introduced the notion of OPEN TEXTURE. *How I see Philosophy*, 1968 (articles, including six-part article on 'Analytic', 1949–53). See also LOGIC.

Weakness of will. See INCONTINENCE.

Well-formed formula. See AXIOM.

Weyl's paradox. See HETEROLOGICAL.

WFF. See AXIOM.

Whitehead, Alfred N. 1861–1947. Born in Thanet, he worked mainly in Cambridge, London and Harvard. His early work was in mathematics and logic, in which he taught, and then collaborated with, RUSSELL. Later he turned more to METAPHYSICS, and developed a philosophy based on processes and events rather than on material objects. His work was influenced by developments in physics then current, and was also relevant to philosophy of science on topics such as laws of nature. *Principia Mathematica*, 1910–13 (with Russell, Whitehead concentrating mainly on the mathematical parts, Russell on the philosophical). *Science and the Modern World*, 1925. *Process and Reality*, 1929 (often regarded as his main philosophical book, but difficult). *Adventures of Ideas*, 1933.

Wisdom, A. John T. D. 1904–   . British philosopher who has spent his working life mainly in Cambridge. Working under the influence of WITTGENSTEIN's later philosophy, he was one of the forerunners of 'linguistic PHILOSOPHY'. He thinks that, while philosophical problems should be attacked by rational methods, light can often be thrown on them, even when they are insoluble, by examining the deeper philosophical motives that led the protagonists to say what they did. This has led him to an interest in psychoanalysis, and has also perhaps been responsible for a certain allusiveness in his style of writing. *Problems of Mind and Matter*, 1934. 'Other Minds' (series of articles in *Mind*, 1940ff., collected with other articles in book of same title, 1952). *Philosophy and Psychoanalysis*, 1953 (miscellaneous essays). *Paradox and Discovery*, 1965 (more essays). See also LOGICAL CONSTRUCTIONS, SCEPTICISM.

J. O. Wisdom is a younger cousin of John Wisdom, who shares some of his interests, including that in psychoanalysis, but writes also on philosophy of science. See also NUMBERS.

Wittgenstein, Ludwig J. J. 1889–1951. Austrian philosopher, born in Vienna, who taught in Cambridge. Both his main works (mentioned below) were leading contributions to philosophical movements, the first to LOGICAL ATOMISM and the second (influential through oral dissemination before publication) to linguistic PHILOSOPHY. In the first he tried to preserve an extensionalist logic, which led him to trace the limits of what could be stated explicitly and what could only be shown. The second revolves around his rejection of the view that there can be words which have meaning by standing for inner experiences private to the experiencer; this led him to think that philosophical puzzlement in general grew out of misunderstandings of how language works. *Tractatus Logico-Philosophicus*, 1921, transl. 1922 and (better) 1961. *Philosophical Investigations*, 1953. See also CRITERION, EPISTEMOLOGY, FINITISM, LANGUAGE GAME, MEANING, POSITIVISM, PRIVATE LANGUAGE, SEEING, SPACE, STRUCTURE, UNIVERSALS, WISDOM.

Z ———————————

Zeno's paradoxes. The surviving paradoxes of Zeno of Elea (see ELEATICS) are mainly in two groups, concerning plurality and motion, though these groups are related.

The idea behind the former group seems to be as follows: to have no size is to be nothing, while to have size is to be divisible (whether in reality or only in principle is left unclear). But the parts resulting from division must themselves either lack size, and so be nothing, or have size, and so be further divisible. Therefore we must end with nothing or with infinitely many parts. If these infinitely many parts lack size they cannot contribute to the whole, but if they have size, however small, the whole they form will be infinitely large.

The paradoxes of motion seem intended to argue that space and time can be neither atomic (made of indivisible points and moments) nor continuous. The *Moving Rows* paradox seems to argue that if both space and time are atomic there is a maximum velocity, namely one point per moment —but anything moving at this velocity relative to one object can always be shown to be moving faster relative to some other object, so there is no maximum velocity. The argument can be made to cover the cases where only one of space and time is atomic. Aristotle, however, who is our source for this paradox, treats it as simply confusing relative and absolute motion. The above version, whether or not historically accurate, is stronger than Aristotle's.

The *Achilles and the Tortoise* paradox argues that if space and time are both continuous, then if Achilles allows the tortoise a start in a race he can never overtake it. He takes at least some time to reach the tortoise's start, during which the tortoise moves at least some distance. While Achilles covers this distance the tortoise moves some more. While Achilles covers this 'more' the tortoise moves again. Clearly the argument can be repeated indefinitely: even though the successive stages get shorter and are covered ever more quickly, at the end of any given stage Achilles is still behind the tortoise. How can he reach the end of an endless series of stages? The *Dichotomy* is a variant of the Achilles. The name The *Stadium* is ambiguous, sometimes meaning the Dichotomy, sometimes the Moving Rows.

The *Flying Arrow* argues that, since at any moment an arrow occupies a definite position, and since between two moments there is nothing but other moments, the arrow can only be *in* positions and never *move* from one to another.

The *Grain of Millet*, on a different topic, argues that a single grain in falling makes no sound, but a thousand grains make a sound, so a thousand nothings become something, which is absurd.

Modern discussions centre on the Achilles, of which many variants have been developed. Its full solution is still disputed.

W. C. Salmon (ed), *Zeno's Paradoxes*, 1970. (Modern discussions, with extensive bibliography.)